THE GERMAN COMPENSATION PROGRAM FOR FORCED LABOR: **PRACTICE AND EXPERIENCES**

Edited by Günter Saathoff, Uta Gerlant, Friederike Mieth and Norbert Wühler
for the Foundation Remembrance, Responsibility and Future

Published 2017
by Stiftung Erinnerung Verantwortung und Zukunft
Foundation Remembrance, Responsibility and Future
Friedrichstr. 200, 10117 Berlin
info@stiftung-evz.de
www.stiftung-evz.de

ISBN: 978-3-9813377-9-2

Coordination: Friederike Mieth, Uta Gerlant
Translation: Cornelia Nuxoll, Friederike Mieth
Editorial support: Anna Lena Vaje, Julia Möller
Copy edit: Kristy S. Johnson
Layout: ultramarinrot, Berlin

© Stiftung "Erinnerung, Verantwortung und Zukunft", Berlin 2017. All rights reserved. Parts of this publication may not be reproduced, stored or transmitted without full attribution.

Contents

Contributors VII

List of Figures and Tables XI

List of Acronyms XII

Preface
Günter Saathoff XIII

Introduction
Friederike Mieth and Günter Saathoff 1

1 Establishing the Program
  Roland Bank 12

2 Eligibility
  Roland Bank 26

3 Funding of the Program
  Susanne Sehlbach 39

4 Organizational Structure
  Susanne Sehlbach 52

5 Outreach
  Dariusz Pawłoś and Norbert Wühler 68

6 Claims Processing
  Norbert Wühler and Dariusz Pawłoś 85

7 Claims Payment
  Norbert Wühler and Dariusz Pawłoś 103

8 Controls and Audit
  Uta Gerlant 114

9   Additional Program Lines
    Norbert Wühler **128**

10 Legal Closure
    Roland Bank **141**

11 Ending the Program
    Uta Gerlant **152**

12 The "Remembrance and Future" Fund
    Ralf Possekel **164**

    Conclusion
    Günter Saathoff and Friederike Mieth **179**

Annex 1: The Law on the Creation of a Foundation "Remembrance, Responsibility and Future" ("Foundation Law") **197**

Annex 2: Joint Statement on Occasion of the Final Plenary Meeting Concluding International Talks on the Preparation of the Foundation "Remembrance, Responsibility and Future" ("Joint Statement") **210**

Annex 3: Agreement Between the Government of the United States of America and the Government of the Federal Republic of Germany concerning the Foundation "Remembrance, Responsibility and Future" ("US-German Agreement") **218**

Annex 4: Statutes for the Foundation "Remembrance, Responsibility and Future" **230**

Annex 5: Overall Funding for the Compensation Program for Forced Labor **237**

Annex 6: Total Payments by Partner Organizations to Beneficiaries **237**

Annex 7: Number of Beneficiaries by Country **238**

Annex 8: Example of IOM Claim Form and Guidelines for Claimants **240**

Annex 9: Excerpt from IOM Document "Evidentiary Guidelines" **252**

Bibliography **258**

Index **264**

CONTRIBUTORS

ROLAND BANK

Roland Bank was the Legal Adviser of the EVZ Foundation during the time when the forced labor compensation program was implemented from the Foundation's early days in the year 2000 until the end of 2004. He was engaged in questions of rights to compensation for violations of international human rights and humanitarian law as a member of the International Law Association's Committee on the Right to Reparation for Victims of Armed Conflict. He held various academic positions, inter alia at the Refugee Studies Centre at the University of Oxford, the Max-Planck-Institute for Public International and Comparative Public Law in Heidelberg and the European University Institute in Florence. He holds a Ph.D. in Law of the University of Freiburg. Currently, he heads the protection unit of UNHCR's representation in Germany in Berlin. The views expressed in the contributions to this book are the author's and are not necessarily shared by the UN or UNHCR.

Email: bank@unhcr.org

UTA GERLANT

Uta Gerlant is a historian who worked for the EVZ Foundation from 2001 to 2016. She worked with the partner organizations in Poland and Ukraine during the implementation of the compensation payments and liaised with all partner organizations regarding the implementation of humanitarian programs financed by leftover funds. From 2008 to 2016 she was advisor to the Board of Directors of the EVZ Foundation. Since the early 1980s, Gerlant has been involved in different peace initiatives and working groups on 'dealing with the past'. After volunteering with Memorial in Sankt Petersburg, Russia, she co-founded Memorial Germany (a member of the International Memorial Network) in 1993 and was part of its executive board for over ten years. Gerlant holds an M.A. in Eastern European History, Philosophy, and Political Science from the Free University Berlin. Currently, she directs the foundation Stiftung Gedenkstätte Lindenstraße, a memorial site at the place of a former prison in Potsdam.

Email: gerlant@gedenkstaette-lindenstrasse.de

FRIEDERIKE MIETH

Friederike Mieth is a social and cultural anthropologist with a specialization in peace and conflict studies. She coordinated the publication of this volume as an external advisor. Her research interests focus on transitional justice, human rights, and social transformation. She has published about everyday practices of dealing with the past in Sierra Leone, as well as the impact and acceptance of transitional justice mechanisms on a broader level. Mieth was a Research Fellow at the Robert Bosch Academy, Berlin, in 2016/17, and previously worked for the International Nuremberg Principles Academy, the Center for Conflict Studies of the Philipps University Marburg, and the United Nations High Commissioner for Refugees. She completed her Ph.D. at the Philipps University Marburg in 2014 and is a co-editor of Transitional Justice Theories (Routledge, 2014).

Email: friederike.mieth@gmail.com

DARIUSZ PAWŁOŚ

Dariusz Pawłoś is the Chairman of the Board of the Foundation "Polish-German Reconciliation" (FPNP) since 2008, having worked for the organization since 1995. Between 1998–2000 he participated in both German and Austrian international negotiations on compensation for Nazi-era forced labor and represented Poland in the Board of Trustees of the EVZ Foundation. In 2007, he launched the Office of the Commissioner of the Minister of Foreign Affairs for Polish-German Cooperation in the Ministry of Foreign Affairs of the Republic of Poland. In 2012, the FPNP was decorated with the "German-Polish Prize", presented by the Foreign Ministers of both countries. Currently, Pawłoś is involved in many dealing with the past mechanisms in Poland: he supervises a documentation program on Nazi terror, participates in efforts to establish a Museum-Memorial Site in Sobibor, a former Nazi-German extermination camp, and engages in educational work with youth. Pawłoś studied German Studies at the Maria Curie-Skłodowska University in Lublin.

Email: dpawlos@fpnp.pl

RALF POSSEKEL

Ralf Possekel is a historian who has worked for the EVZ Foundation since 2000. In 2011, he became Head of Programs, overseeing several hundred humanitarian and educational projects every year. He was born in 1961 in Frankfurt an der Oder. From 1979 to 1984 he studied history at the Moscow State University. From 1984 to 1991 he worked at the German Historical Institute of the Academy of Sciences of the German Democratic Republic in East Berlin and from 1992 to 2000 he conducted research on contemporary German History. Possekel holds a Ph.D. in quantitative methods in American Historiography.

Email: possekel@stiftung-evz.de

GÜNTER SAATHOFF

Günter Saathoff was the Co-Director of the EVZ Foundation from 2003 to 2017. As scientific advisor to the German Parliament he took part in the preparations of the Foundation Law as well as in other initiatives dealing with the acknowledgement and compensation of Nazi injustice and GDR injustice. In 2000, he became head of the compensation program, supervising the implementation of the payments and the cooperation with the partner organizations on behalf of the EVZ Foundation. In 2003, he was nominated Co-Director of the EVZ Foundation, which by then had widened its operations beyond the ongoing compensation of former forced laborers. Saathoff has worked for several non-governmental organizations and is the author of several publications. As an expert on the topic of historical injustice he has given many lectures abroad. He studied politics, sociology, law, and education.

Email: SaathoffG5@email.de

SUSANNE SEHLBACH

Susanne Sehlbach is a lawyer who started working for the EVZ Foundation in 2001. As a head of a control team she liaised with various partner organizations. In 2005, she became the head of the legal advisor's department, which deals with juridical questions concerning the payment process and the funding activities of the EVZ Foundation as well as with questions on data security. Sehlbach has extensive experience studying and working in Eastern Europe and holds a certificate from the German Foundation Academy as a foundation adviser. She currently finalizes a Master of Laws degree (LL.M.) in IT law, focusing on compliance and data protection law. Since 2015 she also works as an independent lawyer.

Email: susanne@sehlbach.de

NORBERT WÜHLER

Norbert Wühler is a lawyer with over 30 years of experience in national and international claims and reparation programs and was the Director of the German Forced Labour Compensation Programme at the International Organization for Migration (IOM). He was Legal Adviser to the President of the Iran-United States Claims Tribunal, Head of the Legal Service of the United Nations Compensation Commission, and Director of the Reparations Department of the IOM. He provided legal and policy advice on the design, and directed the implementation of claims and reparation programs in, inter alia, Bosnia and Herzegovina, Colombia, Guatemala, Iraq, Kenya, Nepal, Sierra Leone, Uganda and Yemen, and he served as a member of the Kosovo Property Claims Commission. He holds a Ph.D. in Law from Heidelberg University and is currently Chair of the Appeal Board of the World Intellectual Property Organization.

Email: nwuehler@hotmail.de

LIST OF ACRONYMS

BADV	Bundesamt für zentrale Dienste und offene Vermögensfragen (German Federal Office for Central Services and Unresolved Property Issues)
BEG	Bundesentschädigungsgesetz (German Federal Law on Compensation)
BMF	Bundesministerium der Finanzen (German Federal Ministry of Finance)
CIS	Commonwealth of Independent States
FPNP	Fundacja Polsko-Niemieckie Pojednanie (Foundation for Polish-German Reconciliation)
GDR	German Democratic Republic (Deutsche Demokratische Republik, former Eastern Germany)
GFLCP	German Forced Labour Compensation Programme of IOM
HVAP	Holocaust Victim Assets Programme of IOM
ICHEIC	International Commission on Holocaust Era Insurance Claims
IMI	Italian Military Internee
IOM	International Organization for Migration
ITS	International Tracing Service
JCC	The Conference on Jewish Material Claims Against Germany ("Jewish Claims Conference")
PESEL-CBD	Official residents' registration system in Poland
UN	United Nations
US	United States of America

LIST OF FIGURES AND TABLES

Figures

Figure 1:	Forced laborers on the factory premises of Daimler in Minsk, September 1942. Source: Mercedes-Benz Classic	4
Figure 2:	Negotiation round on the compensation of Nazi-era forced labor, 1999. Source: Bundesregierung/Engelbert Reineke	16
Figure 3:	Organizational chart of the Foundation for Polish-German Reconciliation (FPNP)	62
Figure 4:	Claimants at the FPNP office in Warsaw. Source: Fundacja Polsko-Niemieckie Pojednanie	77
Figure 5:	First page of a Compensation News newsletter. Source: IOM	82
Figure 6:	Flowchart of the typical stages of the forced labor claims and payment process	92
Figure 7:	The *Ausländerbuch* as a typical form of evidence. Source: Dokumentationszentrum NS-Zwangsarbeit, Sammlung Berliner Geschichtswerkstatt	94
Figure 8:	Festive act of the EVZ Foundation. Source: Bundesregierung/Sandra Steins	154
Figure 9:	Funding of the "Remembrance and Future" Fund	167
Figure 10:	Humanity in Action Poland, Jan Karski Educational Foundation. Source: Stiftung EVZ/Mateusz Gołąb	174
Figure 11:	Encounter program. Source: Stiftung EVZ/Iwan Woshdaenko	176

Annex Figures

Figure A-1:	Example of IOM Claim Form and Guidelines for Claimants	240

Tables

Table 1:	Categories and amounts disbursed by the Foundation for Polish-German Reconciliation (FPNP)	31
Table 2:	Allocated funds and number of beneficiaries of all partner organizations	43
Table 3:	Overview of all program lines and funding	130

Annex Tables

Table A-1:	Overall funding for the compensation program for forced labor	237
Table A-2:	Total payments by partner organizations to beneficiaries	237
Table A-3:	Number of beneficiaries by country	238

PREFACE

How did Germany deal with the historical injustice of the Second World War? It took a long time for the German government, parliament and society to assume full responsibility for the crimes perpetrated by the Nazi regime and acknowledge the suffering of the victims of this regime without reservations. In view of the massive deployment of forced laborers in Nazi Germany and its occupied territories, it is surprising that a compensation program for this victim group was only set up in the year 2000, 55 years after the end of the Second World War. Moreover, the program was not set up by Germany alone, but was the result of protracted and complicated negotiations between international stakeholders, which were themselves triggered by a wave of lawsuits against Germany and German companies. The negotiations resulted in the establishment of the Foundation Remembrance, Responsibility and Future which had the mandate to locate survivors of forced labor and create a process to pay out individual compensations. The establishment of the compensation program for forced labor is thus due, in a large part, to international pressure.

This book is a description of the practical implementation of the compensation program. It is neither a scientific publication, nor a report or handbook. Rather, it provides an insider's perspective to the compensation program for forced labor, written by authors who were directly involved in the implementation of the program, either as employees of the Foundation Remembrance, Responsibility and Future or of its partner organizations during the time of the compensation program. The authors hope that by sharing the experiences and the challenges encountered during the planning and implementation phase of the program, valuable knowledge can be passed on to other practitioners in the field of transitional justice and particularly reparations or compensation programs after mass crimes.

The book seeks to balance carefully between displaying the specific challenges of the German program, which were often due to the unique historical situation, and the information that would most likely be relevant to an international audience. The authors attempted an honest description of the lessons learned in setting up and implementing such a massive program. While the Law on the Creation of a Foundation Remembrance, Responsibility and Future defined the main features of the program, many decisions had to be taken on an ad hoc-basis, as the particular situations were not anticipated. This was also due to the fact that there was no precedent to a program of this size, on which the implementation could be modeled on. By illustrating why and how decisions were taken and how these affected the later phases of the program, the authors hope to provide insights, knowledge, and inspiration for those involved in setting up reparations programs in the future.

This publication addresses policy-makers, activists, victim representatives and others who are in the process of planning or effecting reparations programs or may be so in the future. It is meant for an international audience, including those unfamiliar with the historical context of the forced labor compensation program. At the same time, it is hoped that many of those who were engaged in implementing the program will read the publication.

The reasons for writing such a book are twofold. Over the past years, the Foundation Remembrance, Responsibility and Future received a growing number of inquiries about how the compensation program was designed and implemented. The Foundation noticed that its experience has garnered the interest of a wide range of political, civil society, and other actors from countries that face similar challenges of dealing with the past. At the same time, there is an interest and need of preserving the institutional knowledge of the Foundation Remembrance, Responsibility and Future and the lessons learned from this unique compensation program. At the time of writing, the program ended in 2007, and many of those directly involved in this process no longer work for the Foundation. This book is thus also an attempt to preserve the immense institutional knowledge built up over the years.

This volume is the product of a team of authors that represent different perspectives within the compensation program. As the design and implementation of the program were the common responsibility of the German and international partners, it was important for the editors to not only portray the experiences of the Foundation Remembrance, Responsibility and Future but also those of the partners in an exemplary way. This meant that representatives of the two most "typical" types of partner organizations were asked to contribute to the book. As a team, the editors and authors discussed the overall strategy of the publication, and each chapter in depth. Thus, while all authors accept responsibility for their viewpoints put forth in the chapters, there is nevertheless a shared responsibility for the publication.

Finally, it is not the goal of this publication to arrive at a unified or final evaluation of the forced labor compensation program, but to preserve and showcase the practical lessons learned from it. The authors of this book are conscious that many perspectives that may be relevant, in relation to the compensation program, are not included here. Voices of recipients of the compensation payments, of civil society or governments, of those victims associations that did not agree with the program, or of the other five partner organizations, just to name a few, are not represented in this book. It is thus important to keep in mind that the goal of this publication is not to present a technical analysis or political evaluation of the program, but to put forth the description of practical aspects of effecting such a large compensation program.

Günter Saathoff
Berlin, March 2017

FRIEDERIKE MIETH AND GÜNTER SAATHOFF

INTRODUCTION

This chapter contains:

— Historical background to forced labor under the National Socialist regime
— Germany's long road to facing the crime of forced labor
— General description of the German compensation program for forced labor
— Content and structure of the book

The German compensation program for forced labor under the National Socialist regime was one of the largest and most complex reparations programs worldwide, eventually providing payments to 1.66 million beneficiaries in 89 countries. Running from 2000 to 2007, the program paid out individual compensation amounts to survivors of forced labor during the so-called "Third Reich", in some instances to legal successors of former forced laborers, and to certain other victims of National Socialist persecution.[1] The sum of approximately 5.2 billion Euros for this program was provided in equal shares by German companies and the German State. Together with seven international partner organizations, the Berlin-based Foundation "Remembrance, Responsibility and Future" (*Stiftung "Erinnerung, Verantwortung und Zukunft"* or EVZ Foundation, after its German initials) administered the program. The EVZ Foundation is still active in the field of remembrance, human rights, and intercultural understanding.

How did this large compensation program come to being? How was it possible to raise this extraordinary amount of money from German companies and government? And how was it possible to design and implement such a massive program 60 years after the crimes took place, with no historical precedents? With many civil society actors and transitional justice practitioners advocating for reparations programs today, these questions have become more pertinent than ever before. There are also many practical "lessons" to be learned from this program. For example, one of the main challenges for the decision-makers was to set up a compensation program that would be able to distribute a fixed amount of money to a yet unknown number of beneficiaries, all within a reasonable time frame. Finally, can anything be learned from this program with respect to the impact and acceptance of large-scale individual compensation in other countries and different historical conditions?

This book is an attempt to describe the experiences of the forced labor compensation program from an 'insider's' perspective. It provides an insight into the processes that led to the enactment of a special international agreement and the Foundation Law, on which the program is based, and details the many decisions that had to be taken during the implementation of that law. Many of the challenges faced by this compensation program were of practical nature and appeared during the launch and execution of the program. They revealed that many consequences of the initial decisions on the design and procedure were not fully anticipated during the setup of the program. In this way, the authors of this book wish to share their experiences so that similar difficulties can be avoided or at least anticipated in future reparations programs.

This introduction provides a brief historical background on forced labor under the National Socialist regime and the long road to the recognition of this crime in Germany. It then briefly describes the main features of the compensation program and provides an orientation to the remainder of the book.

---

1 "National Socialism" refers to the general ideology by Hitler's party, the National Socialist German Worker's Party. It is also commonly referred to as Nazism/Nazi.

FORCED LABOR DURING THE SECOND WORLD WAR

Forced labor was one of many atrocities perpetrated during the years of the National Socialist regime, which ruled Germany from 1933 to 1945. The National Socialist party became a powerful force in German politics in the 1920s. Much of their propaganda focused on existing resentments in Germany. Their leader, Adolf Hitler, became German chancellor in 1933 and the party consolidated its power. After a fire in the Reichstag, the seat of the German parliament, the party disabled the opposition by issuing a decree allowing mass arrests of opposition party members. The National Socialists soon started to repress social groups that were deemed "un-German," such as people of Jewish, Roma or Sinti origin, homosexuals, and political enemies. Already in 1933, the regime began to build up a forced labor system within Germany. This was less to exploit forced laborers for economic gains, but to punish and detain in concentration camps or "work-education camps" members of the political opposition and those who were not perceived to belong to the German (racially defined) society. On September 1, 1939, Germany started the Second World War with a military attack on its neighbor Poland. In the following years, German aggression extended to cover large parts of Europe with the aim to establish a German world power. This aggression was the start of an international war that became the deadliest conflict in human history.

The crimes perpetrated by the National Socialist regime remain unparalleled. The regime set up a system of concentration camps all over Europe where inmates were starved to death or killed in gas chambers. More than six million people of Jewish faith and 500,000 people of Roma or Sinti origin were murdered in a systematic genocide. Some 5–6 million Poles and Slavonic people (mostly citizens of Central and Eastern Europe) and other ethnic or minority groups were killed. The regime's ideas of "cleansing" Germany also led them to systematically persecute mentally ill and disabled people, as well as "asocial" individuals and other "unfit" persons, many of whom were murdered or forcibly sterilized. Persons with certain political views such as communists, social democrats, or unionists were also persecuted.

Forced labor became more and more an integral part of the German war economy. While individuals were persecuted by the Nazi regime before the war began in 1939, the practice of German companies and state authorities to systematically force civilians to work under harsh or inhumane conditions began after the start of the war. The goal of such forced labor was two-fold. First, workers were exploited for economic gain; and second, it was related to the plan to eradicate certain population groups by forcing them to work until they died of exhaustion (so-called 'extinction through labor'). From 1939 to 1945, more than 12 million people were forced to work for German industry, agriculture, public sector, and in German households, the majority of whom originated from Poland and the Soviet Union. In addition, more than eight million individuals were deployed in Germany's occupied territories, so that in total more than 20 million laborers were forced to work under the Nazi regime.[2] Many of the

---

2   Mark Spoerer, "Zwangsarbeit im Dritten Reich," Norbert Wollheim Memorial, Frankfurt am Main, 2008, available at www.wollheim-memorial.de/files/993/original/pdf_Mark_Spoerer_Zwangsarbeit_im_Dritten_Reich.pdf (accessed 27 February 2017).

Figure 1: Forced laborers on the factory premises of Daimler in Minsk, supervised by an employee of the German company Todt, September 1942. Source: Mercedes-Benz Classic

individuals deported to Germany or production sites in occupied territories were selected through a highly organized system involving German government institutions, military, and companies. Prisoners of war and people deported to concentration camps suffered particularly inhumane circumstances. By the early 1940s, the German war economy depended on the exploitation of foreign laborers and, as a result, German companies profited significantly.

After the end of the war, Germany was divided into four military zones, each governed by one of the Allied Forces. The United States of America (US), Great Britain and France oversaw zones which later became the Federal Republic of Germany (West Germany). The Soviet Union presided over the zone which later became the German Democratic Republic (GDR; East Germany). The International Military Tribunal in Nuremberg was set up by the Allied Forces to deal with those most responsible for the crimes during the Second World War, and in the decades after the war several other trials of such crimes took place in Germany, other European states and Israel.[3]

---

3   For a general overview of transitional justice in Germany see Sanya Romeike, "Transitional Justice in Germany after 1945 and after 1990," Occasional Paper No. 1, International Nuremberg Principles Academy, 2016, available at www.nurembergacademy.org/fileadmin/media/pdf/news/Transitional_Justice_in_Germany.pdf (accessed 8 March 2017).

GERMANY'S LONG ROAD TO FACING THE CRIME OF NAZI-ERA FORCED LABOR

As early as 1946–47, starting with the Nuremberg trials, forced labor was recognized as a crime and some of the main perpetrators were convicted. The prosecutors of the Nuremberg Trials designated forced labor a charge under the 'crimes against humanity' category and sentenced Fritz Sauckel, the politician responsible for the execution of the forced labor program, to death. However, the tribunal was not responsible for the decision on forced labor victims' right to compensation.

While both German states established compensation legislations for victims of the Nazi regime, they did not include survivors of forced labor. Under the 1953 West German framework of compensation laws and regulations for different groups of victims of the Nazi regime, the *Bundesentschädigungsgesetz* (BEG), persons recognized as persecuted by the Nazi regime such as, for example, "holocaust survivors" were considered eligible for compensation for damages resulting from imprisonment or for health damages, but not for forced labor itself.[4] This framework did not apply to individuals in Central and Eastern Europe, as payments to countries of the Eastern Bloc were politically unwelcome during the Cold War. The GDR also provided pensions to persons persecuted by the Nazi regime, but focused on those who were persecuted for political reasons rather than racial or religious reasons. Here, compensation was not offered to foreign victims of Nazi persecution so that survivors of forced labor were not eligible[5].

Moreover, there was little political will to compensate victims of forced labor. In the 1950s, a time in which the Cold War already dictated international foreign policy, West Germany refused to pay individual compensation payments, citing mainly legal and political reasons: First, it was argued that forced labor was not a specifically National Socialist crime, but rather a most unfortunate consequence of the war. This in turn would be the responsibility between states and/or former conflict parties directly. Second, German companies were not considered responsible for the deployment of forced laborers as they acted solely according to the directions by the Nazi regime. Third, payments to individuals, and to countries under dictatorial rule, which were part of the so-called Eastern bloc, would ultimately lead to strengthening these regimes.

In the same vein, for a long time, German companies also denied their responsibility for forced labor during the Second World War and successfully avoided compensation payments.

---

4   See Federal Compensation Act, Federal Law Gazette, BGBl. I S. 1387, sections 28 to 50, 29 June 1953, last amended 17 August 2015.
5   For an overview of German compensation for National Socialist injustice see Federal Foreign Office "Compensation for National Socialist Injustice" available at www.auswaertiges-amt.de/EN/Aussenpolitik/InternatRecht/Entschaedigung_node.html#doc482342bodyText7 (accessed 15 May 2017).

While a few companies voluntarily investigated their roles in the forced labor system and established compensation schemes for their former 'employees,' the vast majority of companies did not pay any compensation. In some instances companies were sued for compensation, but it was typically argued that companies were forced by the Nazi regime to participate in the forced labor system, thus shifting the responsibility to the government. This argumentation was often followed in the court decisions. One of the notable exceptions was the "Wollheim trial," where the former forced laborer Norbert Wollheim successfully sued the I. G. Farben, a chemicals and arms manufacturer, for compensation. Hence, the vast majority of the survivors of forced labor did not receive compensation in the decades after the war.[6]

It was only decades after the Second World War that the voices demanding compensation for survivors of forced labor grew louder. Particularly after Germany's reunification in 1990 and the dissolution of the GDR, the Green Party in the German Parliament, followed by the Social Democratic Party, and a large number of civil society initiatives (including the Protestant and Catholic Churches) lobbied for taking up the case of former forced laborers. They argued that this was part of accepting the historic responsibility as well as a political and moral settlement with states in Central and Eastern Europe. Eventually, the issue became a priority of the political agenda when a number of class action lawsuits[7] were brought on behalf of survivors of forced labor against German companies in the United States. Together with threats to boycott the businesses and products of German companies in the US, this finally forced Germany to reevaluate its position.

As a result, German companies and the German Government entered into negotiations about a compensation scheme that would explicitly address forced labor. After several rounds of international negotiations among a range of stakeholders an agreement was reached to implement a large compensation program. The negotiators represented all sides — lawyers speaking for former forced laborers, the US and German governments, representatives of governments from countries where the majority of survivors lived (in Eastern Europe and Israel), victims' associations, and representatives of the German companies. Chapter 1 discusses the negotiations in greater depth, as well as the legal, political, and practical challenges that were encountered during this phase.

---

6 See Klaus Körner *"Der Antrag ist abzulehnen" – 14 Vorwände gegen die Entschädigung von Zwangsarbeitern: Eine deutsche Skandalgeschichte 1945–2000* (Hamburg: Konkret Literatur Verlag, 2001). For more information on the Wollheim trial see www.wollheim-memorial.de (accessed 15 May 2017).

7 These are lawsuits that are brought on behalf of a group of claimants rather than an individual. Details are explained in Chapter 1.

THE COMPENSATION PROGRAM FOR FORCED LABOR

In 2000, the EVZ Foundation was established with the aim of immediately putting in place a compensation program. The Foundation was established by the so-called Foundation Law[8] that was the end result of the international negotiations. The German Government and the "Foundation Initiative of the German Industry," an informal body representing the companies, provided the initial assets of the Foundation in equal shares — some 5.2 billion Euros in total. In this way, Germany and its companies finally accepted a measure of accountability towards the victims of forced labor after decades of denying any responsibility for these heinous crimes.

From 2001 to 2007, compensation payments were made through a complex system with the EVZ Foundation as the main administrator and seven *partner organizations* tasked with implementing the program. The partner organizations, defined by the Foundation Law, were five national organizations of Belarus, the Czech Republic, Poland, Russia, and the Ukraine responsible for former forced laborers in these respective countries and a number of other Eastern European states, as well as two international organizations — the Conference on Jewish Material Claims Against Germany (JCC) for Jewish individuals worldwide, and the International Organization for Migration (IOM) for non-Jewish individuals worldwide.

The Foundation Law described two broad *eligibility categories*: survivors of forced labor in concentration camps and ghettoes were to receive up to 7,670 Euros, while individuals who performed forced labor for companies in other confined settings were eligible for payment of up to 2,560 Euros. In order to account for the regional differences, a third 'opening clause' category was mentioned in the Law as well, in which partner organizations could distribute payments to victims of forced labor in other circumstances than the two above, such as to those who were forced to work in agriculture.

The payments were issued in *two installments*. This was because the total amount to be distributed was limited but the exact number of beneficiaries was unknown. While some estimates of the number of forced laborers were available during the negotiations for the program, it was impossible to know how many were still alive after more than 55 years. Paying in two installments allowed the EVZ Foundation and its partner organizations to distribute the overall funds available equally across all beneficiaries, as the exact number of beneficiaries became known after the first installment. Yet, this process created a number of challenges in the administration and implementation of the program, which will be discussed throughout this book.

While the EVZ Foundation's principal task was to make payments to survivors of forced labor and, in some instances, their legal successors, *two additional program lines* were implemented as well. These consisted of compensation payments for so-called "other personal injuries" to

---

8   See Annex 1.

individuals who were particularly subjected to medical experiments, and for "property damages" including personal and business losses, lost bank accounts, losses under insurance contracts etc. In addition, the Foundation Law earmarked funds for so-called "humanitarian programs" for persons who were subjected to particularly harsh suffering. Given the main focus of this book is on the compensation payments for forced labor, these other program lines are only briefly described in Chapter 9.

The German program was not the only compensation program for survivors of forced labor at the time. Parallel to the negotiations with Germany, international negotiations also took place with Austria, which — as a former part of the Third Reich after its annexation by Germany in 1938 — was involved in very similar crimes. Though their design and approach differed in some aspects, the German and Austrian programs often worked with the same partner organizations. The Austrian program will not be described in this book, but it is referred to where comparisons are relevant.[9]

In addition to the compensation payments, a *long-term mandate* of the EVZ Foundation was to preserve the memory of and educate about the lessons of the Nazi injustice, to advocate for human rights as a way of learning from the past for the present and future, and to support humanitarian projects for survivors of forced labor. Toward this aim, a separate "Remembrance and Future" Fund was set up, which supports projects in Germany and a number of other countries. The ongoing work and funding programs of the EVZ Foundation are discussed in Chapter 12.

CONTENT AND STRUCTURE OF THE BOOK

This book discusses a range of aspects of the forced labor compensation program that are deemed most relevant for policy-makers and practitioners who seek to establish and implement reparations programs for mass crimes. Many features of the German program were unique due to the unprecedented scale of the program and the international collaboration. For example, the vast number of potential beneficiaries across many countries posed a number of challenges that do not normally present themselves in a national program. Nevertheless, while every reparations program designed to address certain human rights violations must take the very unique situation into account, there are a number of key aspects and potential dilemmas that have to be resolved by all programs.

The descriptions in this book focus primarily on the experiences of the EVZ Foundation and two of its partner organizations, as a comprehensive description of the work of all seven

---

9   For detailed descriptions of the work of the Austrian Reconciliation Fund that administered the Austrian compensation program, see Hubert Feichtlbauer, *Forced Labor in Austria 1938–1945* (Wien: Austrian Reconciliation Fund, 2005) and www.versoehnungsfonds.at.

partner organizations would have been beyond the scope of this endeavour. By focusing on the work of two typical partner organizations, one operating on a national and one on an international level, this book discusses the challenges of the program in a exemplary way that will be more relevant to the reader.

The program is described in a chronological rather than a stakeholder-centered order, and most chapters are written in a way so that each can be read more or less independently from each other. As the experience of the authors has shown, those who are interested in the lessons learned in other programs often find themselves at a particular stage of a reparations program, e.g. in the advocacy, planning, or implementation phase, and may therefore be interested only in parts of this book. Nevertheless, the authors of this book hope that, even when the historical and contemporary contexts differ, readers may find insights for their specific situation.

Finally, the chapters in this volume do not address the question whether this particular compensation program was the *appropriate* mechanism to address the injustice of forced labor during the Second World War. The EVZ Foundation was set up for the purpose of implementing a law that had already been negotiated and, in this way, many of its activities were already defined. Neither the EVZ Foundation nor its partner organizations were in a position to amend the Foundation Law. However, some thoughts regarding the impact and acceptance of the program are discussed in the conclusion of this volume.

Chapter 1 looks at the process of the international negotiations prior to the establishment of the EVZ Foundation in more detail. Why was the program set up so late? Which stakeholders participated in the negotiations and what was debated? How did they agree on the sum of 5.2 billion Euros made available for the compensation? The chapter also discusses the main provisions of the Foundation Law, which was the result of the negotiations.

Chapter 2 describes in detail the eligibility criteria set out in the Foundation Law. What were the decisions concerning eligibility of claimants? How did the different victim categories come about and how was the amount of compensation for each group arrived at?

Chapter 3 discusses the financial details of the establishment of the Foundation and the planning of the compensation program. It describes how the fundraising was organized from different stakeholders and what decisions had to be taken prior to the implementation with regard to financial aspects. It also addresses administrative costs and the financial management of the large compensation fund.

Chapter 4 outlines the organizational structure of the EVZ Foundation as the main administrator as well as that of two partner organizations. While the overall structure may be unique due to the large number of victims involved and the geographical scope of the program, the different tasks involved in the compensation program are relevant in other contexts as well.

Chapter 5 describes in detail the outreach component of the program, which was a task of the partner organizations. This was a particular challenge for some organizations given the long time that had passed since the crimes and the old age of the potential beneficiaries. The chapter outlines the typical issues that need to be considered during outreach.

Chapter 6 discusses the different stages of the claims processing, including the collection, review and assessment of the claims, the support of claimants, and the most relevant technical processes involved.

Chapter 7 deals with the process of paying out the compensation amounts. It looks at the necessary steps to set up and manage a secure payment system, including creating a financial infrastructure and necessary negotiations with banks.

Chapter 8 describes the controls and audit processes of the program. The EVZ Foundation as the main administrator was tasked with controlling the claims decisions taken by the partner organizations for which it set up separate control teams. The chapter includes a description of the typical challenges in audit processes.

Chapter 9 describes the two other program lines, "other personal injuries" and "property loss," as well as the so-called "humanitarian programs" administered by the EVZ Foundation and the partner organizations, in order to give a full picture of the mandate of the compensation program.

Chapter 10 describes the issue of legal closure in the forced labor compensation program. This did not only involve political decision-making, such as reaching agreements during the negotiations, but also encompassed a range of legal and practical actions that needed to be taken in order to achieve legal closure.

Chapter 11 discusses how "ending" a compensation program needs to be a well-planned process. Many aspects need to be addressed early on in order to allow a smooth completion of such a large program. It describes how some tasks still require dedicated staff after the conclusion of the payment process and how the EVZ Foundation handled the immense amounts of data after concluding the program. The chapter also gives ideas how institutional knowledge can be preserved.

Chapter 12 gives insights into the ongoing work of the EVZ Foundation. The "Remembrance and Future" Fund provides funding for projects that seek to acknowledge the suffering of the victims of National Socialism, foster historical dialogue, support vulnerable survivors, and educate Germans and others in Europe in human rights matters as "lessons of the past."

The *Conclusion* discusses the outcome and impact of the program. Did the EVZ Foundation and its partner organizations achieve the goals of the program? Did the compensation program fulfill the different expectations of the survivors of Nazi-era forced labor, of the initiators and funders of the program, as well as of the wider public? Did it lead to better understanding between peoples or even "reconciliation" between former enemies? The chapter critically looks at successes and challenges of the program, and discusses the significance of the forced labor compensation program in more general terms.

Finally, a few notes on terminology and the use of certain concepts in this book are in order:

Forced labor/slave labor: Elsewhere, the forced labor compensation program has been referred to as "forced and slave labor" compensation program. For this historical context, "slave labor" is not a clearly defined term. Some use it to distinguish the inhumane conditions of forced labor in concentration camps from 'ordinary' forced labor in companies or households. Yet this leaves out forced work in ghettos and other camp-like environments where circumstances were often similar to those in concentration camps. Others understand "slave labor" to describe the forced work by Jewish individuals. The Foundation Law, for various reasons, only refers to the term "forced labor," as will be done in this book as well.

Former forced laborers, victims, and survivors: While it is not uncommon to use the term "forced laborers" in today's language, we found it more fitting to speak of "survivors" or "victims" of forced labor, or former forced laborers. Where used, the word "victim" is not meant to suggest a passive role of the individual in question.

Foundation Law: "Foundation Law" will be used throughout this book to refer to the specific law that allowed the establishment of the compensation program (Law on the Creation of a Foundation "Remembrance, Responsibility and Future," 12 August 2000, see Annex 1). The term should not be equivocated with the federal laws that regulate public or private foundations in Germany.

Reparations/compensation program: In its entirety, the German forced labor compensation program encompasses more forms of reparations than compensations alone, according to the UN guidelines for reparations. Technically, it would therefore justify the label reparation program. At the time, however, the program was called a compensation program, not least because in Germany, "reparations" is a politically sensitive term as it creates a strong association with the earlier, state-level reparations that were part of the obligations Germany had to fulfil after the Second World War. In this book, the term compensation program will be used for reasons of consistency.

ROLAND BANK

CHAPTER 1:
ESTABLISHING THE PROGRAM

This chapter contains:

— Developments leading to the establishment of the compensation program
— Negotiating for a compensation program
— The Foundation Law
— Main features of the compensation program

INTRODUCTION: A MULTI-LAYERED PROCESS

Reparations programs can be established in very different ways, and the form they take depends on the particular historical, legal, and political contexts, as well as the kind and scale of the human rights violations they are meant to address. Some programs are based on a peace accord, some are the result of recommendations by a truth and reconciliation commission, while others are initiated by political actors or as a result of legislation. Many challenges are faced prior to or during the establishment of a reparations program: For instance, which stakeholders should take part in the negotiations for such a program and how can their different interests be balanced? What kind of reparations — restitution, financial compensation, rehabilitation and satisfaction and guarantees — should be covered? How can the necessary funds be raised? Which human rights violations should be addressed and what are the criteria for eligibility? Who are the victims and how can they be reached? How should the procedure be designed to allow for correct determination of eligibility within an appropriate timeframe? A careful design and inclusive process of developing a reparations program are essential for the later acceptance of reparation payments by all stakeholders and for generating an effect of reconciliation and legal closure.

The establishment of the compensation program for former forced laborers was preceded by long and intensive negotiations at the international level involving representatives of the Federal Republic of Germany and German companies, the United States of America, some of the countries of origin of former forced laborers, as well as victims' associations and lawyers who represented victims in US courts. The negotiations took place more than 50 years after the end of the atrocities. Negotiators faced a multitude of challenges, because of the extraordinary magnitude of the crimes, the high number of victims, the number of countries involved and the divergent interests of the stakeholders. Moreover, there was pressure to come to an agreement quickly as possible, as so much time had passed and surviving former forced laborers were very old. Eventually, a compensation program was agreed upon, administered by a public foundation established mainly for this purpose. It was envisaged that the EVZ Foundation would work together with seven partner organizations.

This chapter explains how the compensation program for forced laborers came into being. It first outlines the developments that led to the adoption of the Foundation Law that established the EVZ Foundation, endowed it with the task to administer the compensation program and put the cornerstones of the payment program into German law, and discusses the challenges faced during the lengthy negotiations. It introduces the main features of the program and reflects on how the decisions taken during the negotiations shaped the actual compensation program.

DEVELOPMENTS LEADING TO THE ESTABLISHMENT OF THE COMPENSATION PROGRAM

The establishment of the compensation program in the year 2000 was largely the result of three main developments: the change of the political landscape in Europe after the end of the Cold War; increasing political awareness of the fact that former forced laborers, particularly those in Central and Eastern Europe, had not received any compensation; and finally a number of lawsuits against German companies and the Federal Republic of Germany in the United States of America.

First, the overall political landscape in Europe changed dramatically in the 1990s. The end of the Cold War brought up the issue of compensation payments for victims of the Nazi regime who lived in Central and Eastern European countries, as they had previously not received any or very small payments. This was partly due to the fact that Germany did not want to transfer any payments into these countries, and partly that communist regimes did not allow that citizens of their states received individual compensations. After the fall of the communist regimes in Central and Eastern Europe, there was no longer a political motivation to withhold such payments.

Second, political pressure in Germany grew in favor of creating a compensation program for forced laborers. Throughout the 1990s there was an increasing awareness of the fact that no compensation had been paid to former forced laborers specifically. Forced labor had not formed a criterion for compensation in former programs, neither in German national compensation legislation nor in hardship funds or lump sum agreements with states that had been attacked by Germany during the war. Also, only a few companies who "employed" forced laborers had paid out some compensation to individuals, with amounts varying greatly from one company to another. In the late 1980s and early 1990s, political parties at the national and European level as well as German non-governmental organizations had started a number of political initiatives to achieve compensation for forced labor, but they remained largely unsuccessful. Nevertheless, they brought the issue of forced labor back onto the political agenda.

Particularly, the Social Democratic Party of Germany and the Green Party of Germany (Bündnis 90/Die Grünen) played an active role in creating pressure prior to the negotiations. The Green Party had already promulgated the idea of setting up a foundation for this purpose for several years. This became more specific when, after the 1998 elections, the new Social Democrat/Green coalition government agreed to embark on it in their coalition agreement. After the negotiations started, however, the idea of a compensation program was eventually supported by all parties in Germany. This was partly due to a changing political climate in the 1980s and 90s that became more open in terms of dealing with Germany's Nazi past. The negotiations thus took place with no significant political opposition, which became visible in the wide support of the Foundation Law that was presented to the German parliament after the negotiations.

Third, and perhaps most critical, former forced laborers from different countries had filed lawsuits against German companies and the Republic of Germany in United States courts, which created a lot of pressure to address the issue of forced labor. Starting in 1998, there was a wave of so-called class action lawsuits against those German companies operative in the US that had been involved in one way or another in abuses and exploitation of forced laborers during the Nazi period. The lawsuits were based on the Alien Tort Claims Act that provides for the possibility of a jurisdictional forum in the US even in extraterritorial cases involving the violation of international law.[1] For German companies, these lawsuits not only meant that they could eventually lose the cases and face very large financial obligations, they also had to spend significant sums on legal fees and, probably even more importantly, they got negative publicity in the media. There were, for example, large advertisements in US newspapers that called for a boycott of these German companies. Therefore, these court proceedings had an important impact on the economic performance of the involved German companies in the US. As a direct result of the US lawsuits, German companies had an interest to find a solution that would not only compensate former forced laborers but also protect them against future court proceedings ("legal closure").

NEGOTIATING FOR A COMPENSATION PROGRAM

The years 1998–2000 saw several protracted rounds of negotiations. While there was basic agreement that there should be compensation for forced labor in concentration camps and ghettos as well as for forced labor of persons deported to the territory of the Third Reich, there were a number of issues that were hotly debated during the negotiations. The actual number of potential beneficiaries for these and other potentially eligible groups was highly disputed. The overall amount of funding to be provided to the EVZ Foundation had to be negotiated, as well as the individual amounts for particular historical situations. A major issue was also how to protect German companies as well as the Republic of Germany from further legal action in courts. Negotiations were difficult not only due to the high stakes for all parties involved, but also because there was immense time pressure: the potential beneficiaries were very old and any unnecessary delays would be morally unacceptable. This pressure, along with increasing pressure from the US and German governments and the general public, may well have contributed to finding compromises.[2]

---

1 The text of the Alien Tort Claims Act reads as follows: "The district courts shall have original jurisdiction of any civil action by an alien for a tort only, committed in violation of the law of nations or a treaty of the United States." (28 U.S.C. § 1350). The text was originally adopted as a part of the Judiciary Act in 1789 (1 Stat. 73 (77), § 9). Recently, the law has been changed in a way that would not allow for the kind of lawsuits that were filed against German companies in the late 1990s.

2 For accounts of the course of the negotiations, see Stuart E. Eizenstat, *Imperfect Justice: Looted Assets, Slave Labor, and the Unfinished Business of World War* (New York: Public Affairs, 2003); Lutz Niethammer, "From Forced Labor in Nazi Germany to the Foundation Remembrance, Responsibility and Future," in *"A Mutual Responsibility and a Moral Obligation": The Final Report on Germany's Compensation Programs for Forced Labor and Other Personal Injuries*, eds. Michael Jansen and Günter Saathoff (New York: Palgrave MacMillan, 2009), 15–85; Susanne-Sophia Spiliotis, *Verantwortung und Rechtsfrieden – Die Stiftungsinitiative der deutschen Wirtschaft* (Frankfurt am Main: Fischer, 2003).

Who were the stakeholders?

The negotiations took place with the participation of a large group of stakeholders who all had an interest in the question of compensation for forced labor. The German Chancellor appointed a special envoy tasked to negotiate an overall solution with the Government of the United States and all other relevant governments. The German companies were represented by the Foundation Initiative of the German Industry (*Stiftungsinitiative der deutschen Wirtschaft*), a loose association [3] of those leading German companies that had been involved in using forced labor. The US Government also appointed a special representative for this purpose. The Central and Eastern European countries designated the so-called reconciliation foundations to represent their interests at the negotiating table. These foundations had already been involved in a previous round of German compensation payments in the 1990s, and it seemed natural that they would be the implementing partner organizations for the compensation program for forced labor as well. Many of them already had considerable knowledge of the beneficiaries of the new program and could rely on existing documentation on victims of Nazi injustice. Finally, the victims of forced labor were represented in the negotiations by victims' associations as well as the US law firms involved in the class action lawsuits.

Figure 2: Negotiation round on the compensation of forced laborers, 1999. The partners of the Foundation Initiative for the German Industry meet in the German Foreign Office. Source: Bundesregierung/Engelbert Reineke

---

3   The legal nature of the Foundation Initiative remained somewhat obscure (arguably, an association under German civil law, so called "BGB-Gesellschaft," or a corporation sui generis). This could have raised difficulties: for instance, it would not have been clear who was to be sued if the Foundation Initiative had not raised its equal share of the monetary contributions.

How could the different interests of the negotiators be reconciled? In the following, four of the most important discussion points will be briefly outlined: the number of potential beneficiaries, the overall amount of compensation, legal closure for German companies, and the design of the compensation program.

Who were the beneficiaries?

Knowing the number of potential beneficiaries is crucial when designing a compensation program and, most importantly, for reaching an overall compensation amount. Estimating the number of victims for the forced labor program was particularly difficult as so much time had passed. Yet, in contrast to many other contexts, there were many historical records that could be relied upon, and some of the victim organizations already possessed documentation from earlier compensation programs. In addition, in 1999, European historians came together at a conference in Florence, Italy, that was to provide estimates of the number of potential beneficiaries for the compensation program.[4] Some of the participants in the negotiations also took part in that conference.

At the same time, "forced labor" had to be further qualified during the negotiations. There were different types of forced labor, involving various degrees of suffering. The representatives of the German companies argued that forced laborers in the agricultural sector, who were often placed with small farming companies or family-owned farms, suffered less than those in concentration camps or in industrial forced labor. Therefore, agricultural forced labor was initially excluded from the program. However, Polish victim organizations lobbied successfully for opening the option to include this group in the course of the implementation of the program considering the hardships this very sizeable group had endured. In this case, the fact that victims' representatives were present during the negotiations led to the inclusion of groups that were previously not considered.

The exclusion of certain victim groups was also established early on in the process. In particular, it was decided that a prisoner of war status would not constitute a criterion for eligibility. At the time, this did not give rise to significant controversies among the negotiators who tried to avoid that the issue of prisoners of war would lead to debates in German society on the issue of forced labor by *German* prisoners of war. In order not to put into danger the prospect for a solution regarding civilian forced labor, this aspect remained therefore excluded from the negotiations.[5] However, it became clear during the implementation phase that this exclusion

---

4   Niethammer, "From Forced Labor in Nazi Germany," 60.
5   Niethammer, "From Forced Labor in Nazi Germany," 65.

led to a number of controversies.[6] Long after the conclusion of this compensation program, a specific program for former Soviet prisoners of war was decided by the German Parliament in 2015.[7]

How much money should be allocated for the compensation program and who would pay for it?

The amount of money allocated for compensation programs is often one of the most sensitive topics in negotiations, and the financial aspects were arguably the most difficult part of the negotiations for the forced labor compensation program. There were different lines of argumentation; the overall sum that the German companies were willing to contribute contrasted with calculations based on individual compensation amounts. It was agreed that the program would be allocated a fixed rather than a flexible fund, in particular, in order to avoid incalculable gaps in funding considering the unclear numbers of eligible claimants. Setting a fixed amount for such a complex program was considered the only alternative given the many interested sides that had to agree on this program.[8] Chapter 3 explains in more detail how many consequences this decision had for the design and financial implementation of the program.

In order to arrive at an overall sum, the different stakeholders offered their own calculations based on available estimates of the overall number of beneficiaries and proposals for the amounts of individual payments under the program which diverged drastically in the beginning. While it was initially assumed that the German companies would pay for the program through the Foundation Initiative, eventually the German State agreed to match these contributions, and to establish a public foundation under federal law. After protracted negotiations, the total amount of 10 billion Deutsche Mark (roughly 5.2 billion Euros) was agreed, to be paid in equal shares by the German companies and the German State. This sum must be regarded as a politically informed decision.[9]

---

6 For more information on eligibility criteria, see Chapter 2.
7 It was based on the "guidelines on one-time payments to former Soviet prisoners of war in recognition of their treatment in German detention," established by the German Federal Ministry of Finance. For more information on this compensation program, see www.badv.bund.de/EN/UnresolvedProperty Issues/PaymentToFormerSovietPrisonersOfWar/start.html (accessed 21 February 2017).
8 For more information on the negotiation of the amount of the compensation, see www.wollheim-memorial.de/en/die_stiftungsinitiative_der_deutschen_wirtschaft_1999 (accessed 21 February 2017).
9 There is much documentation available that covers this aspect of the negotiations in depth. See Niethammer, "From Forced Labor in Nazi Germany," 61.

How can German companies be sure that they will not be sued again in the future?

A major point in the negotiations was the issue of "legal closure." One of the main worries of the German companies was that they could still be sued for compensation even if they participated in the compensation program. Therefore, a central demand from the German side was legal closure — which meant that there would be protection from lawsuits in the future. Moreover, German companies expected that the ongoing lawsuits in the US would be terminated upon the establishment of the compensation program — after all, this was one of the main reasons why they were at the negotiation table.

Legal closure is not always an issue in reparations programs as it depends on the nature of crimes perpetrated and on the form of the reparations program (for example, whether former perpetrators or their successors are directly involved in the design and funding of a program or not). However, where such aspects play a role such as in the German case, they are often part of compensation agreements. Guaranteeing legal closure may seem as serving only the perpetrator's side, but it is also a powerful leverage to ensure compliance with such a program.

The German side demanded legal closure as a requirement for the setup of the program and it was decided already during the negotiations that every claimant of the German compensation program would have to waive any future claims against German companies and, in a specified way, against the German State in any matter connected to Nazi-era injustice. It was also agreed that all cases pending before US courts would be terminated before payments under the program would start. This turned out to be quite a significant hurdle for the compensation program to overcome. The specifics of the provision of legal closure in the German compensation program are discussed in Chapter 10.

How should the compensation program be designed?

Finally, the negotiations also covered many legal and organizational aspects. These were important insofar as the program was addressed to claimants all over the world and cooperation was necessary between many political and administrative entities. The stakeholders agreed that a foundation under German public law, combined with the implementation by seven partner organizations abroad, would be the best way to administer the compensation payments. It then had to be negotiated who had the final decision power to approve the claims and the payments, which was to be the EVZ Foundation. It was also agreed that the compensation program would be overseen by a Board of Trustees which largely comprised members who had been participants of the negotiation round (up to this day, for example, the law firms that filed the class actions suits in the US are represented by a member in the oversight body of the EVZ Foundation). These and other aspects will be discussed in more detail throughout the course of this book.

THE FOUNDATION LAW

The negotiation rounds resulted in three main documents that were the basis of the compensation program: a so-called "Joint Statement," an agreement between the German and US governments, and finally, the Foundation Law (see Annex 2, 3 and 1, respectively).

In the *Joint Statement* on the occasion of the plenary meeting that concluded the international negotiations on 17 July 2000, the governments of Germany, the US, Israel and Central and Eastern European States (Belarus, Czech Republic, Poland, Russian Federation, Ukraine), as well as the Foundation Initiative of the German Industry, a Jewish victims' organization (JCC), and a number of victims' attorneys endorsed the basic principles to be included in the Foundation Law. This document is remarkable in that it is evidence of an agreement among very diverse groups of stakeholders. It was an important moment for the program as it symbolized the motivation to come to an agreement and to start the compensation process quickly rather than work on reaching airtight legal solutions. Political will on all sides was crucial.

The *Agreement between the Government of the United States of America and the Government of the Federal Republic of Germany on the Foundation Remembrance, Responsibility and Future* of 17 July 2000 focused primarily on the issue of 'legal closure,' i.e. what was to happen with the class action lawsuits that were pending before courts in the US. It detailed — without binding effect — that these cases should be dismissed by the respective courts as this was in the interest of US foreign policy, and that the compensation program would be the only process in which victims could claim compensation.[10]

The *Foundation Law* is a German federal law that was the legal basis for the establishment of the EVZ Foundation and was enacted on 12 August 2000. The most important elements of the law were comprised in an annex to the US-German agreement.[11] The Foundation Law includes the recognition on the part of the German State and German companies of the historic and moral responsibility for the "severe injustice [committed] on forced laborers, through deportation, internment, exploitation which in some cases extended to destruction through labor, and through a large number of other human rights violations" (Preamble to the Foundation Law, see Annex 1).

---

10 See Annex 3, Annex B.
11 See Annex 3, Annex A.

MAIN FEATURES OF THE COMPENSATION PROGRAM

The Foundation Law already determined many aspects of the compensation program. The main features will be discussed here and in the remainder of the book.

The Foundation Law determined eligibility. Given the enormous variety in individual fates as well as the extremely high number of potentially eligible persons all over the world — it had been estimated that of the persons who were still alive 280,000 had carried out forced labor in concentration camps or ghettos, 623,000 in industry and in the public sector in Germany, 567,000 persons in occupied territories, and 783,000 in agriculture and other types of forced labor[12] — it was decided to establish broad categories of eligibility rather than differentiate between the level and intensity of suffering. These categories addressed the situation of forced labor in a concentration camp, a similarly bad detention camp, or in a ghetto (category A); forced labor in industry after deportation (category B); and an opening clause allowing partner organizations to define additional situations related to forced labor (category C). Even though the primary purpose of the EVZ Foundation was to address the phenomenon of forced labor under harsh living conditions, so-called "other personal injuries" and property losses were also addressed. The inclusion of these other program areas was prompted mainly by lawsuits concerning these other types of situations. These program lines are discussed in detail in Chapter 9 of this book.

The law defined certain maximum amounts for each of the categories of forced labor (first category: up to 15,000 Deutsche Mark [about 7,670 Euros], other categories up to 5,000 Deutsche Mark [about 2,560 Euros]). Within these categories, with few exceptions, partner organizations had discretion to define sub-categories, as well as differentiate in the sums awarded below the maximum amount in order to better reflect the various groups of fates suffered. All aspects of eligibility will be discussed in detail in Chapter 2.

The Foundation Law determined the organizational structure of the EVZ Foundation as well as a number of aspects regarding the workflow and cooperation with partner organizations. The Foundation Law regulated the tasks and functioning of the Board of Directors and the Board of Trustees. Moreover, seven partner organizations were foreseen by the Law to implement the program: organizations for residents of Poland, Ukraine (also responsible for Moldova), the Russian Federation (also responsible for Latvia and Lithuania), Belarus (also responsible for Estonia), the Czech Republic, and international partners for Jewish (JCC) and non-Jewish (IOM) applicants living elsewhere in the world. In addition, the organizations in Ukraine, Russia, and Belarus shared the responsibility for applicants residing in one of the other former republics of the Soviet Union. Cooperation between the EVZ Foundation and the partner organizations was regulated in greater detail in partnership agreements negotiated between the EVZ Foundation and each of its partners. This was necessary because German

---

12 Niethammer, "From Forced Labor in Nazi Germany," 60.

law could not be executed in other states. The central function of the Foundation Law was that, even though the partner organizations had their seat in other states and would not be subject to German law, their decisions on eligibility would have to be in conformity with the German legal provisions. (Chapter 4 discusses the organizational structure and cooperation with partner organizations in detail.)

The Foundation Law further allocated specific amounts for each program and each partner organization. The EVZ Foundation was funded by the German State and the Foundation Initiative of the German Industry with each contributing about 2.6 billion Euros.[13] The full amount of the EVZ Foundation's capital was then allocated to specified purposes. All monies went into the compensation program for forced labor and other personal injuries/damages except the following positions: about 358 million Euros were allocated to a "Remembrance and Future" Fund (see Chapter 12) for financing projects; another 102 million Euros were reserved for administrative costs of the EVZ Foundation responsible for organizing the basic features of the compensation program as well as the costs incurred by the American and German lawyers who had contributed in one way or another to the establishment of the EVZ Foundation. In the following years, the overall fund was also supplemented by about 300 million Euros in interests earned over the course of the program.

Specified total amounts were assigned for specific damages (Section 9 Foundation Law). The largest amount — 8.1 billion Deutsche Mark (about 4.14 billion Euros) — was allocated to seven partner organizations which processed the claims and that were responsible for making available the payments to eligible applicants. It was decided that the responsibility of each partner organization was determined by the place of residence of an applicant on 16 February 1999. The sums were based on the estimates by the historical commission of how many potential beneficiaries lived in the respective countries or areas. However, as a ceiling was established for the total funds allocated to each partner organization, this meant that a partner organization could not spend more than this amount for all eligible applicants within its regional responsibility.

Other programs implemented alongside the forced labor compensation program

In order to address other situations which had formed the subject of lawsuits pending before US courts, some additional cases of eligibility were established. In particular, about 25.6 million Euros were set aside for other personal injuries suffered, in particular, by victims of medical experiments and of homes for children of forced laborers. These claims were also processed by the partner organizations. Another 514 million Euros were reserved for property losses

---

13 All Euro amounts cited here and elsewhere in the book are approximate, as these contributions were paid in Germany's former currency, the "Deutsche Mark". Chapter 3 deals with the question of how the money was raised by the German companies as well as how it was split up exactly between the EVZ Foundation and the various partner organizations.

directly caused by the involvement of German companies, as well as for certain humanitarian purposes, as detailed in Chapter 9.

Another decision was to create a "Remembrance and Future" Fund, at the specific request of the German companies. The negotiators agreed that an important aim of the EVZ Foundation was to uphold the remembrance of the atrocities committed, after having completed the compensation programs. While it was recognized that the compensation program came too late for those who lost their lives in the Nazi era or since, the German legislator declared its intention "to keep alive the memory of the injustice inflicted on the victims for coming generations as well" (Preamble). Therefore, part of the EVZ Foundation's financial resources was allocated to the establishment of a permanent fund

> to foster projects that serve the purposes of better understanding among peoples, the interests of survivors of the National Socialist regime, youth exchange, social justice, remembrance of the threat posed by totalitarian systems and despotism, and international cooperation in humanitarian endeavors. In commemoration and respect of those victims of National Socialist injustice who did not survive, it is also intended to further projects in the interest of their heirs. (Section 2 (2) Foundation Law)

This — permanent — "Remembrance and Future" Fund operated separately from the main compensation program and its work is still ongoing (see Chapter 12).

SUMMARY

The German compensation program for forced laborers was the result of complex negotiations in which many interests and pressure factors were taken into account. The unique historical characteristics of the crime of forced labor which was used almost all across Europe under the Nazi regime during the Second World War as well as the subsequent movements of victims to other parts of the world made the program an international undertaking. The legal framework for the compensation payments bears witness to the special situation in which the negotiators found themselves. Although lawsuits before US courts (that could or could not have turned out to be successful) were among the main factors that triggered the process, the program was a political decision and did not entail a legal right to compensation for potential beneficiaries. To date, it remains the largest compensation program ever adopted. It eventually distributed individual payments to 1.66 million claimants in 89 countries with an overall amount of EUR 4.34 billion Euros.

The decisions taken during the negotiations had a lasting impact on the shape of the later compensation program. As the following chapters show, many features of the program can only be understood when tracing them back to the different interests during the negotiations and in relationship to previous German compensation programs concerning Nazi crimes.

CHALLENGES AND LESSONS LEARNED

- In the case of the forced labor compensation program, it was important to work together with stakeholders representing all relevant parties and groups of victims. The involvement of stakeholders including representatives of the victims' side during the negotiations generated a high degree of acceptance of the program among the stakeholders. In addition, accurate information about the kinds of crimes, the different victim groups and the number of potential beneficiaries is crucial for the design of a reparations program. The establishment of historical facts should not depend on the interests of stakeholders but needs to be accepted on their part. In the case of the forced labor program, acceptance of the estimates of potentially eligible victims and other historical assessments was facilitated by the involvement of expert historians designated by each of the parties involved in the negotiations.

- It was a good practice that the setup of the EVZ Foundation and the implementation of the compensation program were the subject of a law. This gave the involved governments a clear legal responsibility and increased commitment to the program.

- During the negotiations, many specific features were decided upon, and the Foundation Law also contained a rather detailed framework. This had both positive and negative consequences. On the one hand, it served as a predictable framework. However, on the other hand the procedures had to be followed even if at a later stage there would have been better solutions available. For example, the program dealt with extremely large numbers of potential beneficiaries, and yet the Foundation Law already contained very detailed calculations for the total funds allocated to each partner organization. This posed a number of practical challenges during the implementation of the program.

- Including victim groups in the negotiations phase was a good practice. It helped reflect their expectations in the design of the program and may well have increased the overall "acceptance" of the program.

- The fact that many of partners were already participants in the negotiations may have contributed to a rather smooth process of implementation.

- Parties to the negotiations were represented throughout the application of the program in an oversight committee, the Board of Trustees. This way, continuity of commitment and support as well as control and monitoring by negotiating parties was secured throughout the program phases.

- The prospect of legal closure was a central incentive for German companies and for the German state to engage in the negotiations and also led to an increase in the amounts of funding agreed on in the course of the negotiations.

ROLAND BANK

CHAPTER 2:
ELIGIBILITY

This chapter contains:

— Defining eligibility criteria
— Exclusions from eligibility
— Challenges in the application of the eligibility criteria
— The role of evidence in determining eligibility criteria
— Eligibility in case of death of victims of forced labor

INTRODUCTION: THE KNOWN AND THE UNKNOWN

Defining clear eligibility criteria is a cornerstone of all reparations and compensation programs. Eligibility criteria define who shall receive compensatory payments from the program and for which human rights violations the payments are to be made. In many instances, these criteria also define the amount of the compensation for the respective beneficiaries.

In the case of the German forced labor compensation program, a number of the eligibility criteria were agreed on during the negotiations, such as which groups would be eligible for the compensation payments and what maximum amounts would be foreseen for each payment category. The program's eligibility criteria differentiated between different situations involving forced labor and this resulted in two broad beneficiary categories — so-called categories A and B (category A: forced labor in concentration camps, comparably bad detention camps, ghettos; category B: forced labor in industry after deportation). Different amounts were foreseen based on very broad assumptions of the hardship involved; for example, the highest amounts were allocated to former inmates of concentration camps or ghettos. At the same time, it was possible for partner organizations to define additional groups of eligibility (category C, the so-called opening clause). Whereas the definition of categories at the outset provided for transparency and predictability, the flexibility of the opening clause may have increased acceptance of the overall program.

This chapter provides an overview of the main eligibility features of the German program. It outlines the eligibility criteria that were formulated in the Foundation Law and discusses how these provisions impacted the design of the program. It explains how the beneficiary categories of the compensation program relate to the different kinds of crimes in relation to forced labor. Finally, it discusses why some groups were excluded from the program and what compensation was provided in the case of death of eligible beneficiaries.

DEFINING ELIGIBILITY CRITERIA

One of the main challenges of defining eligibility criteria for the forced labor compensation program was that — due to the long time passed since the crimes — potential beneficiaries were very old and finding and collecting evidence for the claims was expected to be difficult. For the drafters of the Foundation Law, this meant that there was an intense time pressure and that expectations of victims would be high. Consequently, it was emphasized repeatedly by the drafters that procedures for determining eligibility had to be non-bureaucratic and expedient. Still, certain delays resulted from the fact that not all aspects were defined predefined by the Foundation Law which hence left open some questions for subsequent interpretation.

The different eligibility categories in the German program were based on broad criteria relevant for the gravity of the situation and the conditions in which forced labor took place. At the time of the negotiations, it was known that forced labor took place practically from the outset of the Second World War in September 1939, when the Third Reich had systematically installed branches of the German employment agencies in newly occupied territories with a view to recruiting workforce. Persons recruited were lured by false promises into labor contracts and their rights were restricted by contracts and ordinances, or they were deported from their homes to other places where they were then forced to work. They were prevented from returning to their region of origin, and were exposed to harsh living conditions in poor barracks or camps, often with insufficient nutrition. When they were held in concentration camps, people mostly were forced to work under atrocious conditions until they died. During the course of the Second World War, more than 20 million persons were forced to work in the Third Reich or Germany's occupied territories, particularly in mining, the war industry, and in agriculture, but also in small businesses, households and other places.

The harsh living conditions were exacerbated for some groups who were specifically persecuted by the Nazi regime. In particular, pursuant to the Nazi ideology, Jews and Sinti and Roma faced "extinction through labor." Slavic peoples, in particular from Poland and the Soviet Union, were regarded as a sub-human race *("Untermenschen")*; they faced extremely harsh treatment in camps and barracks. These issues played a prominent role in the definition of the eligibility criteria.

Provisions of the Foundation Law

The cornerstone of eligibility was the basic historical situation of forced labor for the German industry by persons who were detained or deported. Other situations were added in the course of the negotiations, either following pressure by certain victims groups (for instance, forced labor in agriculture) or in order to extend the reach of legal closure linked to the program (for instance, medical experiments). The scope of the program was, on the other hand, limited by the fact that only victims alive at a specific date were eligible. The various compensation amounts were the result of the negotiations and included the basic premise that victims of forced labor in concentration camps and ghettos should receive a higher sum than those who were subjected to forced labor in other circumstances.

The Foundation Law broadly defined two main categories of eligibility related to forced labor (categories A and B). Questions concerning the interpretation of the eligibility criteria that would arise during the compensation program had to be resolved by the EVZ Foundation and its Board of Trustees. Their decisions were then implemented by the partner organizations.

Category A: Forced labor in concentration camps

Category A comprised beneficiaries who performed forced labor and were detained in a concentration camp, a ghetto, or another place of confinement characterized by inhumane conditions of detention, insufficient nutrition and lack of medical care.

Within this first category, "concentration camps" were designated by reference to a list used in an earlier German national compensation program pursuant to the Federal Law on Compensation (*Bundesentschädigungsgesetz*, or BEG, 1956), which had addressed situations of racial persecution. This was, however, not a comprehensive list, and it was clear from the outset of the forced labor program that there were other comparable camps that would have to be covered under category A.

Camps which were previously not known and the existence of which was revealed in the course of the compensation program could be defined as "other places of confinement" if the nature of their provisions were characterized by inhumane detention conditions, lack of sufficient nutrition, and medical care. In this case, the living conditions in the other places of confinement were considered comparable to those in concentration camps, and survivors of them would be eligible for payment under category A as well. The Foundation Law had foreseen that such classification should be decided by the Board of Trustees of the EVZ Foundation. This proved to be impractical, however, since the Board of Trustees met only twice per year and it also lacked the necessary historical expertise. This task was therefore delegated to the Board of Directors of the EVZ Foundation. Decisions were based on historical expertise and/or information gathered from a relevant number of individual claims for payment and their descriptions of the living conditions in a particular place of detention. In the course of the implementation of the program, more than 3,800 detention camps were thus designated to have been "other places of confinement" for specific periods of time.

Category B: Forced labor in the German industry

Category B included all persons who were deported from their home country, kept in detention, detention-like or comparable "harsh living conditions" and forced to work. It referred to all types of work except in agriculture and households.

The deportation criterion suggested that only persons who were forced to *leave* their home area against their will qualified, but not those who were not allowed to *return* after they had arrived voluntarily in Germany. In practice, however, particularly for workers from Eastern Europe, there was no differentiation between those who were able to show that they were transported away from their home country against their will and those who had agreed formally with this transfer as long as there was no clear indication for collaboration. This was based on the fact that people transferred from Eastern Europe frequently were forced to act as a "volunteer" by exerting pressure on their family or village. Moreover, these people were completely misled as to the conditions awaiting them in Germany or its occupied territories. It was therefore clear that, typically, there was no real consent given to the transfer. Also, there was no difference in exploitation and harsh conditions of life and work between the deported and these "volunteers" in the Third Reich.

In addition, certain differentiation within the legal categories was possible by the creation of sub-categories for category B. The Foundation Law allowed partner organizations to establish sub-categories in which they could determine a different compensation amount according to the severity of suffering.[1]

The opening clause (Category C)

The situation of forced labor during the Second World War was very complex and it was already clear during the negotiation phase that the two categories A and B would not cover a number of people who were also victims of forced labor but did not fall into these categories. A large number of Polish and other citizens, for example, were forced to work in German agriculture, but were not eligible in either category A or B.

Therefore, it was necessary to expand the eligibility criteria in order to find a solution for the (potentially) large number of people who would fall outside the core categories but had suffered from forced labor. This was done by creating a so-called "opening clause" that allowed the partner organizations to allocate certain amounts of money to eligibility categories they could establish themselves according to their specific context. It is important to point out that the inclusion of the opening clause was in large parts due to the initiative of victims' organizations that were present during the negotiation phase. This shows the importance of including different stakeholders in the design process of a compensation program. Thus, in addition to the two main categories, the opening clause became part of the Foundation Law.

The opening clause did not mention "forced labor" specifically and left the definition of details mainly to the partner organizations implementing the program. In fact, the wording of the Foundation Law provided little guidance on which other groups of victims of Nazi injustice could be defined as eligible by the partner organizations. Only by way of example, forced laborers in agriculture were mentioned. The only limitation to the potential scope of the clause was the requirement of a minimum similarity with one of the criteria underpinning the categories defined by Foundation Law (detention, deportation, or forced labor). The opening clause also required the consideration of certain financial limitations, which meant that partner organizations would only include the opening clause if they had sufficient money in the funds allocated to them. Thus, the option to define criteria for additional categories under the opening

---

1   See Annex 1, Section 9 (8) of the Foundation Law.

clause meant that cases not involving any kind of forced labor could also be covered by this provision if another type of persecution, deportation, or detention existed.

In practice, a broad interpretation of similarity with the legally defined criteria was applied. For instance, with regard to persons who went into hiding, it was accepted that this implied detention-like living conditions. Other examples were children who were deported with their parents but did not perform forced labor, persons who were detained under appalling conditions without being forced to work, or persons who were forced from their homes to another area within the same country.

An advantage of the opening clause was the flexibility it allowed the partner organizations to address particular situations that had not been specifically addressed during the negotiations. Partner organizations could thereby react to or avoid pressure from the public or victims organizations and cover situations which did not fall under any of the other categories but which were important for their context. This, in turn, improved the acceptance of the program in the public discourse in the respective country.

Categories and amounts disbursed by the Foundation for Polish-German Reconciliation (FPNP)			
	Total amount in €	1. installment € (75 %)	2. installment € (25 %)
Legal categories*			
Category A Prisoners in concentration camps and ghettos	7,669.38	5,752.03	1,917.34
Subcategory A Prisoners in "Polish camps" in Silesia, in penal camps and ZALJ, in AELs and penitentiaries/prisons (other place of confinement)	7,269.37	5,452.03	1,817.34
Subcategory A Prisoners of the camp Lebrechtsdorf (including satellite camps in Thorn and Smukula – other place of confinement)	4,218.16	3,163.62	1,054.54
Category B Deported forced laborers in the commercial and public sector	2,249.68	1,687.26	562.42

* Inside the legal categories and the opening clause the categories are ordered hierarchically by amounts.

Categories and amounts disbursed by the Foundation for Polish-German Reconciliation (FPNP)			
	Total amount in €	1. installment € (75 %)	2. installment € (25 %)
Opening Clause			
■ Children up to the age of 16, who were detained in a transit camp for at least 180 days ■ Prisoners from prisons and detention centers ■ Persons who were persecuted on racial grounds (outside ghettos, concentration camps and "other place of confinement")	2,556.46	1,917.34	639.11
Forced laborers who lived outside the administrative borders of Poland that were implemented for the period of occupation and who were dislocated and had to work in an industrial or another commercial enterprise or in the public sector	2,249.68	1,687.26	562.42
Deported and dislocated forced laborers who worked in the agricultural, forestry and service sector or in private households	1,124.84	843.63	281.21
Children up to the age of 12, who were deported or dislocated with their parents or who were born while subjected to forced labor	1,124.84	843.63	281.21
Children up to the age of 16 forced to work in the heavy and armament industry at their place of residence	1,022.58	766.94	255.65
Children up to the age of 16 who were detained in a transit camp for at least 180 days	562.43	421.82	140.61

Table 1: Categories and amounts disbursed by the Foundation for Polish-German Reconciliation (FPNP) as an example of how partner organizations were able to include different groups of victims according to the context. Note: Chapter 3 explains more in detail the two-installments system.

The different partner organizations could set different priorities when including particular victim groups in the compensation program. For example, in Ukraine and in Poland, the inclusion of forced labor in agriculture was crucial. The JCC, which was responsible for Jewish victims worldwide, on the other hand, chose to forgo the possibility of the opening clause in order to maximize benefits for those who performed forced labor in labor camps. The significance of the opening clause is illustrated by the fact that almost half of the 1.66 million beneficiaries received compensation through the opening clause, constituting almost 22 percent of the financial resources of the compensation fund.

However, there were also practical consequences of the opening clause which were not intended. In the forced labor compensation program, delegating the decisions on the opening clause to partner organizations had the consequence that, to a significant degree, eligibility depended on the geographical responsibility for an applicant. What is more, whether a partner organization was able to use an opening clause depended not only on its political will but also on the level of its funding. As explained in Chapter 3, each partner organization received a fixed amount for implementing the program, which was based on estimates of the numbers of beneficiaries. Depending on how accurate those estimates were, some partner organizations had funds available to incorporate extra eligibility categories, whereas others did not. In practice, this meant that claimants who had suffered the same fate, but were living in different countries — and therefore under the responsibility of different partner organizations — received different compensation amounts, or in some cases no compensation at all. Also, the opening clause posed serious challenges for outreach activities: not having all the criteria for eligibility clearly defined at the start of the program risked turning away potential beneficiaries too early, or on the other hand raised expectations which were not met in the implementation of the program.

EXCLUSIONS FROM ELIGIBILITY

Eligibility criteria may also entail provisions that exclude certain groups of people. Even though the German compensation program focused on victims of forced labor, there were certain individuals who fit this criterion but were nevertheless excluded from compensation. For example, one principle of the German program was that prisoners of war were not eligible for payment: "Eligibility cannot be based on prisoner-of-war status," as stated in the Foundation Law (Section 11 (3)). However, the Foundation Law included those who were prisoners of war at some point, but were subsequently either forced to work *as civilians* or who were persecuted on racial grounds. This situation applied to many Polish prisoners of war who were detained at the beginning of the war and then "released" into a civilian status and forced to work under that status.[2]

2   As mentioned in Chapter 1, this was an issue of much debate during the negotiations and it was finally excluded from this program for political considerations. It was feared that if prisoners of war were made eligible for the compensation program, German prisoners of war could ask for compensations as well. In the end, the debate on this issue continued until in 2015, fifteen years after the Foundation Law, a compensation program was set up by Germany for both foreign and German prisoners of war forced laborers.

CHALLENGES IN THE APPLICATION OF THE ELIGIBILITY CRITERIA

Even though the eligibility criteria seemed very straightforward at the beginning of the compensation program, challenges in their interpretation and application arose in the course of program implementation.

First, when establishing eligibility criteria, it is important to review the historical context thoroughly. For example, the wording of the Foundation Law defined "deportation to the territory of the German Reich in its borders of 1937 or to territories occupied by the German Reich" as a criterion for eligibility. Problems arose concerning the application of the criterion in cases where applicants had been deported not to an area within the German Reich or its occupied territories but to the territory of a State *allied* to the German Reich, for instance Romania or Slovakia. A similar question in this context was how to address situations where persons were deported from their home area not to another country but another area within their home country. Due to the unequivocal phrasing of the Foundation Law, individuals with this fate were not eligible for compensation.

Second, the specific nature of the crime should be adequately reflected in the eligibility criteria. "Harsh living conditions" was another significant criterion in those cases under the second category (category B) where workers were not detained. With respect to the interpretation of this term, it is important to note that the Foundation Law is underpinned by the purpose to deliver a gesture of late justice in particular to victims in Central and Eastern Europe after they had been cut off from any compensation scheme for several decades, due to political reasons. To this end, according to the explanatory reports in the legislative process, the term "harsh living conditions" was aimed at reflecting the systematic discrimination of people of Slavic origin.[3]

Consequently, the criteria were interpreted as not covering forced laborers of "non-Slavic origin" which many saw as unfair. As a result of this decision, Western Europeans an other persons considered to be "non-Slavic" under the ideology of the Third Reich were found not to be eligible under the program for lack of deportation and discriminating living conditions. This was applied in an undifferentiated manner irrespective of harsh treatment in practice and led to problematic exclusions. For example, the particularly degrading conditions of Greek forced laborers were not covered in the program, and advocates for these groups continue to date to ask for compensation. By contrast, the Austrian Reconciliation Fund applied a comparably low threshold for including forced laborers originating from Western Europe in their compensation scheme. For example, bombing raids also had affected a lot of Western European workers in Germany and were accepted as a sufficient example of harsh living conditions in the Austrian program.

---

3   See explanations on Section 11 (1) of the draft of the Foundation Law, Register of the German Parliament, BT-Drs 14/3206, p. 15, http://dipbt.bundestag.de/doc/btd/14/032/1403206.pdf (accessed 30 March 2017).

Third, eligibility criteria itself need to be applied consistently and fairly throughout the implementation period. The example of the so-called Italian Military Internees (IMIs) illustrates that inconsistent interpretation of eligibility criteria may not only have led to frustration of claimants but also caused more work and costs for the compensation program itself. Large numbers of Italian soldiers were detained and forced to work by German troops after Italy agreed on concluding a cease-fire agreement with the Allied Forces in 1943. At the time they were denied prisoner of war status even though it was clear that they were prisoners of war under applicable international law. Yet, even though these IMIs were forced to work, had a civilian status and were exposed to very harsh conditions, they were not recognized as eligible in the compensation program with the reason that they were prisoners of war. Moreover, this decision was taken after some 100,000 compensation claims of all IMIs were already registered under the forced labor compensation program. This meant that the already filed applications had to be rejected with the consequence that many members of the group were deeply frustrated and many of them filed appeals against these rejection decisions. The matter was brought before the courts in Italy as well as before the International Court of Justice (see Chapter 10). Such experiences show that it should be clear from the outset of a program, not only who is responsible for determining and interpreting eligibility, but also that such decisions are taken in a transparent, predictable, and fair way.

EVIDENCE

During the process of designing eligibility criteria, it is quite important to take into account what evidence is available to support the claims. It would be meaningless to establish elaborate eligibility criteria when they are difficult to prove or at least to be made credible. As experience of other programs shows, the standard of proof has an important impact on the balance between individual justice and expediency of the process: strict evidentiary standards will increase accuracy whereas more relaxed standards will increase expediency. One example of how availability of evidence, or lack thereof, influenced eligibility criteria in the forced labor compensation program was that no distinction was made between different *lengths* of the suffering by victims of forced labor. In none of the categories was thus a differentiation made between, for instance, a person who was subjected to forced labor for years and a person only detained for a few months. This decision also was made in anticipation of a lack of evidence in this respect.

Generally, the German forced labor compensation program provided for a *relaxed standard of proof* because it was conscious of the fact that much time had elapsed since the historical events and that the type of injustices which the program addressed were difficult to prove. Moreover, the long time since the events also implied that the survivors had a very advanced age. Against this background, it was a matter of fairness not to rely on documentary evidence or public records only and that applicants were allowed to support eligibility with a variety of evidentiary means, including credible statements. Chapter 6 describes in detail which evidence was accepted in the program and how it was evaluated.

ELIGIBILITY IN CASE OF DEATH OF VICTIMS OF FORCED LABOR

In every compensation program, provision needs to be made for the case that a claimant passes away during the process. Also, it should be decided early on, if and how descendants of victims are eligible for compensation. In the case of the German program, many of those subjected to forced labor had already passed away before the start of the program. Also, as the majority of the survivors of forced labor were very old, it was likely that many would not be alive when the payments would be made.

The compensation program took a pragmatic stance, in this respect, by focusing in principle on compensating individuals who were still alive at a certain date. This meant that, generally, descendants and family members of former forced laborers were not eligible for compensation. However, during the negotiations the German delegation announced on 16 February 1999, the date of the establishment of the Foundation Initiative of the German Industry, that all persons who were alive on that day would be eligible for compensation. On a practical level, this meant that in all cases where victims of forced labor passed away after this "inclusion date," certain close relatives were eligible to apply for compensation. Notwithstanding a more fundamental discussion if such a strategy is fair to the families of already deceased victims of forced labor, this was a sensible decision at a time when it was not clear how long it would take to finalize the negotiations.[4]

What the program still had to do was to define which legal successors would be eligible in case of death of a victim. The Foundation Law stated that only certain close relatives or heirs under a will were so eligible:

> In a case where the eligible person has died after February 15, 1999, (...) the surviving spouse and children shall be entitled to equal shares of the award. If the eligible person left neither a spouse nor children, awards may be applied for in equal shares by the grandchildren, or if there are no grandchildren living, by the siblings. If no application is filed by these persons, the heirs named in a will are entitled to apply. (Section 13 (1))

With this, the Foundation Law established a so-called "self-contained regime" with its own definition of "legal successors" which could, and in a number of cases did, differ from national inheritance laws. This system was not uncontested since it meant disappointing persons who were heirs according to their respective national inheritance law including those who were designated as a beneficiary in the will of the deceased person. However, given the large number of beneficiaries, the system avoided the challenge of having to establish first, which

---

4   It was also a solution lobbied for by the victims' associations. If descendants were made eligible for compensation payments, the amount of individual compensation payments would have been drastically reduced.

national inheritance law applied, and then who was an heir under such national inheritance law. It would have been very difficult, time consuming, and costly for the partner organizations to identify and then apply different national inheritance laws, particularly for those partner organizations that covered a large number of countries, like the IOM and JCC.

The above provision, together with the "inclusion date," made sure that eligibility would not cease in case of the death of a potential beneficiary. It also prevented any impression that, by delaying the negotiation process, the negotiators had tried to "save money." However, some partner organizations decided to maximize the sums to be paid to victims still alive by establishing sub-categories for legal successors with reduced compensation amounts. This benefitted the elderly survivors, but also gave rise to criticism by the affected heirs.

SUMMARY

Eligibility criteria for the German compensation program had to keep in mind the need for expedient procedures. Therefore, broad categories were established rather than detailed criteria that would have allowed for multiple differentiations of fates. Moreover, while some of the groups to be covered — and the criteria for their definition — were agreed on rather easily, in the international negotiations, regional expectations sometimes varied as to which additional groups were supposed to be covered under a program addressing the injustice of forced labor. Rather than addressing all these by the definition of detailed legal criteria, an opening clause was adopted allowing for some regional flexibility. The need for expediency of the process also paved the way for a relaxed standard of proof. Finally, the decision to focus on those victims still alive allowed for maximizing the individual sums while keeping with the overall ceiling amount. And lastly, by defining for the program itself who would be the legal successors in case of death of a claimant, the intricacies of adhering to numerous inheritance law systems in a worldwide compensation program were avoided.

CHALLENGES AND LESSONS LEARNED

- Many aspects of a large scale compensation program, such as criteria for eligibility, standards of proof, deadlines for applications need to be carefully chosen in order to strike a fair balance between addressing individual injustice and achieving overall fairness for the claims program as a whole.

- The definition of eligibility criteria impacts on the expediency of the process and, thereby, on the acceptance of a program. Clear definition of eligibility criteria is important for expectation management and for providing a fair chance to submit a claim.

- A certain flexibility in the eligibility criteria can be helpful, particularly in cases where the historical situation is complex and regional expectations may not be foreseeable comprehensively at the time of the establishment of the program. However, such approaches should be allowed for only with great caution as they bear the potential of unequal treatment and dissatisfaction by partner organizations or beneficiaries. Moreover, such flexibilities complicate outreach.

- The possibility of establishing an opening clause may have contributed to preserving a positive image of the program in the countries which had been affected most severely.

- Since not every issue is foreseeable at the outset of a program, it will be helpful to have a monitoring body which has the authority to decide questions that arise only during the implementation phase.

- In the case of death of a potential beneficiary, eligibility criteria should be clear from the outset of a program. Particularly in the case of transnational programs, it will be useful to adopt a "self-contained regime" that avoids the application of national inheritance laws, thereby preventing unnecessary delay and costs.

SUSANNE SEHLBACH

CHAPTER 3:
FUNDING OF THE PROGRAM

This chapter contains:

— A fixed fund vs. continuous payments
— Fundraising for the compensation program
— Allocating funds for partner organizations
— Administrative costs
— Compensation payments in two installments
— Financial management

INTRODUCTION: EVEN A LOT WAS NOT ENOUGH

Securing sufficient funding is often the biggest challenge when establishing a reparations program. The type of funding of such a program, for instance by a one-time fixed sum or continuous payments, shapes the entire claims processing and payment process. This is why it is important to gauge different funding possibilities to find solutions that best address the specific context and purpose of a reparations program.

One of the main challenges of the forced labor compensation program was that, while a fixed overall amount for the program had been agreed during the international negotiations phase, the exact number of beneficiaries was not known. In addition, the fact that the fixed sum had to be split up among different partner organizations made the compensation program highly complex. Among other measures, one way to ensure that all eligible persons would receive compensation was that the payments were issued in two installments. This way, it was assumed, the exact number of beneficiaries would be known after the first installment and the remaining amounts could be calculated to meet the overall funding amount. This guaranteed that the funding allocated overall and for each partner organization was not exceeded but it meant that the final amount granted to an eligible applicant in a certain category was not fixed from the outset.

This chapter describes how the funds for this program were raised and distributed and how the administrative costs were managed. It explains how the compensation payments were issued in two installments as well as the many consequences of this decision. The chapter also discusses other aspects relevant to funding, such as dealing with different currencies and financial management.

A FIXED FUND VS. CONTINUOUS PAYMENTS

A reparations program can be financed by regular (e.g. yearly) contributions from a government or donors, or by establishing a one-time fixed fund. It is also possible to mix these options by agreeing to provide additional funds if necessary. In the forced labor compensation program, the decision on funding depended primarily on the interests of the stakeholders involved, particularly with a view to the overall amount that had to be raised in order to grant appropriate individual compensation amounts. Negotiators who represented the victims' side, such as victims' associations, argued that the sum had to be based on the number of potential beneficiaries and the severity of the suffering ("bottom up"). The German negotiating side — i.e. those who had to provide the funds — centered this decision on the question of how much money they would be able to raise in the first place ("top down").

In this case, it was decided early on that the compensations would be paid out of a fixed fund. The representatives of the German companies argued from the beginning that they would only be able to raise a fixed sum in a one-time effort. An ongoing responsibility by German companies in supplying funds to the program would not have been realistic.[1] At the same time, the negotiators felt that a fixed fund was necessary to terminate the class action lawsuits in the US against German companies. Finally, a fixed fund was a means to negotiate for a *one-time solution*, which was in the interest of all negotiators.

The commitment to a fixed fund, which would have to be collected only once, thus became the main determinant of the design of the program. At first sight, it was a real disadvantage that there was no possibility to correct the overall compensation amount according to the needs during the program. Yet, there were also clear advantages of this solution. The program would be independent from political will: Starting from the moment that the required amount was collected, the donors would no longer be interested in holding back funds. From the beginning of the program, protracted re-negotiations were excluded and all stakeholders concentrated on the common goal: to pay out compensation to the beneficiaries as fast as possible. Last but not least, a fixed fund would generate interest, which, in this case, would amount to considerable sums.

FUNDRAISING MORE THAN 5 BILLION EUROS

It was agreed during the negotiations that the German State and German companies would each pay an equal share of the agreed sum of approximately 5.2 billion Euros. While the State was able to provide its share immediately from the federal government budget, raising the money from German companies proved to be much more difficult.

The "Foundation Initiative of German Industry" represented German companies during the negotiations and was now tasked to fundraise roughly 2.6 billion Euros from many different companies with rather heterogeneous interests. The initiative itself was established by a group of 17 founding companies, mainly large manufacturers, banks, and insurance companies, which pledged that they would guarantee for any open balance of the companies' share.[2]

The Foundation Initiative organized a widespread fundraising campaign. The main message of the campaign was that all contributions were voluntary and that the Initiative would not make public which amount was contributed to the fund by a specific company. Rather, this concerted effort would serve the reputation of German companies generally, irrespective of the involvement of contributors to injustices during the National Socialist era. Indeed, after the final amount was known, a large number of companies contributed to the fund.

---

1   This option is more realistic for a fully state-funded program, as, for example, *the Federal Foundation for the Examination of the Communist Dictatorship in Eastern Germany,* which was set up by Germany in 1998 and is largely based upon an annual budget.
2   For more information on the Foundation Initiative of the German Industry and the companies it represented see: www.wollheim-memorial.de/en/die_stiftungsinitiative_der_deutschen_wirtschaft _1999 (accessed 12 April 2017).

However, it was soon clear that more mobilization was needed. The actual contributions remained very low and generating funding was also much slower than anticipated. To this end, a liaison office was established, with support by leading industry associations. Some 200.000 companies were asked to contribute in newspaper adverts, mailings, and individual correspondence. Additional pressure came from so-called "negative lists" in the media, which listed companies who had used forced laborers during the time of National Socialism but had not yet contributed to the compensation fund. Accompanying these lists were calls to the ethical conscience of the companies and even threats of boycott. Eventually, the founding companies issued a guarantee that they would provide any missing funds to the overall fund.

Still, the expectations of the founding companies were not fulfilled. The 17 founding companies contributed about 60 percent of the ca. 2.6 billion Euros, with the result that 94 percent of the overall amount was provided by four percent of the contributing companies.

ALLOCATING FUNDS TO PARTNER ORGANIZATIONS

Not only was the overall amount for the compensation program decided during the negotiations phase, but also the fixed allocation for each partner organization. All but one of what later became the partner organizations already had stakeholders in place for the negotiation process. Five countries with so-called reconciliation foundations, later responsible for administering compensation payments in Central and Eastern European countries, and the JCC, later responsible for Jewish claimants outside these countries, took part in the negotiations. Only the IOM was appointed to administer payments for non-Jewish claimants outside of Central and Eastern Europe after the overall sum was divided into sub-funds.

Different from the negotiations about the overall amount, conflicts during the division of that sum arose not between 'donor' and 'receiving' sides, but between the representatives of different countries and victims associations on behalf of potential beneficiaries. It can be assumed that the respective size of the seven fixed funds for the compensation of victims of forced labor also resulted from the negotiation skills and assertiveness of the various stakeholders.

Consequences of fixed funding for partner organizations

Similar to the case of the overall fixed amount, there were many implications from fixing the funds available for each partner organization so early in the process. On the positive side, each of the partner organizations could work according to their own capabilities and speed, as the funds available were secure and independent from those of other organizations. For example, some of the partner organizations could draw on existing knowledge about the potential beneficiaries. With a fixed sum they were able to quickly develop a decision practice according to their knowledge and available evidence without impacting the work of the other partner organizations. The independent funds also allowed partner organizations to consider particular victim groups in the framework of the 'opening clause' (see Chapter 2).

A more negative consequence of fixed funds was that some of the estimates, on which the partner organization funds were based, turned out to be inaccurate. While certain replenishing mechanisms were devised in the case of underfunding of a particular partner organization for claims in categories A and B, payments under the opening clause depended entirely on funds available within the respective partner organization. This had the consequence that some groups of beneficiaries were not treated equally throughout the program, due to the different funding situation of the partner organizations.

Partner organization	Initial fund (in million Euros)	Final fund (in million Euros)	Number of recipients
Belarus	355	355	129,485
Czech Republic	216	217	75,769
IOM	276	431	88,784
JCC	1,059	1,197	158,097
Poland	926	1,011	483,287
Russia	427	444	252,543
Ukraine	881	883	471,167
All partner organizations	4,141	4,535	1,659,132

Table 2: Table showing the initial and final allocated funds for each partner organization, as well as the number of beneficiaries. Note: All Euro amounts are rounded. The detailed table can be found in the final report on the compensation program, submitted to the German Parliament (http://dipbt.bundestag.de/doc/btd/16/099/1609963.pdf; accessed 15 May 2017), pg. 5.

Replenishing fixed funds of partner organizations

Early in the process it became clear that the fixed funds for some of the partner organizations were not sufficient, as they received more applications from eligible persons than anticipated. The missing sums were to be provided by the EVZ Foundation from interest that accumulated over time from the unused part of the overall fund, as well as from donations given to the

EVZ Foundation after its establishment.[3] Yet, the Foundation Law did not specify how these additional funds should be distributed. Options would have been to do this in proportion to each partner organization's agreed fixed fund or according to the respective interest accrued. Foreseeing the need of a regulation of this issue, however, a provision was included in the Foundation Law that the Board of Trustees was responsible for distributing any extra funds to partner organizations, and that these funds should as a priority be used to restock missing funds for compensation of category A and B claims. This allowed the interest accrued and further donations received by the Foundation to become a means to make up for insufficient funding of the partner organizations.

In practice, a formula was developed that linked the allocation of additional monies to a calculation of missing funds consistent for each partner organization. Once the exact number of claims in categories A and B for all partner organizations was known, it became clear that the funds of the JCC, the IOM, as well as the Russian partner organization needed restocking (see Table 2). However, in the end, the interest did not cover the restocking completely and the partner organizations dealt with this through differentiation in the amounts paid in the various sub-categories.

ADMINISTRATIVE COSTS

Every reparations program has to allow for a certain portion of the money to be used as administrative costs. The administrative costs of the EVZ Foundation itself were allotted from the overall compensation fund. The administrative costs of each partner organization, however, had to be covered from the fixed fund allocated to the respective organization. One consequence of this was that the partner organizations had a lot of pressure to keep administrative costs low.

Generally, the EVZ Foundation and all partner organizations had to adhere to three main principles: expenditures had to be judged by their necessity, efficiency, and that they were as economic as possible. Given that higher administrative costs had a direct impact on the amount available for the compensation payments to the beneficiaries, the Foundation Law and partnership agreements emphasized the responsibility to use the means that were set aside for administrative costs in the most economical way. As detailed in Chapter 8, auditors commissioned by the EVZ Foundation regularly reviewed the administrative expenditures of partner organizations.

---

3   The EVZ Foundation centrally managed the large overall fund and only transferred the amounts necessary for the payment of so-called "tranches" (definite lists of beneficiaries) after the partner organizations had submitted them for the EVZ Foundation's approval. That way interest could accumulate and rather significant additional funds became available with time.

The partner organizations required different levels of administrative costs. This was due to several reasons. Some partner organizations had more knowledge about the total number of claims to be expected. Also, the review and evidentiary situation was more complex for some partner organizations than for others. For example, in the case of IOM, it was uncertain, for a considerable time, how many claims would be filed and how resource-intensive the processing and review of the claims would be. There were also large differences in staff and non-staff costs between the various countries where the partner organizations operated. This meant that some partner organizations had clear advantages due to external factors that made the implementation less costly.

Each partner organization's calculation of administrative costs was reviewed together with the EVZ Foundation and the final percentage was specified either in the formal partnership agreement or in other frameworks. In most cases these costs were lower than three percent of the partner organizations' fixed funds.

COMPENSATION PAYMENTS IN TWO INSTALLMENTS

Even though the overall fund had been divided among the partner organizations, the problem of calculating the specific compensation amounts remained a task yet to be determined. How could a fixed amount be divided into an unknown number of beneficiaries and into different categories of claims? One option would have been to wait for all claims to be processed and decided before starting to pay out any compensation. The other extreme would have been to simply start paying out compensation without knowing whether the funds would be sufficient to pay the same amount to all eligible beneficiaries in a category. During the negotiations, there was wide agreement that the compensation payments should start as quickly as possible so that as many beneficiaries as possible would benefit from the compensation program, as they were already very old. The solution adopted was to make the compensation payments in *two installments*, which was already foreseen in the Foundation Law.

The beneficiaries thus received a first installment as an advance payment. The Foundation Law contained the provision that the advance payment should be at least 50 per cent for category A and at least 35 per cent for the other categories. A partner organization also had the possibility to increase the amount of the first installment with the approval of the Board of Trustees, if they could demonstrate that the allocated funds would not be exceeded. With time, all of the partner organizations used this possibility to different extents.

The second installment would be paid out only after all claims were processed, giving partner organizations the possibility to calculate the entire amount needed. With the exception of category A, which was always the maximum compensation amount, the amount of the second installment then depended on the overall number of eligible claimants in each category as well as on the amount available for the respective partner organization.

However, the two installment system had many consequences that went beyond merely calculating and paying out the compensation amount in two installments. While the negotiators had agreed on this system as the most appropriate way to administer the compensation, it made the implementation extremely complex. In the following, some of these challenges are described in more detail.

Cut-off dates

The two installment system required the setting of a cut-off date for the filing of claims, as this was the only possibility to know in due time the exact number of eligible claimants (as the program was not open-ended). Therefore, it was agreed that only the claims that were received within a certain time frame were eligible to benefit from the program. Initially, the cut-off date was set for April 2001, which was eight months after the enactment of the Foundation Law. Soon it became clear that this date was too early and it was extended to 31 December 2001.[4]

In addition to the cut-off date for filing claims, more cut-off dates were needed to implement the two installment system. As described in Chapter 2, the Foundation Law had clear provisions for the situation when claimants passed away after 15 February 1999 and legal successors became eligible for the payments. In practice however, to secure eligibility claimants only had to file a claim before the cut-off date. In case of death of the claimant, legal successors could have waited years to claim the compensation payments. To account for the exact number of beneficiaries within a reasonable time, a cut-off date was thus also established for legal successors to make themselves known, namely within six months of the death of the initial claimant. This led to many misunderstandings since some legal successors were not even aware that their family members had filed a claim for compensation under the program.

Procedural challenges

While the cut-off dates were the legal requirements for the implementation of the two installment system, a number of questions arose as to how to carry out the transition to the second installment at the practical level. The Foundation Law regulated only a few parameters: the second installment could begin immediately after all claims had been processed; to pay out the second installment earlier, the partner organizations were also allowed to reserve up to 5 percent of their funds for open appeals. Thus, the basic assumption of the Law was that, after the first installment all claims would have been decided upon (e.g. in which category a claimant would fall), and that the remaining amounts needed could therefore be precisely calculated.

---

4   In fact, the payout of the first installment tranches in June 2001 proved to be a major factor for the outreach of the program, as described in Chapter 5.

In reality, however, the transition to the second installment became very complicated because there were unanticipated developments. For example, in some cases potential beneficiaries did not respond to inquiries after sending their initial application. The Foundation Law did simply not anticipate this, but since the claimants fulfilled the basic eligibility criteria, their cases remained open. Contacting each of these claimants absorbed a lot of time and resources of the partner organizations. Eventually, an overall completion date had to be imposed for finalizing all payments (31 December 2006).

Also, more procedures had to be completed before calculating and paying out the second installment. First, it was necessary to wait for the outcome of many appeals. As described in Chapter 6, the claims process entailed the possibility to file an appeal in cases where the claim was rejected or where claimants were not satisfied with the amount of the compensation. This meant that the final compensation amount in these cases could still go up as a result of the appeal decision. The Foundation Law foresaw that partner organizations could establish a reserve of up to five percent for open appeals, but it did not prescribe specifically for which cases this reserve was to be set up, and neither how much this should entail per open appeal. In the end, the partner organizations came up with a very complex calculation that took into account the success rate and average additional amount granted in appeals that were already dealt with.

Second, the emergence of new historically relevant information slowed down the claims processing, as some of this information had an effect in which category a certain claim would fall. This was particularly the case with so-called 'other places of confinement,' which were internment camps comparable to concentration camps in which the detainees were forced to work. Over the course of the program, about 3,900 additional places of confinement were discovered and the verification of this information turned out to be more complex than anticipated.

Third, partner organizations had some challenges with identifying legal successors, which also impacted the transition to the second installment. In some cases, legal successors had to be found, which delayed the payments. For many reasons, this was not easy: partner organizations could not know if the claimant was still alive and simply sent out the notification for the second installment. If this notification was then received by legal successors who did not contact the partner organization within six months of the death of the initial claimant, they were no longer eligible to receive the payment, which understandably led to much frustration. Such cases were also complicated for partner organizations that had set a lower compensation amount for legal successors (by classifying them as a sub-category), as the amount had to be recalculated.

Leftover funds

Even with the rather complex calculations and the two installment system, the forced labor compensation program still produced *leftover funds*. Here, the goal was to keep these leftover funds as small as possible, and to find ways to still make them available to the beneficiaries. Already in the Foundation Law it was stated that the Board of Trustees should decide how these leftover funds should be spent, which set up a number of humanitarian programs (see Chapter 11).

To conclude, the system of two installments was meant as a solution to the initial problem of the fixed amount of money available for an unknown amount of beneficiaries. The two installments allowed the partner organizations and the EVZ Foundation to calculate as precisely as possible the exact amount needed for compensations without overstretching the overall fund. Also, the approach allowed payments to start rather quickly and at a point in time where the exact number of beneficiaries was not yet known. Therefore, all claims by eligible persons received compensations. Yet, in hindsight, this solution was extremely complex and laborious, and many practical consequences only emerged during the implementation of the program.

Finally, the two installments also impacted on the acceptance of the compensation program. Both the EVZ Foundation and its partner organizations received negative feedback from beneficiaries particularly about the two installment system, which was one of the main causes for misunderstanding and frustration. While the system was practically unavoidable from the program's point of view, from the perspective of the beneficiaries it was difficult to understand why the compensation could not be paid out at once, especially given the old age of the claimants. In addition, the partner organizations and the EVZ Foundation received feedback criticizing the long wait between the two installments.

FINANCIAL MANAGEMENT

Different currencies

Depending on the context, reparations programs may also have to deal with different currencies. This was the case for the forced labor compensation program, which was administered in Germany, but payments were to be made in many countries through partner organizations, of which some operated on a national and some on an international level. At the outset of such a program, two considerations are therefore particularly important in this respect: (1) will the issue of different currencies arise (i.e. when funds are in one currency and payments are in another); and if so, (2) who will bear the risk of currency fluctuation? In the case of the

German program, these issues were relevant for the partner organizations that received funds from the EVZ Foundation in one currency and paid out compensations in another currency, as well as for the calculation of the actual compensation amounts to be paid out in different currencies to beneficiaries. Therefore, it had to be decided that either the EVZ Foundation or the partner organizations themselves would have to carry out a currency conversion. Where necessary, these provisions were included in the partnership agreements.

Still, the issue of currency conversion led to a major misunderstanding during the compensation program, which demonstrated that the organizations involved did not take into account all practical aspects of currency conversion, as well as the issue of clear communication. In June 2001, the EVZ Foundation converted the entire fixed fund for the Polish partner organization from Deutsche Mark into Polish Złoty with the intention to avoid negative effects of rising exchange rates for a stronger Złoty. In reality, however, the exchange rates for the Złoty went down significantly in the following months and it would have been possible to generate higher sums if the conversion had taken place later on and/or separately for each tranche. The overall loss was estimated at about ten percent — which meant that less money would have been available for the Polish partner organization.

This incident led not only to accusations between the Polish partner organization FPNP and the EVZ Foundation. Given the historical context of this compensation program, this was by no means a mere technical mishap, but became a palpable tension at the political level as well. The case was for some time the subject of external review. The intensive consultations that followed this incident took longer than six months, during which both sides tried to mend the damage. Eventually, the issue was closed with an agreement on 7 January 2002, which detailed that additional amounts would be made available for the Polish partner organization. These would be taken from interest rates accrued from both organizations, which prevented any losses for the beneficiaries. The incident highlights not only the necessity of clear regulations of financial aspects but also the importance of good communication and well-coordinated processes.

Managing investments

Particularly in the case of such a large compensation program, funds not yet needed for compensation should be used for investments — during various stages of the program — so that they generate as much interest as possible. At the beginning of a program it should therefore be estimated how much interest will likely accrue, what it should be used for, and where relevant, how it should be distributed. These questions were very relevant in the case of the forced labor program as the overall sum was made available right at the start of the program and thus could generate a rather significant amount of interest that was then available to the program in addition to the original sum.

In addition, the question here was *where* interest should accrue — under the auspices of the EVZ Foundation or with each partner organization? It was decided that the EVZ Foundation would manage the fund centrally, as this would eventually benefit all partner organizations and the risks would be lower. To maximize the interest on the original fund, as well as to minimize risks due to the volatility of Eastern European banks, it was decided that partner organizations would receive the overall amount allocated to them in several stages, as so-called 'tranches.' After the EVZ Foundation approved a list with beneficiaries that a partner organization submitted for payment, it calculated the necessary amount and transferred the required funds to the partner organization. The partner organizations were then to transfer the payments to the beneficiaries as fast as possible so that no interest would accrue in the banks effecting the payments. The EVZ Foundation, as described in Chapter 8, controlled this process.

To adequately manage the fund, the EVZ Foundation had its own financial management department. The main priorities of the financial strategy were security and liquidity. To avoid currency risks, the fund was managed first in Deutsche Mark and later Euros. The portfolio consisted of different products, such as call money, time deposits, and also short-term bonded loans. Banks that satisfied the criteria of deposit guarantee were regularly asked for relevant offers. Due to the large overall amount and the good situation in the markets in the early twenty-first century, the EVZ Foundation was able to generate interest in the amount of approximately 337 million Euros.[5] From this sum (together with additional donations), about 318 million Euros could be used for compensation payments. The rest was then used for humanitarian projects.[6] At no point during the program did financial management decisions delay the payment of compensation.

SUMMARY

The design and implementation of the forced labor compensation program cannot be separated from the ways it was financed. In fact, the financial model influenced the design of the program significantly. The system of two installments seemed to offer a simple way to distribute a given amount of money to an unknown number of beneficiaries. However, the many difficulties that this procedure entailed only emerged during the implementation of the program. One of the particular difficulties turned out to be establishing whether the requirements were met for paying out the second installment. This chapter further highlighted a range of aspects related to financing that need close consideration when setting up similar programs, such as administrative costs, currency issues, and financial management.

---

5   See Michael Jansen, Günter Saathoff and Kai Hennig, "Final Report on the Compensation Programs Carried Out by the 'Remembrance, Responsibility and Future Foundation'," in *"A Mutual Responsibility and a Moral Obligation": The Final Report on Germany's Compensation Programs for Forced Labor and Other Personal Injuries,* eds. Michael Jansen and Günter Saathoff (New York: Palgrave Macmillan, 2009), 141.

6   See Chapter 11.

CHALLENGES AND LESSONS LEARNED

- The advantage of having a fixed fund is that it is predictable, no further fundraising is necessary, and once the funds have been made available, the program would be independent from political will.

- Separate fixed funds for different partner organizations can allow them to operate independently from another. However, without a mechanism to even out imbalances of the funding between different partner organizations, one risks inequalities in the evaluation of claims and subsequent compensation payments.

- The two installment system is a possibility to begin with the compensation payments before knowing the exact number of beneficiaries.

- Paying out compensation in two installments has several advantages: the first installment can be paid out rather quickly, while still calculating the overall amount. This procedure prevents large leftover sums and maximizes the amount used for individual compensation.

- A disadvantage of the two installment system is that it can make procedures very complicated and cause more work. Also, when the time span between the first and second installment becomes too long, contact to claimants can be lost. Because of the old age of the claimants in this program, there was also the danger of claimants passing away in the meantime.

- Another serious disadvantage of such a system is that eligible applicants may have difficulties in accepting payments in two installments and may be disappointed in case the second installment turns out to be smaller than expected.

- Fixed cut-off dates for claims and deadlines for paying out compensations facilitate the overall claims process, but can have an impact on the acceptance of the process if not communicated well.

- Financial management should focus on liquidity and security as well as produce new funds where possible.

- Operating in different currencies can have advantages and disadvantages. This should be considered early on.

SUSANNE SEHLBACH

CHAPTER 4:
ORGANIZATIONAL STRUCTURE

This chapter contains:

— The "foundation model": a public-law foundation for compensation payments
— The EVZ Foundation as the central coordinator of the program
— The responsibilities and structure of the partner organizations
— Coordination between the EVZ Foundation and partner organizations

INTRODUCTION: BUILDING THE HOUSE

Generally, the organizational structure of reparations programs must cover the following functions:

- Policy-making, i.e. the overall decision making process and oversight
- Claims processing
- Administration

Which organizational type is most suitable to administer a reparations program? Which organizational organ should cover which functions? What are the relations between the different departments and responsible managers, and how should they operate in practice? These and others are questions guiding the establishment of any organization tasked with the implementation of a reparations program.

All of these aspects were also considered when setting up the forced labor compensation program, but the particular situation of having the program negotiated in an international arena, as well as the sheer scope of it, led to many particularities. Already during the negotiations, it was decided there should be one overarching body — the EVZ Foundation — that should be responsible for shaping and overseeing the program's implementation, as well as for the overall coordination of the partner organizations and for the administrative and financial management. The Foundation was thus established to fulfill these tasks. The actual claims processing was performed in a de-centralized manner by the partner organizations, some of which already existed and had been active in similar processes before.

This chapter outlines the organizational structure of the EVZ Foundation and of two exemplary partner organizations and explains how cooperation worked between the different organizations. The particular structure of the forced labor compensation program was largely due to the international negotiators' desire to have continued influence in the program. In this way, the successful implementation of the program should also be measured against its ability to anticipate and deal with the conflicts that arise from such a setting.

THE "FOUNDATION MODEL"

The overall organizational structure of the forced labor compensation program was quite unique. Its Board of Trustees, wherein the main participants of the negotiations were represented, was the key organ for policy-making. As introduced earlier, the EVZ Foundation, based in Berlin, took on the main coordination of the program. The bulk of the implementation, however, was done by the Foundation's partner organizations that processed the claims, decided their eligibility and carried out the actual payments all over the world.

The EVZ Foundation as the central organization of the program was a non-profit foundation regulated by German public law. As such, it was an independent entity with dedicated assets for a particular purpose and not limited in the timeframe of its operation. To establish such a public law foundation was decided early on in the negotiations process since it had clear advantages over a foundation governed by private law.[1]

By establishing a public-law institution, the German State could express the shared responsibility it held together with the German companies for the crimes that took place during the Second World War. The public law status guaranteed an authority and reputation necessary for implementing the compensation program beyond the German borders, which did have a notable effect during the implementation of the program. Yet, the credibility of a public institution is only given when the involvement of the government itself is perceived as integer, both on the national and international level, and when the intention to deal with historical injustice seems earnest. In the case of the German compensation program, this was manifested by the Foundation Law in which the tasks of the EVZ Foundation were essentially declared as the duties of the state.

A foundation under German law was also in the interest of the German negotiators. Only a setup that included guarantees of the German State for the compensation program could justify the demand for legal closure sought by German companies. Establishing an institution under public law was a prerequisite for the US Government during the negotiations, which would otherwise not have agreed to support the withdrawal of the class actions pending before US courts. Furthermore, the Foundation Law contained a clause that this program would be the only forum for settling any claims for forced labor compensation. For the German side, this ensured that future claims for compensation in German courts would be excluded.[2]

However, since all functions and bodies of its organization were established by a law, the EVZ Foundation was, in special dimensions, also relatively inflexible. Changes in the organizational structure or of the basic claims process could in a lot of cases only be carried out by changing first the law, which was a rather lengthy and complicated process. The possibility to make certain smaller amendments was reserved in the law for the respective bodies.

Being a public-law institution, the EVZ Foundation had to adhere to the requirements of the German Federal Budget Law and was controlled by the German Federal Court of Audit. These control mechanisms were a significant aspect for the negotiators and were already included in the US-German Agreement (see Annex 3).

---

1   The "foundation model" had already been used in Germany in 1971, when a public-law foundation was established to eliminate the possibility of future claims for compensation for damages by the Contergan medication. The sleeping pill was sold in the late 1950s and early 1960s by the Chemie Grünenthal GmbH company and contained the component Thalidomid, which caused deformations and disabilities in unborn children. In the law that established a foundation to pay compensation to the affected families, any future claims against the company were excluded. This was declared as constitutional by the German Federal Constitutional Court (BverfGE 42, 263) on 8 July 1976.
2   See Chapter 10 for information on legal closure.

The German Ministry of Finance was responsible for the legal supervision of the EVZ Foundation, which meant that it supervised whether the Foundation acted according to the respective applicable laws (see Chapter 8). While the EVZ Foundation was otherwise an independent organization that took its decisions autonomously, the Ministry of Finance used its supervisory power on occasion quite broadly, and the EVZ Foundation felt at times that it had to comply with the Ministry's instructions even when it held a different view.

THE EVZ FOUNDATION AS THE CENTRAL COORDINATOR

As the main coordinating body of the compensation program, the EVZ Foundation was responsible for a wide range of tasks:

- Coordination and supervision of the implementation of the program by partner organizations;
- Decision on common guidelines regarding the compensation payments;
- Decision on the inclusion of so-called 'other places of confinement,' i.e. inclusion of more places of confinement in eligibility categories;
- Administration and financial management of the overall compensation fund;
- Distribution of accrued interest and additional donations;
- Decision about how to use leftover funds.

The following tasks were not part of the Foundation Law but evolved during the implementation of the compensation program:

- Coordination and financing of archive research and search for evidence (in cooperation with professional archives);
- Archiving of the waivers to secure legal closure.

The EVZ Foundation's organizational structure consisted of several components: the Board of Trustees, the Board of Directors, and the Foundation office run by the Board of Directors that will be described in the following.

Board of Trustees — policy and oversight

As the law establishing the EVZ Foundation did not specify all aspects of the compensation program, establishing an overarching policy organ was of fundamental importance. The main responsibility of this Board of Trustees was to decide on basic policies and to oversee the work of the EVZ Foundation and its partner organizations. The importance and the tasks of the Board of Trustees can thus be seen in a political and in a functional way, both of which could not always be carried out in a tension-free manner.

The main *political goal* for establishing the Board of Trustees was to ensure the continued influence of the negotiating partners on the implementation of the negotiated agreements. The Board of Trustees had 27 seats, the majority of which were reserved for participants in the negotiations. The distribution of these seats — like all other fundamental aspects of the program — were discussed during the negotiations and were then included in the Foundation Law (Section 5 (1)). The distribution insured a balancing of interests between the 'victim' and the 'perpetrator' side.

Since the EVZ Foundation was a German public-law institution, it was deemed necessary that Germany should be adequately represented in the Board of Trustees. Eventually, it was agreed that the German State and companies hold 14 of the 27 seats of the Board of Trustees. Also, the German Chancellor chose the Chairman of the Board of Trustees who had to be a person of "international reputation,"[3] underlining the political weight of the board.

The main *function* of the Board of Trustees in the compensation program was to provide guidance and control:

- It selected the members of the Board of Directors and supervised their work;
- It decided on the annual budget of the foundation and its annual accounts;
- It took decisions concerning a number of important substantive issues as laid down in the Foundation Law; and
- It issued basic guidelines for the claims process.

The Board of Trustees drew up its own rules of procedure; its members did not receive compensation for their work.

Despite the many advantages of a Board of Trustees that represented the many stakeholders involved in a program, there were also practical challenges. The designation of representatives proved difficult, for instance, there were some seats that had to be filled by representatives jointly appointed by several organizations. In the case of a seat allocated to representative organizations of the Sinti and Roma, for example, the organizations were not able to find a common representative, which led to the seat being vacant for 14 years. It was also questionable whether the large number of (interested) members was still needed after the compensation program was completed in 2007, as some stakeholders' interests no longer related to the remaining tasks of the "Remembrance and Future" Fund. The founding documents foresaw the possibility of a reduction in the membership of the Board of Trustees. This was discussed in the Board of Trustees when the completion of the compensation program came closer, but in the absence of any guidance in the founding documents, no agreement could be found on such a reduction. The result was that possibilities of influence for all board members as well

---

3   See Annex 3: US-German Agreement, Annex A (2).

as international acceptance were prioritized over an advisory function to the program activities. Finally, it turned out that unclear boundaries between executive and controlling function of the Board of Trustees was not practical and, in fact, contradicts the German Corporate Governance Codex.

The size and multilingual setup of the Board of Trustees allowed a broad participation of all stakeholders but was also a permanent and significant cost factor for the EVZ Foundation. In response to the international character of the Board of Trustees, it was decided to establish three working languages: German, English, and Russian. All documents were translated into the three languages and all meetings were simultaneously interpreted. The costs for the Board of Trustees amounted to almost 15 percent of the Foundation's non-staff administrative costs.

Board of Directors — management of the program

The day-to-day management of the EVZ Foundation was the responsibility of the Board of Directors. This body — in contrast to the Board of Trustees — worked full-time and was therefore capable of acting on short notice. The Board of Directors consisted of three members; after the completion of the compensation program its membership was reduced to two members.

The main tasks of the Board of Directors in relation to the compensation program were:

- Day-to-day management of the EVZ Foundation;
- Preparation of Board of Trustees meetings and decisions;
- Preparation of the annual budget and the yearly accounts;
- Planning of the allocation of funds; and
- Conclusion of the agreements with the partner organizations and supervision of the partner organizations (during the compensation program only).

The decisions taken by the Board of Directors were recorded and forwarded to the Chairman of the Board of Trustees who kept all members of the latter informed about important decisions. This way, the supervisory function of the Board of Trustees was secured.

The Board of Trustees elected the members of the Board of Directors with a simple majority. Until 2006, candidates were suggested freely, but after that year, a process based on public advertisements was established. The composition of the first Board of Directors thus highlighted the political interests in this function and it was considered whether a particular candidate had enough political 'weight' and integrity to carry out the EVZ Foundation's work and enforce the process in a way that would be acceptable to all stakeholders.[4]

---

4 Henning Borggräfe, *Zwangsarbeiterentschädigung: Vom Streit um „vergessene Opfer" zur Selbstaussöhnung der Deutschen* (Göttingen: WallsteinVerlag, 2014), 385–387.

The term of office of each member of the Board of Directors was four years. Directors could be appointed for more than one term, which happened in some cases. Over the years, the board's management tasks shifted according to the changing nature of the work of the EVZ Foundation. After the end of the compensation program in 2007, the board was reduced from three to two members by changing the respective passages in the law. In the event of a tied vote, the chairman of the Board of Directors casts the deciding vote. From that time onwards the work of the EVZ Foundation focused mainly on implementing the "Remembrance and Future" Fund (see Chapter 12).

The EVZ Foundation Office under the Board of Directors

For the duration of the compensation program, the EVZ Foundation had to apply both political and practical principles that were not always easy to combine. Politically, the work of the Foundation was met with the high expectations that it would carry out the program by designing a process that was fast and flexible and could satisfy the interests of both the victims and the donors. This required the ability to react quickly and work with a minimum amount of bureaucracy, while at the same time showing empathy towards the claimants. On the other hand, as a foundation under German public law it had to comply with a number of administrative law provisions.

Moreover, the departments of the EVZ Foundation had to be established under great time pressure. In the public perception, the EVZ Foundation existed from the moment when the media reported widely on the negotiations, and when the Board of Trustees met shortly after the enactment of the Foundation Law in August 2000. At that time, however, the actual office of the Foundation only existed on paper.

Almost immediately, there was a multitude of tasks that required a functioning office, first and foremost the financial management of the large fund and the negotiation of the agreements with the partner organizations. Also, the EVZ Foundation already received many inquiries, applications, and other correspondence from all over the world. Also the administrative, legal, historical, and public relations tasks had to start. For this, only a few departments were formed, such as a financial and IT department, while other legal or historical issues, among others, were responded to in a collaborative way by members of different teams.

Some of the tasks of the EVZ Foundation also required creating very specific departments. A typical task with regard to the databases that were used to record the claims was that their content had to be managed. While there was an IT department that dealt with the technical aspects of the databases, and a financial department that used the databases for paying out funds to partner organizations, the actual content was managed by staff who were familiar with the claims processing. For example, each beneficiary had to be allocated the correct payments, while double payments had to be avoided. This task could be allocated in either the IT or the financial department; within the EVZ Foundation, however, a separate "compensation payments team" developed. Also, to ensure controls of the claims decisions by partner organizations, so-called 'control teams' were formed later on (see Chapter 8).

During the height of the compensation program, the EVZ employed approximately 40 professionals.

The various responsibilities of the EVZ Foundation office required different priorities with regard to the profile of employees. The departments directly concerned with the compensation program needed to establish a quick and flexible procedure to oversee a victim-friendly implementation of the Foundation Law. Many of the professionals were familiar with the historical situation and could start working directly. Thus, in the respective decisions, priority was given to those persons who had relevant historical or legal expertise, who possessed intercultural competencies, and spoke relevant languages, as practice showed that difficulties arose when there was a lack of intercultural competences. However, in the beginning, the importance of understanding administrative procedures was underestimated.

For the administrative department, the EVZ Foundation oriented itself on typical federal administrative structures. Importantly, the EVZ Foundation received support from several federal authorities and ministries. These were mainly experts of administrative matters who knew the federal regulations well and who could help build capacities of EVZ employees.

In general, the different working styles and purpose of these two types of approaches led to tensions within the EVZ Foundation. The departments dealing directly with the compensation program worked rather flexibly and unconventionally, and, in the beginning, did not have a consistent approach to basic administrative principles. This repeatedly led to internal tensions with the administrative department.

After the completion of the compensation program, most of the main activities of the EVZ Foundation were no longer applied. The respective departments were reduced in size and, where possible, dissolved. Some of the employees could transfer to the "Remembrance and Future" Fund, the only activity that would be continued by the EVZ Foundation. Finally, even though the compensation program was officially concluded in 2007, the Foundation still had to supply capacities to respond to the many inquiries concerning the compensations.

PARTNER ORGANIZATIONS

The main procedures of the compensation program were carried out by the partner organizations. As described in earlier chapters, some of the partner organizations already existed at the time of the negotiations and had already been involved with earlier compensation programs. The following partner organizations were part of the compensation program:

National organizations:

- Belarus: National Foundation "Understanding and Reconciliation," also responsible for Estonia;
- Czech Republic: "German-Czech Future Fund";
- Poland: Foundation "Polish-German Reconciliation" (FPNP);
- Russia: National Foundation "Understanding and Reconciliation," also responsible for Latvia, Lithuania, and so-called CIS states;[5]
- Ukraine: National Foundation "Understanding and Reconciliation," also responsible for Moldavia.

International organizations

- Conference on Jewish Material Claims Against Germany (JCC) for Jewish claimants worldwide, except those living in the countries named above;
- International Organization for Migration (IOM) for non-Jewish claimants worldwide, except for those living in the countries named above.

The Foundation Law names only the two international organizations directly, while the national partner organizations were expected to be nominated by their respective governments, which indicated that they were at least expected to cooperate. There was no option in the Law for the case of a partner organization unwilling to implement the program, neither were there any provisions in the case of a cancellation of an established partnership after the start of the program. This illustrates that the cooperation of the partner organizations was already expected during the negotiations, just as the coordinating role of the EVZ Foundation. However, since partner organizations were not directly bound to the Foundation Law, the EVZ Foundation also had to negotiate partner agreements detailing the process.

Generally, the partner organizations were responsible for outreach, processing of the claims (including the search for supporting evidence), appeals process, payment, as well as coordination with victims' associations, as detailed in the Foundation Law. These activities will be discussed in detail in Chapters 5, 6 and 7.

The functions that each partner organization had to fulfill were thus much broader than those of the EVZ Foundation. On the one hand, they were required, per the partnership contracts, to strictly implement the Foundation Law. On the other hand, they were closely connected with the claimants. This situation often produced tensions during the program, which were experienced to different degrees by the respective organizations. In the best case,

---

5 The Commonwealth of Independent States (CIS) formed when the former Soviet Union dissolved and consist of Armenia, Belarus, Kazakhstan, Kyrgyzstan, Moldova, Russia, Tajikistan, and Uzbekistan as member states, with Turkmenistan and Ukraine as associate states. In the case of the compensation program, Belarus and Ukraine had their own partner organizations and were not covered by the Russian partner organization.

such tensions could be mitigated by a careful distribution of the roles of the EVZ Foundation and partner organizations. Clear guidelines from the EVZ Foundation and the results of the claims audits could, for instance, help the partner organizations better explain reasons for the rejection of claims.

Organizational structure of the partner organizations

The following describes the setup of new working structures to implement the Foundation Law by the FPNP, the Polish partner organization, representing the situation of a national partner organization, and the IOM exemplifying the work of an international partner organization.

Due to the fact that the organization had already implemented a compensation program for victims of Nazi persecution in the 1990s, the Polish partner organization FPNP already had a working organizational structure. Paying out the compensations for survivors of forced labor was the highest priority during the respective years, and practically the entire organizational structure and staff were oriented towards this goal.

According to the statutes, the following organs of the Polish partner organization were responsible for deciding on content-related issues:

Foundation Board: The members of the Foundation Board acted pro-bono. The tasks of the board were to evaluate the activity of the Board of Directors, to advise on the overall guidelines of the organization's mandate, to evaluate the administration of the financial means of the organization, and to review and verify the financial reports. The funder (the Polish Ministry of Treasury) nominated the members of the Foundation Board.

Board of Directors: The Board of Directors managed the activities of the organization, represented it, and administered the funds. The funder nominated the members.

Review and Verification: This department, at peak times employing close to 60 staff, processed the incoming claims and reviewed/verified them according to the Foundation Law.

Appeals Committee: The appeals committee decided on claims where an appeal was filed, corresponded with claimants, and informed about the ways in which the claims were evaluated.

Supporting organs were:

Information center: As described in Chapter 5, the information center provided information about the eligibility under the Foundation Law and about the status of the claims. The center provided service to individuals who came in person, as well as corresponding via hotlines and letters.

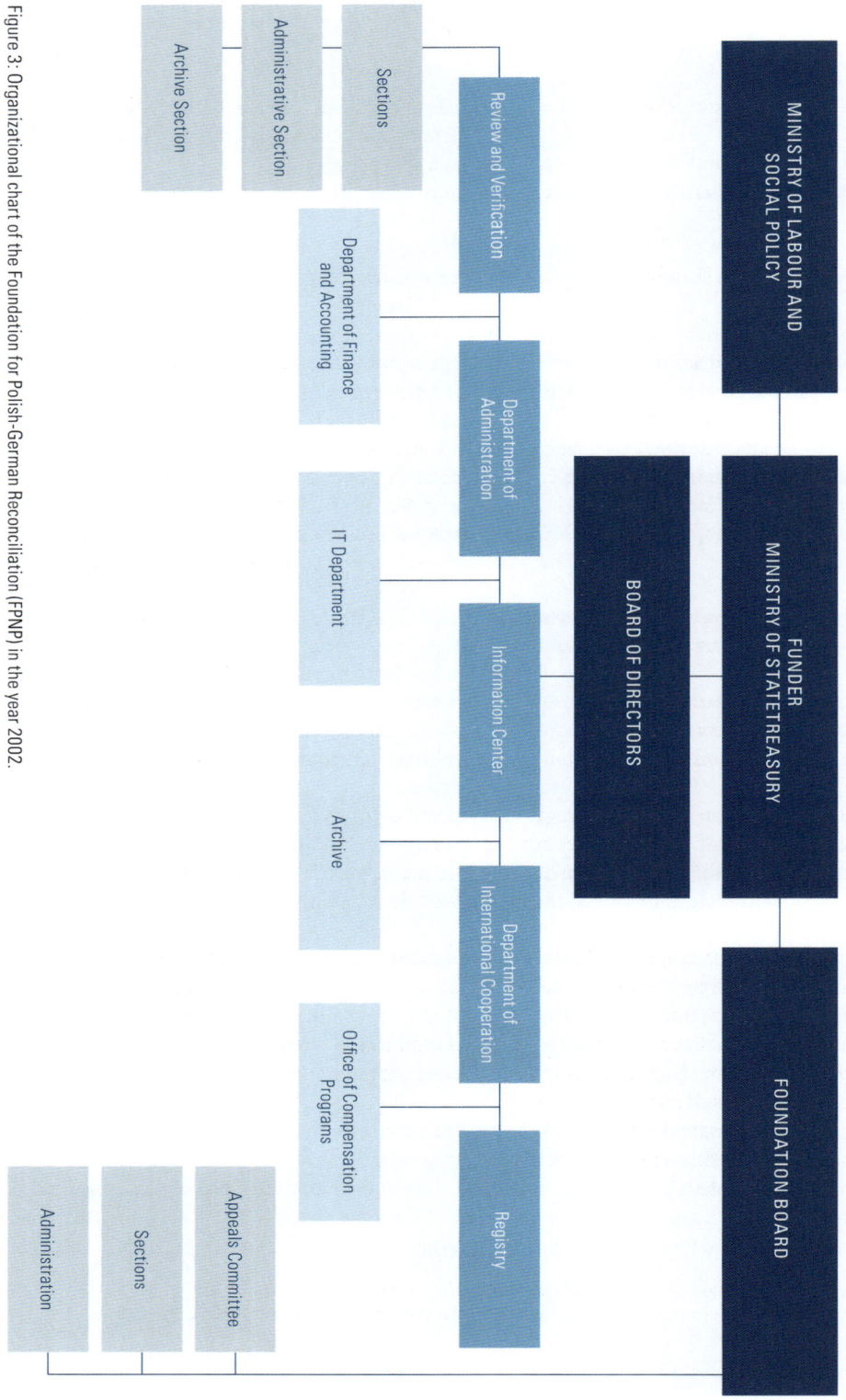

ORGANIZATIONAL CHART OF THE FOUNDATION FOR POLISH-GERMAN RECONCILIATION

Figure 3: Organizational chart of the Foundation for Polish-German Reconciliation (FPNP) in the year 2002.

Archive: The archive collected all submitted claims. It also corresponded with claimants and sent back documentation where requested.

Registry: This department registered all correspondences, as well as logging times and dates of correspondence electronically.

Finance and Accounting: This department was responsible for all accounting tasks of the organization and processed all checks for the successful claims.

Various state-level authorities in Poland strictly supervised the work of the FPNP. It was controlled three times by the national auditing authority, three times by the inspection office of the Council of Ministers, and two times by the Ministry of Work and Social Welfare. A professional auditing firm reviewed the financial report of the organization, which is a process prescribed by law. Reports about the activity of the FPNP were shared with the register court, the Ministry of Treasury, the Ministry of Work and Social Welfare, as well as the chairmen of the *Sejm* (Polish Parliament) and the Senate. The FPNP liaised closely with victims' associations throughout the program.

An important aspect of the organizational structure of the Polish partner organization was the establishment of an independent appeals committee. This role was taken up by an existing appeals body, which, to comply with the Foundation Law, had to be moved from under the supervision of the Board of Directors to under the supervision of the Foundation Board directly. Also, the rules of procedure had to be changed in order to incorporate that the appeals committee would act independently and not be subjected to any directives.

The IOM had, in contrast to the other partner organizations, no experience with previous compensation programs for victims of Nazi injustice and was forced to establish new working structures from scratch. However, the organization could rely on its existing country offices for the processing of claims from all over the world.

The *German Forced Labour Compensation Programme* (GFLCP) was established as a separate project within the larger organization. The first step was to put together a core team made up of two senior IOM staff members, plus four experts with experience from other claims programs who were recruited from outside. Based on the best assumptions it could make at the time about IOM's claims population and the program's workload, the team first developed a work plan with process flows, targets, and an organizational structure, then defined staff and non-staff resources and budget. Based on this work plan and the budget approved by the EVZ Foundation, IOM then undertook several tasks in tandem; it recruited staff; procured office space, equipment and other non-staff resources;[6] developed and started the outreach and

---

[6] In its start-up phase, the program could make use of office space and other non-staff resources that IOM made available at its headquarters in Geneva.

public information campaign; and it designed and distributed the claim form. The core team also recruited the program staff at IOM's headquarters in Geneva, and arranged for the recruitment of dedicated program staff in more than 40 IOM country offices worldwide that were responsible for the intake and registration of the claims. At its peak, a total of 120 staff worked in the Geneva office, and over 1,200 staff worked in country offices worldwide.

The program staff in Geneva — responsible for the supervision of staff in the field offices, review of and the decision on the claims, as well as for their payment — was organized into the following teams: management, registry, forced labor, personal injury, property loss, appeals, public information and hotline, IT, and admin and finance. The largest team was the one reviewing the forced labor claims, followed by the team dealing with claims for property losses. The positions for the forced labor compensation program were advertised like other IOM posts and the selection of candidates followed the standard procedures. Experience in the respective work area was a requirement, along with language skills as an extra qualification, as IOM had to handle claims in 27 different languages.

GFLCP had to follow general personnel, budget, procurement, and IT rules of IOM, it was audited by the (external) IOM auditors, but as a very large separate project the program was otherwise managed and funded independently of the wider organization.

Cooperation with victims' associations, which was called for by the Foundation Law, was especially relevant for IOM, given the geographical scope of its responsibilities and the fact that it first had to establish its claimant group. Early on, IOM therefore established a "Steering Committee of Most Involved Victims' Associations" for which it asked the largest victims' associations in the major claimant countries to agree on a manageable number of representatives. The program drew on the knowledge of Steering Committee members about relevant historical facts and situations of claimants, and it could also rely on the assistance of the Steering Committee in the distribution of information about the program, including its limitations, to (potential) claimants. Several IOM country offices also cooperated closely with national advisory councils composed of victims' associations. This was done on the basis of a model cooperation agreement developed by the team in Geneva. As a result, 15 victims' associations assisted in information dissemination, claim intake and registration, depending on whether the victims' association could do the job more efficiently and cost-effectively than the IOM country office.

Appeal committees within the partner organizations

According to the Foundation Law, all partner organizations were required to set up appeal committees, which should be able to independently decide on appeals made against the initial decisions by the respective partner organization. This procedure was agreed upon, in detail, in the partnership contracts. Claimants could appeal within three months after receiving a decision for their claim (see Chapter 6).

The informal inclusion of victims' associations in these procedures was already expected during the negotiations and in the justification of the Foundation Law. Most of the partner organizations gave representatives of victims' organizations the opportunity to take an active part in the compensation program, not least so that they could gain insights into the decision-making process of the partner organization. However, it had to be considered that most of the victims' associations only represented particular victim groups. There were instances when contemporary witnesses who were part of the appeals committees based their decisions too much on their own experiences rather than considering more broad historical knowledge available.

The independence of the appeal committees was a measure to secure a fair procedure. However, in practice in some partner organizations the independence was compromised structurally, as some of the employees with historical expertise who supported the appeal committees had previously worked in the main claims processing department. In any case, it was excluded that an employee could work in both departments simultaneously. There were some arguments in cases where the appeals committee had a fundamentally different opinion for a decision on particular claimant groups. In this case, the partner organizations had no structural option to control the decisions of the appeals committee.

COORDINATION BETWEEN THE EVZ FOUNDATION AND PARTNER ORGANIZATIONS

Communication and cooperation between the EVZ Foundation and the partner organizations took place on all hierarchy levels in order to implement the tasks set out in the partnership agreements. In all departments, via the respective managers, the employees in 'matching' positions worked directly together. There were also regular meetings of the control teams of the EVZ Foundation with the claims processing staff in partner organizations, as well as the financial and information management departments. The requirements for this close cooperation were the deep knowledge of the roles of each organization, both according to the Foundation Law and the partnership agreement, and a feedback system within the respective organizations. This way, the separation of responsibilities, and control and implementation functions was maintained.

While EVZ Foundation regularly sent out information bulletins with general guidance on the interpretation of the Foundation Law, there was a need of multilateral exchange between the EVZ Foundation and all seven partner organizations. This was particularly fruitful to gain an overview of the interpretation of the Foundation Law, particularly with regard to claims decisions. These coordination meetings were often called before a meeting of the Board of Trustees. As some of the representatives of the partner organizations were themselves members of the Board of Trustees or were in close coordination with the respective representatives of their country or organization, the coordination meetings could thus also be used to prepare decisions by the Board of Trustees: in the coordination meetings the acceptance of certain practices could be gauged; and the different organizations had the possibility to exchange their views. Based on the good experiences with these meetings, meetings of the appeal committees were also organized, albeit with less frequency.

Both the EVZ Foundation and partner organizations included, formally or informally, victims' associations in their work. During meetings and in letters they were informed about the ongoing developments of the program. This was the case for the general timeline of the payments as well as more detailed descriptions of the inclusion or exclusion of particular victims' groups. This intensive exchange strengthened the general understanding for the decisions by the EVZ Foundation and its partner organizations. The main aim of this exchange was less to receive support for disappointing results (such as the exclusion of certain victim groups) but to make transparent the decisions and to prevent misunderstanding and mistrust by the affected groups.

SUMMARY

The organizational structure of the compensation program for forced labor, as laid down in the Foundation Law, was complex and involved several layers of bodies and responsibilities. The overall structure of the EVZ Foundation comprised a supervisory and an executive board. The main function of the former, the Board of Trustees, was to provide general guidance on the interpretation of the Foundation Law by deciding on major questions that arose during the program. The latter, the Board of Directors, managed the program and was supported by the office of the Foundation in Berlin. It also supervised the implementation of the program by partner organizations. The partner organizations carried out the bulk of the work of the compensation program, and had to create their own organizational structures for outreach, claims processing and payment, as well as an appeals process. Due to this complex organizational structure of the compensation program, there was a significant need for cooperation and continued communication between the EVZ Foundation and its partner organizations.

CHALLENGES AND LESSONS LEARNED

- The inclusion of the negotiation partners in a supervisory body of a reparations program can reduce tensions between the 'victim' and 'perpetrator' sides and contribute to the acceptance of the program.

- When changes in overseeing bodies are anticipated, such as a reduction in size over the course of the program, clear guidelines are necessary and need to be set up during the design of such a program.

- When deciding about the functions of the different boards of an organization, there should be a clear distinction between supervisory and executive functions.

- International boards without a binding business language will generate high costs due to simultaneous translations and document translations.

- Training office staff in administrative procedures can minimize tensions and create more effective workflows. At the same time, to encourage commitment, administrative staff can be made aware of the greater purpose of their work.

- When responsibilities are shared between organizations — such as in this case between a central foundation and implementing partners — there is a need for close and continuous communication, as well as for clearly defined roles of each involved organization.

- Cooperation activities have to be sufficiently planned and budgeted for.

DARIUSZ PAWŁOŚ AND NORBERT WÜHLER

CHAPTER 5: OUTREACH

This chapter contains:

— Outreach at the start of the program
— Interaction with claimants
— Ongoing communication needs

INTRODUCTION: MORE THAN PROVIDING INFORMATION

Public information and outreach are critical for every large-scale compensation program. The goal is to reach as many potential claimants as quickly as possible and provide comprehensive and reliable information to them about the program. An active search for potential claimants was particularly important in the case of the forced labor compensation program, considering the long time that had elapsed since the events giving rise to the claims; the advanced age of the claimants; their often difficult access to public information; and the wide geographical distribution of the program. The importance of outreach was recognized already in a provision in the Foundation Law (Section 10 (2)), and the EVZ Foundation stipulated in its agreements with the partner organizations specific obligations in this respect.[1]

The main goal of the outreach was to provide information concerning the following:

- Who is and who is not eligible to claim and receive benefits?
- What are the conditions of eligibility/the categories of claims?
- Where and how should applications be filed?
- What are the filing deadlines?
- Where can claimants obtain claim forms?
- What should claimants submit together with the claim forms?
- What is the process of the resolution and payment of the claims?

Providing this information was particularly important at the beginning of the program in order to announce its existence and to allow claims to be submitted within the filing deadline. Yet a continuous provision of information was also required throughout the implementation process to answer queries of claimants and the public, to address new circumstances and to inform about important requirements and milestones, such as the extension and end of deadlines, or the requirements for legal successor claims.

This chapter focuses more specifically on the outreach activities of the partner organizations, as they mirror the typical situation in a reparations program. The following description concentrates on the practice of the Polish partner organization as an example of a national partner organization and the IOM as an example of an internationally operating partner organization. While each of the seven partner organizations addressed a specific situation and faced particular challenges, the Polish partner organization and the IOM are sufficiently representative for the two main types of situations during the German compensation program.

---

1   For example, the partnership agreement concluded with the Polish partner organization provided that in accordance with Section 10 (2) of the Foundation Law, the Federal Foundation and its partner organizations are responsible for the adequate publicity of eligible benefits according to the Foundation Law. It further stated that rather than launching their own public information activities, the EVZ Foundation would financially assist partner organizations in their outreach activities.

OUTREACH AT THE START OF THE PROGRAM

Outreach was primarily the responsibility of the partner organizations, as they would be handling the claims process. However, the EVZ Foundation also undertook general outreach and public information activities. In cooperation with the German Federal Government and all diplomatic representations abroad (embassies and consulates general etc.), the EVZ Foundation could publicly announce the existence of the program and asked for the dissemination of information on the application procedure and the principles of eligibility through these channels. German diplomatic missions published the corresponding information on their websites, held press conferences, and provided consultancy services. When they received further questions, inquiries were directly being forwarded to the EVZ Foundation. Within Germany, the EVZ Foundation launched a comprehensive information campaign. In countries most affected by forced labor practices during the Third Reich, the EVZ Foundation held press conferences, at times in cooperation with partner organizations. Partner organizations received an additional five million Euros from the EVZ Foundation to implement outreach activities.

The five Central and Eastern European partner organizations in Belarus, the Czech Republic, Poland, the Russian Federation, and the Ukraine were each responsible for the claims from former forced laborers (or their legal successors where applicable) residing in their respective country.[2] The JCC and the IOM, on the other hand, were responsible for Jewish and non-Jewish survivors of forced labor residing in any country of the world outside the responsibilities of the five organizations listed here. Both the JCC and IOM, therefore, had to reach potential beneficiaries worldwide.

In the 1990s, four of the five Central and Eastern European countries received lump sum payments from Germany for distribution to Nazi victims, many of whom also became claimants (and beneficiaries) under the forced labor compensation program. Only the Czech partner organization was not part of the earlier 1990s program and had no previous records of potential beneficiaries. All five Central and Eastern European partner organizations, however, possessed considerable historical knowledge about Nazi injustices committed in their respective areas of geographical responsibility. From its fifty years of managing a variety of compensation programs for Holocaust victims, the JCC had wide experience with the history of Nazi injustices and persecution, and it also had extensive records of such victims from its earlier programs.

This varied geographical scope presented a range of challenges for these two types of partner organizations. The five Central and Eastern European partner organizations could limit their

---

2   The Russian partner organization was also responsible for claimants residing in Latvia and Lithuania, the Belarussian partner organization for claimants residing in Estonia, and the Ukrainian partner organization for claimants residing in Moldova. Claimants from Armenia, Azerbaijan, Georgia, Kazakhstan, Kyrgyzstan, Tajikistan, Turkmenistan and Uzbekistan fell under the responsibility of one of the respective partner organizations that were now responsible for the country they were originally deported from into the German Reich. (Many survivors of forced labor did not return to the countries they were once deported from.)

outreach to their respective country; they were able to use familiar national communication channels; could operate in their own language; and could obtain information from and cooperate with governmental and non-governmental organizations, with many of which they had prior working relationships. Conversely, the JCC and IOM had to find and reach out to survivors of forced labor (and their legal successors, where applicable) in many countries worldwide, use large numbers of national and international communication channels, operate in a variety of languages,[3] and seek information and cooperation from governmental and non-governmental organizations, some of whom they dealt with for the first time. The conditions for the IOM were especially challenging since its country offices were the only existing resources it could rely on, which had up to that point, however, not been involved in any matters concerning survivors of Nazi injustice or persecution. The JCC could rely on its offices in a number of countries relevant for the forced labor program, as well as make use of a network of Holocaust survivors and support organizations with whom it cooperates in other programs.

On a general note, the compensation program was to be accessed by claimants directly, without any legal advice or any administrative costs involved.

Example of an outreach campaign of a national partner organization

In Poland, the Foundation for Polish-German Reconciliation (*Fundacja Polsko-Niemieckie Pojednanie*, FPNP) was entrusted with implementing the compensation program. Prior to this program, the FPNP had already worked with Nazi victims and therefore possessed extensive knowledge about these groups. Organizational structures, technical equipment and an experienced team were already in place. Stretching four kilometers long, the FPNP's archive stored documentation on former forced laborers during the Third Reich, including an extensive database holding recorded and already processed claims filed by forcefully displaced people and detainees of concentration camps who had been held for the purpose of forced labor.

The FPNP worked closely with victim associations and other organizations representing persons affected by National Socialist persecution. The FPNP set up contracts with some of these organizations that then served as branch offices. They disseminated general information, provided claim forms to affected parties and assisted with the application process. Particularly, members of victims' associations were able to file an application with their own organization. However, the majority of claimants filed their applications with the FPNP in Warsaw.

Although the implementation of an information campaign within a single country, in this case Poland, may seem a rather straightforward undertaking, there were a number of challenges. First of all, the sheer number of interested parties was overwhelming. In Poland, more than

---

3   IOM operated the compensation program in 27 languages.

one million informal and official claims were submitted to the FPNP, which exceeded those of any other country. This was due to the course and extent of the Second World War, where Poland was severely affected.

As this was the first large-scale compensation program for survivors of forced labor in Poland, it was highly anticipated and from the outset received considerable social, media, and political interest. Already during the course of international negotiations with the German Government and companies, numerous Polish residents sought information regarding potential compensation. Thus, the Polish partner organization, which was from the start involved in the international negotiations, was faced with enormous societal expectations.

The FPNP established an information center that was responsible for outreach activities and was the first point of contact for affected individuals. The information center, which was a separate department within the organization, maintained close contact with victims and was the essential source of information for interested parties. Its scope of activities was rather vast and included:

- Contact with the media
- Dissemination of information sheets and forms
- Collaborations with victims' associations
- Personal and phone support for interested parties
- Reception of claims
- Correspondence with (potential) claimants and their families.

Apart from the ongoing work of the information center, the FPNP initiated a coordinated and professional information campaign for the forced labor compensation program. The Polish partner organization devised the campaign and implemented it in coordination with the EVZ Foundation. The campaign began as soon as the partnership contracts were signed and a claim form was designed in coordination with the German side. Primarily through mass media channels, the FPNP then informed about how the forms should be completed and what the deadlines for the application were. The FPNP also informed competent Polish Government authorities, victims' associations, official media channels, municipal authorities and gave information to supra-local media, including television, e.g. by holding press conferences.

The importance of the program in Poland was mirrored by the scale of public interest:

- In October/November 2000, the thirteen largest weekly and daily newspapers of all political colors as well as regional papers placed paid advertisements informing about the compensation program. Regional and trade press also published information on the program free of charge, as they expected that this would increase their readership.

- News about the official start of the compensation program on 28 June 2001 appeared in all available media channels. These reports were not only used to disseminate information on the compensation program, but they also published guidelines on how to fill the claim forms along with complete printed sample forms. Regional and national press published articles explaining the application procedure step by step. National and regional television and radio stations broadcast special information programs.

The Polish partner organization sent out tens of thousands of application forms to potential beneficiaries who had already registered with the organization through previous assistance programs. Thus, the FPNP database already held hundreds of thousands of potential beneficiaries of the program. Of course, claim forms were available at the FPNP information center and were distributed to victims' associations as well. A sample claim form was published on the FPNP website.

In order to optimize outreach activities, the Polish partner organization collaborated with a number of civil society organizations. In Poland there were nearly one hundred organizations and associations that represented war veterans, former prisoners (of ghettos, Nazi prisons, and concentration camps), victims of forced labor or other Nazi injustices. Most of them were regionally active and focused on a particular victim group whereas others were operating nationally throughout Poland, holding a number of departments and branch offices.

Given the fact that the FPNP did not have any branch offices, the collaboration with these organizations in terms of reaching victim groups proved to be all the more important. For example, associations and their branches could make use of offices throughout the whole country. Through them, the FPNP sent out thousands of claim forms and corresponding guidelines. The associations' heads had more or less unrestricted access to claim forms and all other information circulated by the FPNP. The FPNP made sure that the victims' associations knew all details of the program so that they could in turn support their members and potential claimants.

That said, collaboration with victims' associations did not always run smoothly. Not all victim groups were entitled to compensation payments, and organizations representing these groups consequently voiced their disappointment and discontent explicitly. This protest was not only directed at the Polish partner organization, but also at the EVZ Foundation and Polish authorities. Similarly, the media reacted to these protests and in most cases took the side of excluded victim groups. In other cases, some of the victims' associations were displeased with the program. Some of them believed they had better ideas; some started using unauthorized claim forms; others challenged the decisions on some of the claims and criticized the eligibility criteria.

For the aforementioned reasons, regular contact with major and, particularly, representative victims' associations was of utmost importance. Based on these contacts, a permanent consultative body was established. This committee was comprised of the heads of the six largest and most important victims' associations and proved immensely helpful in terms of interpreting the Foundation Law and in disseminating crucial information among their members and other victims of Nazi injustice throughout Poland.

Other factors weighed in positively to help inform the Polish society and potential beneficiaries about the program. During the parliamentary election campaign (Sejm and Senate, the two chambers of the Polish parliament) in 2001, a number of candidates from all political parties disseminated information material and claim forms. With the help of the press, more than 1.3 million claim forms were distributed. More than 150,000 of these forms went to the offices of Sejm- and Senate delegates, but they were also sent to veteran organizations for the purpose of forwarding them to potential claimants. This also illustrates the political importance of the program in Poland.

Example of an outreach campaign by an international partner organization

IOM's outreach efforts were faced with considerable challenges regarding communication and logistics. IOM was responsible for processing the claims of all non-Jewish applicants worldwide, except in those Eastern European countries that were covered by other partner organizations. IOM was chosen for this task because it had, through its normal operations in the fields of migration and humanitarian interventions, offices in most countries of the world.

There was relatively little knowledge about former forced laborers residing in the so-called "non-Jewish, rest of the world" for which IOM was responsible. Estimates spoke of 75,000 to 100,000 potential beneficiaries, but figures on surviving spouses or children, i.e. legal successors, were not available. At the beginning, and in contrast to the other partner organizations, the size, composition, and geographical distribution of IOM's group of claimants was therefore largely unknown. IOM's most important and pressing task was thus to organize and manage a strong and visible public information and outreach campaign in order to locate the claimants and reach out to as many potential beneficiaries as possible. In addition, IOM established local helplines and support services to assist with the distribution and completion of claim forms for potential claimants and to provide additional information. In the end, the number of claimants seeking compensation within IOM's program significantly exceeded the initial estimates preceding the Foundation Law.

In July 2000, upon the adoption of the Foundation Law, IOM established its own sub-program called "German Forced Labor Compensation Program" (hereafter GFLCP). It issued a press release informing the general public, national governments and victims' associations about the establishment of the program. Based on the feedback from this first outreach effort, IOM arrived at an estimate of the size of its group of claimants and their locations. IOM then launched a global public information and outreach campaign with the dissemination of a one-page notice (Public Service Announcement) through its international network of country offices, the German Federal Ministry for Foreign Affairs and its affiliated embassies, as well as relevant Permanent Missions in Geneva. The response from more than 80 IOM offices together with the data received from historians and victims' associations was used to determine 46 core countries in which the majority of IOM's claimant population resided and to develop an appropriate communication strategy. This information was also an important factor in the determination of the budget for IOM's outreach.

The information campaigns followed a two-track strategy. First, IOM continuously disseminated multilingual[4] general information about eligibility criteria and claims procedures, mainly through mainstream media, with a special effort to reach out to target communities globally. IOM closely cooperated with victims' associations, the other partner organizations, media, international organizations, national governments, local authorities, minority representatives and other partners. IOM coordinated the dissemination of brochures, flyers, posters, and fact sheets on the program through IOM's field offices and other partners.

Through an international bidding process, a Czech advertising agency was selected to develop a campaign logo and to provide the layout and graphic design of printed information material. More than 1,400 print advertisements were, in cooperation with a US company selected through another bidding process, placed in major newspapers and target group media in 40 countries. IOM arranged for the production and worldwide broadcasting of multilingual radio and TV spots, organized 40 press conferences in 30 countries, published 24 press releases, and created web banners and a special webpage that was updated on a regular basis. The support of a multitude of international and national partners including media companies such as CNN, Deutsche Welle, Swiss Radio International, and UN Radio was enlisted. IOM staff around the world gave numerous interviews to the press and other media and frequently participated in local radio and TV programs. In general, large print media had the widest reach, but depending on the country, TV spots, and radio programs were also successful information tools. Weekly reports from more than 40 IOM country offices involved enabled the management team of the program in Geneva to closely monitor the impact of its information campaigns and to obtain an increasingly more accurate picture of the size and geographical distribution of IOM's claimant group.

The expenditures for IOM's information campaign could partly be covered by a special outreach budget made available by the EVZ Foundation in acknowledgement of the particularly difficult task assigned to IOM, given the geographical scope of its responsibilities and the fact that it

---

4   Information material that was first drafted in English was translated into the other program languages. For forced labor claims, they were: Albanian, Croatian, Bosnian, Bulgarian, Danish, Dutch, Finnish, French, German, Greek, Hungarian, Italian, Macedonian, Norwegian, Slovak and Slovenian; for property loss claims, they were: Czech, German, Hebrew, Hungarian, Polish, and Russian.

first had to establish its claimant group.[5] In the end, the number of claimants seeking compensation within the different components of the GFLCP significantly exceeded the initial estimates preceding the Foundation Law: IOM received more than 332,000 claims for forced labor instead of the estimated 75,000–100,000.

However, the general information campaign did not reach all target groups, and IOM reinforced its outreach activities with special information campaigns focusing either on a certain component of the program or reaching out to a specific target group. These included, for example, targeted campaigns for Sinti and Roma survivors of Nazi persecution. In Central and Eastern Europe, Sinti and Roma survivors often lived in remote communities, and many elderly victims were either illiterate or did not speak the respective national language. To reach them, IOM developed specific outreach activities, assigning a prominent role to local Roma organizations and Roma media including radio and television programs.

In May 2001, IOM held a meeting with Roma representatives at its headquarters in Geneva to discuss the scope of the program and the best approach for a coordinated outreach effort. Campaign strategy and draft information materials were shared and adapted in accordance with feedback from the representatives and other experts on Roma issues who participated in the meeting. Materials were printed not only in local languages but also in Romani. In 17 countries, IOM cooperated with a specialized company that also provided outreach services to the Roma community in similar programs in close cooperation with local IOM offices.[6] The special outreach campaign for Sinti and Roma included a radio spot broadcast in Romani and local languages, a brochure and a flyer published in Romani, English, German and other local languages, a print advertisement placed in Roma newspapers and magazines and web banners uploaded on numerous Roma websites. In addition, local IOM staff participated in talk shows on Roma television and radio programs.

INTERACTION WITH CLAIMANTS

Particularly during their initial outreach, the partner organizations had to balance creating awareness of and providing comprehensive information to a broad public while avoiding raising excessive expectations, especially among victims who would not be covered under the program. This proved challenging since the eligibility of a number of victim groups was not clarified until later in the program.

---

5   The EVZ Foundation allocated approximately 1.28 million Euros for IOM's global outreach activities. More than 50 percent of these funds were spent on paid print advertisements in major newspapers across the globe.
6   These countries were Belarus, Bosnia and Herzegovina, Czech Republic, Croatia, Estonia, the Former Republic of Yugoslavia, Hungary, Latvia, Lithuania, Macedonia, Moldova, Poland, Romania, the Russian Federation, Slovakia, Slovenia, and the Ukraine.

After a large scale information campaign in Poland, the information center staff as well as FPNP staff in general was tasked with providing information on all aspects of the program, such as eligibility criteria and the procedures of the compensation program. Claimants could visit the FPNP and contact it through service hotlines, via e-mail, or in writing.

Even the best press release could not make up for the direct and personal contact with affected parties. For this reason, the personal service in information centers was received very positively. The claimants expected to have their cases dealt with on an individual and personal basis, have all questions answered and remaining doubts dispelled. The staff members of the information center also advised on how to provide evidence of Nazi persecution, how to authenticate documents and how to complete claim forms. In fact, many forms were completed in situ with the help of FPNP staff. Interested parties (victims, family members, friends, even neighbors and representatives of victims' associations) came from all over Poland throughout the year and often had to accept long waiting hours and standing in queues. On average, more than 5600 people were received per month.

Figure 4: Claimants at the FPNP office in Warsaw. Source: Fundacja Polsko-Niemieckie Pojednanie

The interaction with claimants was needed throughout the program. Whenever updated information was available and new regulations were in place, public interest notably increased. Already in 1999, when the German Government announced that it would set up a compensation fund, inquiries to the FPNP increased by 67 percent compared to the previous year. In 2000, the number of people being serviced in this manner increased by another 50 percent. Inquiries increased again when the deadline for submitting claims drew closer. By the end of 2001, numbers peaked. Notably, on the last day of claims acceptance, on 31 December 2001, more than 800 people visited the information center; many of them spent New Year's Eve with FPNP staff members.

As was the case for other partner organizations, conversations with claimants were not only informative but also often very personal and almost therapeutic. Many came to the information center with traumatic past experiences, and many of the elderly lived in impoverished living conditions and had to deal with chronic physical and psychological illnesses. Almost all claimants wanted to tell their unique life story and share their experiences of suffering. There were critical moments that required a gentle but determined way of solving issues; for instance, when claimants realized that they would not receive benefits immediately; that they might have to wait for a considerable amount of time; that documents were missing information; or that they were in fact not entitled to receive any compensation payments. Upon realizing this, a few people fainted, and there was one case where a person died of a heart attack.

It was clear that staff members of the FPNP should treat each claimant with respect, dignity, and patience. In order to be more prepared, the staff of the information center received periodical training in assertiveness and attended psychological and first aid training. Additionally, the information center was equipped with a first aid kit.

Finally, the sheer number of claimants had also consequences for the space of the FPNP office. The high numbers of claimants in 2001 who stood in long lines at the FPNP office affected the work at the Ministry for State Security, where the Polish partner organization had its office on the second floor. Eventually, the information center was separated from the FPNP and relocated. The new information center offered a spacious and comfortable waiting area and sufficient space for consultations. Air-conditioning, automated assigning of one number per claimant, large information boards, information material on compensation payments, along with additional amenities were made available in the new building. The waiting area also held an information desk where claimants obtained only the most essential information and could hand in their claims without long waiting times. With the establishment of 14 professional contact points made available to interested parties and with 11 phone helpdesks, more than 250,000 claimants could be assisted in 2001 alone.

Finally, despite the effectively implemented information campaign, a few thousand people failed to submit their claims within the fixed deadline and were as a result not entitled to receive potential compensation payments.

In the case of IOM, direct interaction with claimants took place basically in two ways. Personal contact occurred in the already existing country offices when claimants submitted their claims or when they visited the office to enquire about the program or the status of their claim. Often it was important for claimants not only to receive advice and information concerning their eligibility and the submission of the claim, but also to be able to tell their stories and express their feelings towards the program. While the formal and practical aspects of claim submission did normally not create problems, when large numbers of claimants attempted to file their claims simultaneously, logistical and security challenges could arise for an office and its staff.

The IOM office faced with the biggest of such challenges was IOM Rome. This had to do with a particular aspect of the (non-) eligibility of many of the Italian claimants. It was not until after the process of receiving and registering claims by so-called Italian Military Internees (IMIs) was completed, that the EVZ Foundation managed to have their ineligibility clarified (see Chapter 2). By that time, IOM Rome had no choice but to accept for further processing the over 100,000 claims by IMIs, with the prospect that they all might have to be rejected — which later turned out to be the case. Had the status of the IMIs been clarified at the inception of the program, the filing of such a large mass of eventually ineligible claims could have been avoided, including the stress on IOM and its staff in dealing with these claimants and, importantly, the disappointment of the IMIs when they received the rejection of their claims. This emphasizes the need to communicate clear eligibility criteria from the very start of a program.

The other way that interaction with the claimants occurred was through the telephone hotline established at IOM headquarters. Upon the expiration of the filing deadline and the gradual phasing out of the involvement of IOM country offices in the program, a Geneva-based hotline became the most important source of information for IOM's claimants. Multilingual staff operated in three shifts to attend to queries from claimants and other interested parties 12 hours per day, Monday through Friday. Additional hotlines were kept operational in Berlin and The Hague almost to the end of the program in order to attend to claimants residing in Germany and the Netherlands, respectively.[7] Callers sometimes called regularly because they appreciated that the hotline staff listened to their stories of the past and their current concerns. Other callers, on the other hand, used the opportunity to vent their anger about what they saw as the limitations of the program, the long time that the process took or the small compensation amounts.

In addition to the two examples described thus far, the case of the Ukrainian partner organization is noteworthy as it also made use of local authorities to disseminate information and accept claims. The organization held its own offices in the largest governorates that informed the general public, distributed claim forms, received and processed claims and assisted

---

[7] The cost incurred by the hotline service in The Hague, Netherlands, was covered exclusively by funds provided by the Dutch Government as a voluntary contribution.

with the completion of forms. Also, conversations about injustices suffered and present living conditions of affected parties formed part of the daily work routine. Yet, as district capitals were hard to reach for many potential claimants, it was organized that social welfare offices would fulfill the functions on a local level. The majority of claimants, however, could make their way to the Ukrainian foundation's head office in Kiev to hand in their forms and clarify relevant questions in person. The examples show that accessibility needs to be considered in an attempt to reach all eligible persons of such programs.

ONGOING COMMUNICATION NEEDS

While outreach typically is an activity in the beginning of a compensation program, communication and interaction with claimants is often needed on a continuous basis, and indeed even until the end of the program, sometimes beyond.

In the case of the Polish partner organization, contacts with victims were neither limited nor concluded after a certain date. The information campaign was continued throughout the program. The compensation program was the most important program in the post-war history of German-Polish relations and, therefore, it was often prioritized over other running projects the FPNP implemented around the same time.

Communication needs could be divided into three phases. During the first phase, claimants mostly needed information on the application procedure and about the payment of the first installment. The second phase was related to the fact that the compensation payments were paid out in two installments. During this phase, the FPNP dealt with disseminating information on paying out second installments and, due to the fact that a number of beneficiaries had passed away in the meantime, about the procedures regarding legal successors. The final step on the outreach agenda was the completion of payments. At that time, several institutions within the Polish partner organization played a role in providing further information, for instance the appeals committee and the department that dealt with cases of legal successors.

The public interest in German compensation payments lasted for many years. Although the deadline for submitting claims had expired, those who had submitted their claims in time could still hand in missing documents and evidence past the submission date. For this reason, many people continued to visit the Polish foundation. A number of issues remained of great interest until the completion of compensation payments: providing evidence of persecution, appeals, resolving doubts, dealing with the issue of deceased beneficiaries' legal successors. With the completion of compensation payments, queries shifted towards other humanitarian projects that the FPNP had established largely with funds from the EVZ Foundation.

Upon expiration of the final filing deadline on 31 December 2001 and the start of the first payments, the focus of IOM's public information activities shifted from targeted outreach and awareness raising to general public information related to the status of program implementation and to helpline services for claimants, their representatives, media, and other interested parties. Large groups who had submitted claims to IOM and who did not meet the eligibility criteria of the Foundation Law needed special attention and information. Also, the limited scope of the Foundation Law as well as sporadic and isolated attempts to deceive elderly and defenseless victims about the purpose of the program and relevant deadlines required targeted public relation activities, as illustrated in the following examples:

- In Serbia and Montenegro, in early 2003, IOM had to take steps to counter rumor that the filing deadline for the program had been extended. A special press release was distributed to all relevant national media and IOM staff participated in several TV programs and reunions of victims' associations. In addition, all late filers received a standard response postcard.

- A similar situation developed in Bosnia and Herzegovina towards the end of 2003 after former detainees of the Jasenovac camp had received their first payment. IOM received a huge number of late attempts to file a claim. To discourage individuals, representatives, and organizations that insisted on filing claims at this stage, IOM disseminated a special fact sheet and a press release, contacted victims' associations involved, and established a special hotline number with a Bosnian-speaking staff member.

- In 2004, in many republics of the former Yugoslavia, rumors were spreading that IOM was paying compensation for damage caused by the NATO bombardment in 1999 or awards for children born after the bombardment. To set the record straight and to avoid abuse and the raising of false expectations of a vulnerable group of people, IOM initiated an intensive media campaign including the publication of public service announcements and background media reports, the dissemination of a targeted fact sheet and the participation of IOM staff in topical TV programs and meetings with victims' associations.

On the other hand, IOM had to stop time-consuming and costly individual correspondence in response to high numbers of queries received by post. In some countries, including Bosnia and Herzegovina, Romania, and Serbia and Montenegro, the high influx of unwarranted mail and late requests was provoked by rumors, systematic misinformation and even attempts to defraud. IOM created special response postcards containing the basic information on program deadlines in the respective languages.

In order to keep claimants, partners and the general public abreast of program implementation, new developments, procedures, decisions by the EVZ Foundation etc., IOM made use of a broad range of information tools. These included regularly updated *fact sheets*, periodic responses to frequently asked questions (*FAQs*), a bi-annual newsletter *Compensation News*, and regular contributions to the IOM magazine *Migration,* published four times a year in English, French, and Spanish and distributed to governments, embassies and IOM country offices worldwide. *Press conferences* were organized to mark major milestones of the program and *press releases* were issued in English and local languages to raise awareness of new developments and to ensure broad and continuing press coverage by international and national media.

Figure 5: First page of a *Compensation News* newsletter, Issue 2, 2002, IOM.

Towards the completion of the program, public information activities focused on the expiration of final deadlines, the need to provide death notifications for deceased claimants in timely fashion and to submit missing information.

SUMMARY

A thorough on-going and wide-scale information and outreach campaign is crucial to reach, inform and attend to as many potential beneficiaries as possible. The chapter sheds light on information channels used, measures taken, and challenges faced during the campaign, as well as on the central role local partner organizations played in processing thousands of incoming claims.

CHALLENES AND LESSONS LEARNED

- Outreach is not a one-time shot at the beginning of a claims program. Together with general public information activities, it should continue throughout program implementation, and to a certain extent even beyond.

- Outreach requires significant efforts and resources that must be foreseen in the planning and funding of a program.

- Outreach must be targeted towards the conditions and infrastructure in the country or countries concerned. It should employ the communication means that are best suited to reach the largest numbers of claimants. It should also use existing organizations and networks, such as victims' associations, social and other public offices, banks, medical cabinets, etc.

- Outreach should be clear, easily understandable, "barrier-free," and also available to vulnerable groups and people with impairments.

- A difficult balance needs to be struck: on the one hand, the outreach should find as many potential claimants as possible and provide them with comprehensive information about the program; on the other hand, it should make clear who is *not* eligible under the program to avoid wrong expectations and subsequent disappointment and resentment. To achieve this goal, the eligibility criteria must be clearly defined at the outset of the program.

- Even the most efficient and comprehensive outreach and information campaign will not reach every single potential claimant or convince each one to file a claim.

- The personal contact with the claimants should be respectful and take into account, as much as possible, their specific needs. This will also contribute to the overall acceptance of the program.

- An outreach that targets not only direct beneficiaries, but also their family members, neighbors, similar victims, as well as associations and organizations which accompany the victims in their daily lives, can help prevent isolation of old and vulnerable victims and sensitize society for their needs.

- The best outreach is to begin paying out compensation, as this assures those expecting payment that the program actually takes place. This is another reason why payments should start as soon as possible, and claims processing and payment should occur on a rolling basis.

- Outreach turns into continuing communication with clients, as information needs to be provided during the later phases of the program. This should be considered in planning for capacities and budget.

- Even when reparations programs have deadlines, ongoing communication needs to be anticipated for a certain time after the end of the program, requiring appropriate institutional capacities.

NORBERT WÜHLER AND DARIUSZ PAWŁOŚ

CHAPTER 6: PROCESSING AND RESOLUTION OF THE CLAIMS

This chapter contains:

— Different starting points of the partner organizations concerning the claims process
— Claims processing
— Decisions on the claims and approval of the EVZ Foundation
— Processing of legal successor claims
— Appeals

INTRODUCTION: THE "HEAVY LIFTING"

In terms of time and resources required, the processing and resolution of claims typically constitutes the largest part of the implementation of a reparations program.[1] Even though the implementation phase of the forced labor compensation program was preceded by lengthy and complex negotiations and was followed by a similarly long payment phase, the claims processing was still the most time-consuming and resource-intensive part of the program.

As explained in Chapter 4, the EVZ Foundation itself did not undertake the actual processing of the claims, but this was rather assigned to the seven partner organizations.[2] This principle was laid down in the Foundation Law, whereas the details were set out in the respective partner agreements that the Foundation concluded with each of the partner organizations.

Since the general eligibility criteria were specified in the Foundation Law and the funding for each partner organization was also fixed, the work of the partner organizations could start as soon as these legal bases were in place. Beginning with outreach and public information campaigns as explained in Chapter 5, the processing and resolution of the claims comprised within each of the partner organizations the following:

- Collection and registration of the claims, including their recording in a database;
- Review and verification of the claims;
- Decision on the claims, including where applicable, on appeals; and
- Preparation and organization of the compensation payments.

While the partner organizations performed the typical activities of large-scale claims programs, the EVZ Foundation played a direct role in overseeing the claims processing. Most importantly, the EVZ Foundation provided continuing and detailed guidance concerning the interpretation of eligibility criteria and performed regular audits of the partner organizations' review of and decisions on the claims.

This chapter describes stages of the claims process that, to different degrees, all large-scale claims programs have to deal with, and that have in some form or other been performed by all the partner organizations of the EVZ Foundation. This description focuses primarily on the practice of the Polish partner organization and the IOM, aware of the fact that each of the

---

1   For examples, see Pablo de Greiff, ed., *The Handbook of Reparations* (Oxford: Oxford University Press, 2006); and Norbert Wühler and Heike Niebergall, eds., *Property Restitution and Compensation: Practices and Experiences of Claims Programmes* (Geneva: International Organization for Migration, 2008).
2   "[T]he partner organizations [...] formed the backbone of the entire payment process," see *"A Mutual Responsibility and a Moral Obligation": The Final Report on Germany's Compensation Programs for Forced Labor and Other Personal Injuries*, eds. Michael Jansen and Günter Saathoff (New York: Palgrave MacMillan, 2009), 115.

seven partner organizations had its specific situation and faced its particular challenges. The Polish partner organization and the IOM are sufficiently representative for the two types of situations and approaches described earlier.

DIFFERENT STARTING POINTS OF THE PARTNER ORGANIZATIONS

Throughout the processing and resolution of the claims, the different "starting points" of the various partner organizations impacted on their operations. As described in Chapter 5, most of the partner organizations already implemented other compensation programs for victims of the Nazi regime in the 1990s. While the earlier compensation programs did not concern forced labor, these partner organizations still had acquired considerable institutional and historical knowledge. They were in a better situation than IOM to understand the situation of the potential beneficiaries and some could even turn to previous records, as many previous beneficiaries were also eligible for compensation under this program.

Other organizations, particularly the IOM, learned about their claimants only during the outreach and claims processing phases. As IOM had not been involved in any matters concerning survivors of Nazi injustice or persecution prior to the Program, the processing of the claims (i.e. their collection, review, and verification) was, at least initially, considerably more difficult and consequently more time-consuming than for the other six partner organizations. IOM did not only have to find and reach out to all potential claimants, but there was also no institutional knowledge in the organization about these constituencies and the conditions of their forced labor under the Nazi regime. IOM therefore needed to acquire this knowledge as quickly and comprehensively as possible to be able to process and evaluate its claims in a fair and efficient way.

There were two main consequences flowing from the different situations of the partner organizations. First, the international partner organizations, and in particular IOM, needed more time than the national partner organizations to reach their worldwide claims populations and to collect the claims under their responsibility. Second, the verification of the claims by the Central and Eastern European partner organizations and the JCC could in view of their document and knowledge base involve a more individualized review of the circumstances of each specific case, whereas IOM had to rely to a greater degree on the grouping of similarly situated claims and their assessment against the historical and factual patterns of the group. These different approaches are explained in the following sections.

CLAIMS PROCESSING

The following sections deal with the processing of forced labor claims. Chapter 9 discusses the additional program lines, i.e. personal injury claims, and in the case of IOM also property loss claims.

Organizational requirements for the claims process

While the organizational set up of the partner organizations is described in more detail in Chapter 4, a number of structural requirements are particularly relevant for the claims process. Most importantly, as claims processing and resolution consists of several separate steps, the organizational structures should mirror these. There has to be a department that performs the initial processing of the claims and verifies them by examining the evidence or by other verification measures. This work is ideally checked by some form a review mechanism. Finally, in instances where claims decisions are not accepted by claimants who file complaints, there must also be structures in place to deal with this, such as an appeal commission.

Designing a claim form

A well designed claim form is an important part of an efficient claims process that must strike a difficult balance. On the one hand, the form should be standardized, as much as possible, to allow easy entry of the information in a database and its computer-assisted processing; for this, simple fields, ideally with tick boxes or drop-down menus, should be used. On the other hand, the claimants also must have the opportunity to tell their individual stories, and this requires free-text space whose content is much harder to capture. Prior to its use, the claim form should be tested for ease of understanding and comprehensiveness. In IOM's case, for example, this was particularly important not only in view of the age of the claimants, but also because of their distribution over many countries, cultures, and languages.[3]

As an example, the original IOM claim form with the accompanying guidelines that were distributed to claimants is included as Annex 8.

Claims collection and registration

In the case of the Polish partner organization FPNP, the initial period of collecting the claims was challenging simply because of the great number of applicants. After implementing a large-scale information campaign, the Polish foundation had to deal with enormous amounts of letters flooding in. Claim forms and all kinds of inquiries (so-called informal applications) came in by the thousands. Although the office of the Polish organization somewhat expected a rush, the number of incoming mail exceeded all expectations.

Some of the first official applications using the authorized claim forms reached the FPNP in November 2000. By the end of 2001, the numbers of incoming claims had peaked. At the end

---

[3] IOM also designed and distributed separate claim forms for personal injury claims and property loss claims.

of the same year, the official deadline for submitting claims ended which prompted many thousands to hand in their forms. All kinds of letters and even postcards coming in before the end of December 2001 were accepted as informal applications meeting the deadline.

For the FPNP office it was a time of intensive work. All personal data and categories needed to be collected in a database, including:

- information on the nature of persecution (forced labor);
- what kind of evidence was submitted to prove persecution;
- assigning a country code to each case reflecting where the claimant was deployed as forced laborer (Germany, Austria, or occupied countries); as well as,
- assigning a code for the type of persecution suffered, the names of involved companies or what type of company it was.

The incoming mail was registered and forwarded to the relevant department.

In IOM's case, the majority of the claims were received in IOM's country offices. They were submitted on the standard claim form that IOM had made available during its outreach. The claims were either sent by post or they were submitted by the claimants in person. Where claimants asked for this, the dedicated program staff in the country offices assisted them in filling out the claim forms. A number of claims were received by post in the central program office at IOM's headquarters in Geneva. In total, IOM received more than 332,000 claims for forced labor.[4]

The program staff in the country offices also registered the claims and archived the claim files. Through a web-based software application, they entered the information from the claims relevant for their processing and verification directly into the specially designed claims database which was maintained in the central program office at IOM Geneva. To the extent that a claim was not complying with the formal submission requirements, the country office would request the claimant to rectify the deficiency.[5] The claim forms and attached documents were scanned and consolidated into a documents database that was centrally managed at IOM Geneva.

From the first day of claims intake, the core team at IOM Geneva received questions from the country offices concerning the program. The questions covered a wide spectrum of issues,

---

4   Within two other program lines, IOM further received approximately 42,000 claims for personal injury, and 35,000 claims for property losses. For details of these program lines, including the claims processing, see Chapter 9.
5   One issue was whether so-called "informal" claims not submitted on the claim form would be treated as claims received, and, if so, for how long after the end of the filing deadline they could still be completed and turned into formal claims.

including the formalities of the claims submission; eligibility requirements, especially concerning claimants or claimant groups not covered by the program;[6] evidentiary issues; and technical questions relating to the registration of the claims and the cooperation between the central program office at IOM's headquarters in Geneva and the respective country office. Some of the questions were specific to claimants or claimant groups from a particular country; others were of a more general nature applicable to many or all types of claims in the program.

In order to ensure compliance with the legal requirements of the program by the country offices and consistency in their work, including the replies and the advice they gave to (potential) claimants, the program introduced weekly "Question & Answer" communications from the core team in Geneva to all country offices. These communications provided answers to those questions that had been raised by the country offices during the week and that were relevant for more than one or for all of the offices. The staff in the country offices were also provided with claims intake and registration guidelines drafted by the core team in Geneva, and regular trainings of country office staff were held in the largest country offices and at IOM Geneva. The overall approach was that claims would not be rejected at the intake or registration stage, but that the decision on their acceptability would be taken by the core team in Geneva.

This 'division of labor' was also adopted by other partner organizations, particularly those that operated in vast territories. The Ukrainian partner organization, for example, worked together with local social welfare offices and regional offices run by partner organizations that accepted claim applications, advised claimants and helped them with the completion of their application forms, while the main office in Kiev controlled the overall procedure and took decisions on claim applications.

Review and verification of the claims

In the case of the Polish partner organization, the processing of the claims was done by a review and verification commission, which had already been established during earlier compensation programs. As part of the commission, eight smaller teams operated as review committees, usually a team of four plus a team manager. Depending on the incoming number of claims, the size of these review committees would be increased or reduced accordingly. In early 2001, the FPNP established an archive section that was responsible for searching relevant documents to verify the claims, including research in Polish and international archives.

---

6   To understand and comply with the legal regime governing the compensation of former forced laborers was for another reason particularly difficult for claimants falling under the responsibility of IOM. Simultaneously with the forced labor compensation program, IOM implemented part of the Swiss Bank Settlement under which many of the same claimants were entitled to compensation that were also entitled under the compensation program. The claims under this parallel Holocaust Victim Assets Programme (HVAP) were received and processed in many of the same country offices as the compensation program claims, and the staff of the two programs had to coordinate closely to assist and advise potential claimants properly.

From 2000 onwards, reviewing and verifying claims took place in accordance with the Foundation Law, its legal specifications and the review principles stipulated by the FPNP board. Determining internal rules, regulations and instructions was crucial in terms of standardizing the decision-making process for audit departments. Also, the EVZ Foundation could gain insight into the decision-making processes of its partner organizations which made the overall procedure more transparent.

The review committees checked the claim forms in form and content and filed them per category. The staff filled in internal review forms before compiling all data in the database. For audit purposes, data records were forwarded to the EVZ Foundation (see Chapter 8).

When a claim could not be verified, the Polish foundation would contact the claimant and ask him/her to produce the necessary evidence, but it would also start its own research in Polish and international archives for documents that confirmed persecution. In January 2001, the review and verification commission reached its highest level of employment with 83 staff members.[7]

Out of the more than 650,000 claims for compensation for forced labor, the review committee approved more than 590,089 claims as formally correct, out of which 485,216 were approved and 104,973 were rejected. On 23 June 2003, the phase of reviewing and verifying forms was concluded.

In IOM's case, the review of the claims and their verification was done centrally by the program team at IOM Geneva. This involved a number of actions. An important first step was the verification of the claimant's identity and of the authenticity of his/her signature.[8] Preliminary checks were performed on the claims database to identify claimants who had submitted the same claim more than once, possibly in different country offices and/or at IOM Geneva. Through regular electronic exchanges with the EVZ Foundation, it was also checked whether claimants had submitted the same claim with more than one of the partner organizations. Claims that did not fall within the responsibility of IOM but within that of one of the other partner organizations or of the Austrian Reconciliation Fund were transferred to that organization, and corresponding claims from the other partner organizations and the Austrian Reconciliation Fund were received and introduced into the IOM program.[9]

---

7 The high number of staff members was also due to additional tasks, such as the review and verification of forms claiming compensation payments from the Austrian Reconciliation Fund, the processing of claims regarding other program lines as explained in Chapter 9, and the processing of claims regarding other aid projects for victim groups not eligible according to the Foundation Law.

8 While the claimants did not need to be represented by a lawyer but could file their claims free of costs themselves, in cases where a claimant was represented by a lawyer or another person it was sometimes difficult to ascertain the authenticity and authority of such a representative.

9 Foundation Law, Section 11 (1), sentence 2 provided: "... persons who because their forced labor was performed primarily in the territory of what is now the Republic of Austria can receive payments from the Austrian Reconciliation Foundation." For information on the Austrian compensation program, see www.versoehnungsfonds.at (accessed 6 April 2017).

The following *Figure 6* is a flowchart of the typical stages of the claims processing of the partner organizations of the EVZ Foundation.

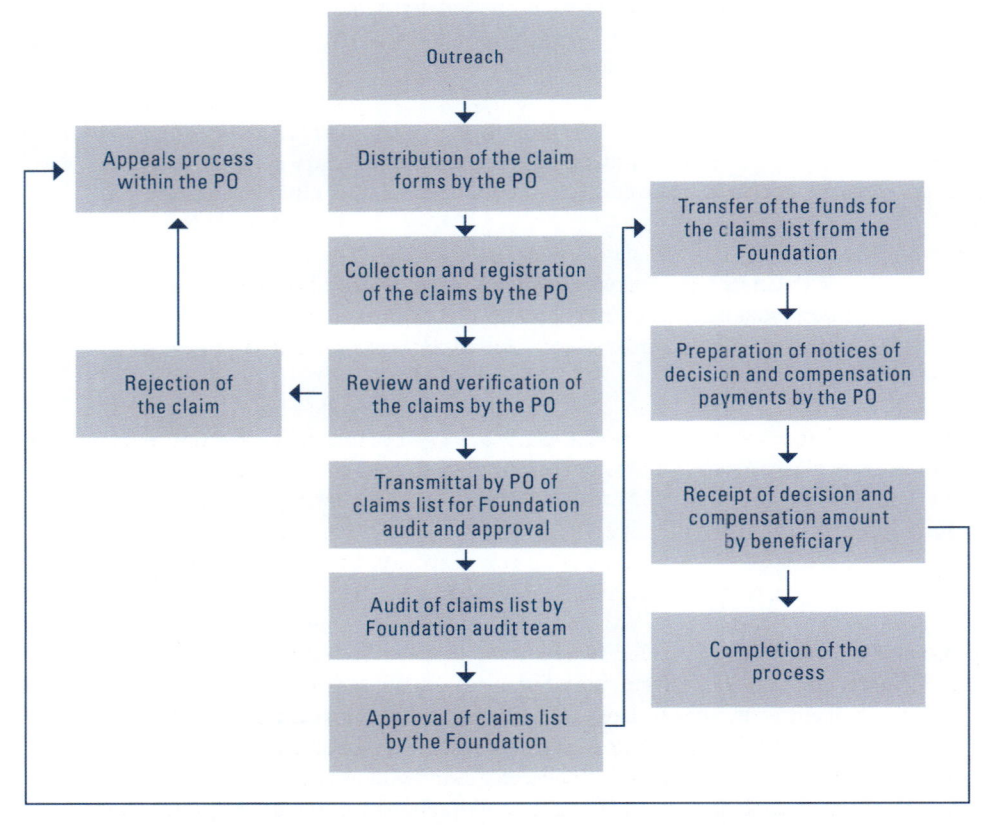

Figure 6: Flowchart of the typical stages of the forced labor claims and payment process. The process varied slightly depending on the different situation of a partner organization. Note: PO refers to partner organization.

The methodology used in the substantive review and verification of the claims followed several key principles. The most important of these was the decision to group together as much as possible similarly situated claims so that four goals could be achieved, which included:

- information and documents from some of the claims could be used to verify other claims in the group that were lacking information and/or documentation;
- information from the claims in the group contributed to a more comprehensive picture and better understanding of what had happened to that group of claimants;

- the review of claims together in groups made their processing more efficient; and
- all of the above resulted in greater consistency and thus fairness to the claimants in the group than an individualized one-by-one review would have achieved.

The grouping was primarily done based on information in the claims database concerning items such as origin of the claimants; place and/or conditions of their confinement; company or entity that used the claimants as forced laborers; evidence (or lack thereof) in the claims; known historic facts about the claimants in the group and their conditions at the time; and other factors.

In order to maximize the benefits of group processing, the review staff at IOM Geneva was organized into teams who 'specialized' in one or more claimant groups and in that way became experts for the group and their particular situation.

As laid down in the Foundation Law (Section 11 (2)) and described in Chapter 2, the program applied relaxed evidentiary standards. Claims could essentially be verified in three ways: either they contained sufficient documentary evidence, or they were verified in external archives, or they were determined to be credible. This was in line with the practice of other claims programs dealing with situations that occurred in a distant past and where the victims, because of the circumstances of the crimes, could not be expected to possess significant documentary evidence.[10]

Faced with a great variety of evidentiary documents, IOM had to find ways to ensure consistency in the assessment. IOM's claimant population was very diverse and submitted different types of documents. To ensure consistency in the review, the program management provided guidelines to the various review teams that contained an annex showing photocopies of each document submitted in the claims and describing its evidentiary value. This "GFLCP Book of Evidence" was a living document that in the course of the claims processing grew to include more than 200 documents.[11]

Because it lacked the type of knowledge about its claims population that the other partner organizations had from earlier programs, and since it quickly realized the scarcity of documentary evidence in its claims, the core team at IOM Geneva was from an early point on looking for outside archives against which it could match the information in the claims in order to verify them. This was in line with its experiences in other claims programs where such archive searches had been used successfully.[12]

---

10 For examples in other programs see Heike Niebergall, "Overcoming Evidentiary Weaknesses in Reparation Claims Programmes," in: Carla Ferstman et al., eds., *Reparation for Victims of Genocide, War Crimes and Crimes Against Humanity* (Leiden: Koninklijke Brill NV, 2009), 145–166.
11 For the table of contents of the GFLCP Book of Evidence see Annex 9.
12 For instance, by the Commission for Real Property Claims in Bosnia and Herzegovina and the Housing and Property Claims Commission and the Kosovo Property Claims Commission in Kosovo.

Figure 7: Typical form of evidence: The German employment offices issued an "Arbeitsbuch" for foreign laborers in which all work stations were to be documented. (The example above is the inner side of the Arbeitsbuch of an Ukrainian (born 1924) deported to German-occupied Poland; with the insignia of the employment office in Linz; a Gestapo photo was cropped to function as a passport picture). Source: Dokumentationszentrum NS-Zwangsarbeit, Sammlung Berliner Geschichtswerkstatt

Later on in the German compensation program, when the partner organizations had exhausted the pool of claims which they were able to verify themselves based on documents, the EVZ Foundation assisted in setting up a process whereby each of the partner organizations could match claims against information at the International Tracing Service (ITS) in Bad Arolsen, Germany, the largest archive of Nazi Second World War documents and records. These searches were performed periodically through the exchange of electronic lists pursuant to an agreed standard protocol, and many of IOM's claims could be verified in this manner.

In addition, the EVZ Foundation financed the creation of an "Archives Network" in which over 350 German national, state and municipal archives and archives maintained by companies[13] and concentration camp memorials, as well as archives from other countries participated.[14] Archive searches were thus one of the most important manifestations of the victim-friendly nature of the program which had been stipulated in the Foundation Law when it obliged the partner organizations to assist the claimants in supporting their claim (Section 11 (2)).

---

13   A few German companies had earlier granted access to their archives for purposes of the program.
14   For the role of the German Federal Archive and the "Archives Network" beyond the completion of the claims program, see Chapter 11.

Claims that lacked sufficient documentary evidence and could not be verified in archives or against other external records were still compensable if they were otherwise credible.[15] At IOM, a claim was essentially deemed credible if the information and the personal story of persecution provided by the claimant corresponded to that of other claimants in a group or category which was recognized as eligible under the compensation program. The grouping of claims was therefore particularly relevant for these types of claims, and since it used this technique from the outset, IOM started working on these types of claims early on. It then became apparent that for a number of such groups of claims additional historical research was needed since the respective categories of former forced laborers had not yet been covered by earlier research.[16] The category of IOM claimants that was the most difficult to deal with and to verify, and where grouping and credibility were therefore most relied on, were Sinti and Roma claimants especially from South Eastern European countries.[17]

DECISIONS ON THE CLAIMS AND APPROVAL BY THE EVZ FOUNDATION

The reporting of the partner organizations' decisions to the EVZ Foundation and their control by and eventual approval through the Foundation was the same for all the partner organizations. Once a partner organization had completed its review and decision-making on a group of claims ("tranche"), it put together an electronic list of the tranche which contained standard data on the claims as agreed with the EVZ Foundation. This was the case both for tranches of approved and rejected claims.

The controlling of the tranches was performed by so-called "control teams" that the EVZ Foundation had created for this purpose. When an electronic tranche from a partner organization was received by the Foundation, a control team would select a sample of claims which it would then, together with the partner organization's decision, examine on site at the partner organization. Chapter 8 describes in detail the control process, including the resolution of any disagreements between the partner organizations and the EVZ Foundation.

Upon the completion of the controls, the EVZ Foundation would send back to the partner organization the electronic tranche list with the decision as approved for each claim contained in the list. For tranches containing claims approved for payment, the EVZ Foundation would transfer the required funds to the partner organization that would make the payments to each claimant. Details of the payment process are discussed in Chapter 7.

---

15 Section 11 (2) of the Foundation Law provided in this respect: "If no relevant evidence is available, the claimant's eligibility can be made credible in some other way."

16 This was the case, in particular, for former forced laborers in the Balkans and in Greece. IOM cooperated with several reputed historians in Germany and in South Eastern European countries in this respect. Additional historical research was also performed or commissioned by the EVZ Foundation itself.

17 As stated earlier, in its claims processing activities, IOM used synergies between the German compensation program and the program that it implemented simultaneously under the Swiss Banks Settlement. Target groups, including Sinti and Roma, were partially identical and many potential claimants were eligible under both programs. Hence, for a number of individual claims and for certain groups or categories of claims, historical and "group" evidence could be used for the verification under both programs.

LEGAL SUCCESSOR CLAIMS

As described in Chapter 2, the Foundation Law provided for a self-contained regime of eligibility of legal successors (Section 13 (1)).[18] Legal successors in this hierarchy could only be paid compensation if the deceased person would have been eligible to receive it. Consequently, the compensation program had two types of legal successor claimants:

(i) Those who filed a claim as successors of former forced laborers who were alive on 15 February 1999 but died before they could file a claim; and
(ii) Those who took over the claim application as the applicant passed away while the process was still ongoing.

Before a legal successor's claim could be reviewed on substance, the legal successor had to prove that the former forced laborer died on or after 15 February 1999, which was the cut-off date decided during the negotiations. Legal successors of deceased claimants had to notify the partner organizations of their legal succession within six months after the death of the initial claimant or their entitlement to receive payment would expire.

The various partner organizations essentially used two different approaches for the communications with legal successors and the processing of their claims. Both had advantages and disadvantages, and both presented different processing challenges. In the first approach, all legal successors making a claim for the same deceased person had to agree on one of them as their representative in the compensation process. This had the advantage for the partner organization of having to deal with only one legal successor per affected family. Communications in this case only took place between the partner organization and the legal successor representative, and the total payment for all eligible legal successors was also made only to that representative who was in turn obliged to pay out the respective shares to each of the other eligible legal successors. It was possible in this case that not all eligible legal successors would participate in the process because the partner organization relied on the other legal successors, and in particular the legal successor representative, to communicate properly with all legal successors. There was thus also the risk that the legal successor representative would not pay out one or more shares of the compensation he or she would receive on behalf of all eligible legal successors since the partner organization relied on the legal successor representative in this respect as well.

In the second approach, the partner organization tried to identify and communicate with all (potentially) eligible legal successors of a deceased person, and it made payment of the respective share of the compensation awarded directly to each eligible legal successor. This approach put a higher processing burden on the partner organization. It also exposed the partner organization to the risk of attempts to be held liable by legal successors that it did not find or include in the process or to whom it did not pay out their share of the compensation. On the other hand, communications and payout did not depend on the ability or honesty of one or more of the legal successors, but was in the domain and control of the partner organization itself.

---

18 The exclusionary levels of legal successors were: spouse and children; grandchildren; siblings; and a will.

The processing of legal successor claims by a national partner organization

During the course of paying out the first installments, the FPNP already established a separate department for defining basic principles regarding payments and procedures for legal successors. By calling into existence a department that dealt with special inheritance cases and legal successors of compensation payments, the FPNP foundation board sanctioned the work of this newly established team in October 2002. The department's main task was the distribution of compensation payments among legal successors in accordance with the Foundation Law and internal FPNP regulations.

As a result of cooperating with the Polish Ministries for the Interior and Administration, the Polish partner organization gained access to the central database PESEL-CBD, the official residents' registration system in Poland, in May 2004. Having access to this database sped up the process of payments considerably, e.g. the time that was previously needed to divide payments among legal successors could almost be shortened by half. Moreover, time-consuming written correspondence for the sake of completing personal data could be reduced. The PESEL database was used to determine dates of death, PESEL-reference numbers, addresses of legal successors and their degree of relationship with deceased beneficiaries. This collaboration also resulted in considerable cost savings on the part of the FPNP. However, only the Polish partner organization was permitted to access this useful tool while other partner organizations could not benefit from it.

Nonetheless, processing claims of legal successors became a challenge for all partner organizations. This was also the case in Poland, where payments made to legal successors on the basis of the Foundation Law often did not correspond to national inheritance law. Due to the fact that payment dates were repeatedly postponed and beneficiaries were generally quite old, some claimants were no longer alive to receive the second installment payment. Moreover, legal successors often contacted the foundation with considerable delay and sometimes failed to meet the six-month deadline within which they were supposed to get in touch with partner organizations after the death of the eligible claimant in their family. Many only learned about this procedure when they were notified about the second installment payment.

Therefore, the FPNP approached the EVZ Foundation to request a favorable interpretation of both the Foundation Law and the six-month deadline for legal successors. In this regard, a joint meeting of all partner organizations with the EVZ Foundation in Warsaw in March 2004 proved very fruitful. It was agreed that until 15 May 2004, all partner organizations would accept all applications in the name of claimants who met the initial deadline to submit their claim (31 December 2001) but who had passed away before receiving the complete amount of compensation payments. In these cases, the partner organizations decided to approach legal successors directly, instead of waiting for them to get in touch.

The resolution facilitated securing thousands of "belated" legal successors compensation payments in Poland. In April 2004, the FPNP launched a large-scale information campaign for the media and victim's associations, sending out nearly 50,000 letters which informed about the procedure in the event of a beneficiary's death and which included the corresponding application form. Ultimately, more than 45,000 legal successors, most of whom did not know that they could claim compensation, contacted the partner organizations.

The processing of legal successor claims by an international partner organization

The processing of legal successor claims by IOM followed the second approach described above. Once the eligibility for payment was determined for the former forced laborer, IOM identified all claims relating to the case. If they were submitted by different individuals, IOM determined which individuals could be considered as eligible legal successors and grouped them together as part of the same "family group."[19] Where individuals had not submitted separate claims but were identified by IOM as legal successors for the same deceased person, IOM included them in the related family group. IOM sent requests to all identified legal successors in each family group for proof of identity and relationship to the deceased victim so that their eligibility could be confirmed as within the hierarchy pursuant to the Foundation Law. A person claiming a legal successor right needed to provide a recognized certificate of death and recognized proof of the relationship between the person asserting the right and the deceased victim.[20] Only one certificate of death, however, was required for each family group. In all instances, legal successors had to show that they were in the highest level of relationship to the deceased person on whose behalf they were claiming. So long as identified eligible legal successors at a higher relationship level had survived the deceased person, legal successors at a lower level were not eligible for payment.

Similar to the claims by forced laborers, IOM required that all identified legal successors also signed a waiver stating that they would not make any further claims against the German State and companies. IOM also required that eligible legal successors agree in writing to share among all unidentified eligible legal successors at the same relationship level, in case IOM had not received notice of all equally entitled eligible legal successors prior to distribution of payments.

All identified legal successors in each family group received decisions from IOM explaining whether their legal successor claims were considered to be eligible and, if not, for what reasons they were rejected. The controls and approvals by the EVZ Foundation and the payment process for legal successor claims were basically the same as those for claims by former forced laborers themselves.

---

19 The identification of a "family group" was done primarily with the help of the information in the GFLCP database.
20 Since IOM was dealing with legal successors residing in many different countries, it had to process a great diversity of death certificates and heirs' documents. To ensure consistency in their assessment, IOM put together a "Book of Heirs Evidence" with evaluation guidelines similar to its "Book of Evidence" for claims by former forced laborers.

Among the 330,000 forced labor claims processed by IOM, approximately 11,000 were legal successor claims. Some 40 percent of these were claims filed originally by claimants who subsequently died, and some 60 percent were claims filed by legal successors. The number of legal successors included in these claims was approximately 22,000, which meant that on average each claim represented two legal successors.

APPEALS

A claimant who was not satisfied with the decision on his or her claim could make an appeal to an independent appeals commission within the partner organization which had decided on the claim. An appeal could be made against the rejection of a claim or against the amount of compensation awarded, for instance when the claimant was assigned a lower eligibility category than expected. Appeals could be made by victims of forced labor or their legal successors entitled to compensation payments. The deadline for making an appeal was within three months and seven days after the decision by the review and verification commission was sent out.

Appeals were examined by independent appeals commissions.[21] While the appeals commissions were independent in their review of the earlier decisions on a claim and drew up their own rules of procedure, they were still bound by the legal framework of the Foundation Law and the binding regulations and interpretations of the EVZ Foundation. The EVZ Foundation performed similar audits on decisions of the appeals commissions as it did on the initial decisions of the partner organizations. When disagreements existed between an appeals commission and the EVZ Foundation, they attempted to find a common position.

Appeals commissions were not allowed to change a first instance decision to the disadvantage of the claimant, except in cases of proven fraud or other obvious abuse of power. The decisions made by the appeals commissions were final. The Foundation Law explicitly stated that there was no further legal action possible to object the decision of the appeals commissions.

Claimants who had been awarded some compensation appealed on the following grounds:

- Dissatisfaction with the amount of the compensation; the claimant found that the compensation amount was too low and did not accurately reflect nor compensate for the suffering endured;
- Dissatisfaction with only the partial payment (first installment) of an already small amount;
- Dissatisfaction with unfavorable exchange rates, particularly in the case of Poland (see Chapter 3);
- Non-consideration of the duration of forced labor and the age of victims in the amount of compensation;

---

21 As defined in Section 19 of the Foundation Law on appeal proceedings and in the respective partnership agreements, partner organizations were required to establish independent appeals organs.

- Dissatisfaction with assigning the suffered repression to an inaccurate category; particularly controversial was that detention sites had to be on the so-called "BEG-list"(drawn from earlier compensation legislation for victims of Nazi injustice), and later had to be classified as so-called "other places of confinement";
- Dissatisfaction with the evidentiary requirements.

Groups of claimants who appealed because the claims of their group were rejected:

- Individuals who did not meet the requirement of deportation beyond the national borders of 1937 (these were individuals who were forced to work in their place of residence as well as relocated individuals);
- Prisoners of war who were also used as forced laborers;
- Italian Military Internees (IMIs);
- Individuals who had failed to file their claim within the legal deadline or who had failed to claim legal succession within the deadline.

In the case of the Polish partner organization, the foundation board entrusted the review of appeals to an already existing appeals committee within the organization. It resumed its work as part of the forced labor compensation program in November 2001. After lengthy consultations with the EVZ Foundation, the existing committee was restructured into the appeals commission and internal principles were defined to ensure that the review of appeals was in accordance with the Foundation Law and the partner agreement.

Members of the appeals commission acted independently in the matter of reviewing appeals. They made their decisions in accordance with applicable regulations and on the documentation provided by the claimant or evidence gathered by the FPNP. Based on the partner agreement, the FPNP was required to determine the composition of the appeals commission in agreement with the EVZ Foundation. Members of the appeals commission, as required by the German side, could not dually be board members of the Polish partner organization, nor could they in any way be involved in the first instance decision-making.

The Polish appeals commission was also in contact with state archives and assisted claimants in providing the necessary evidence that would prove their persecution. It also made use of the possibility of authenticating incomplete evidence of repression in order to help a larger number of eligible persons to claim compensation and to actually receive it. This is also reflected in the percentage ratio of positive and negative decisions of which more than 70 percent were in favor of appellants.

Also the FPNP negotiated several times with the EVZ Foundation on whether its appeals commission could review complaints filed later than the three months' deadline initially agreed upon. The aim was to try to pay out as many beneficiaries as possible within the overall existence of the compensation program, even if claimants were formally no longer eligible as they had missed the deadlines. The terms of these negotiations were formally recorded in amendments of the partnership agreement between the EVZ Foundation and FPNP.

When it searched for candidates for its appeals commission, IOM consulted with its "Steering Committee of Most Affected Victims Associations."[22] As spelt out in the partner agreement, the appeals commission had to consist of three members. As a result, IOM chose, as two of the members of its appeals commission, candidates recommended by the Steering Committee who brought particular knowledge of victims' situations and relevant historical background into the work of the Commission. The chairman of the appeals commission was a judge at the European Court of Human Rights who brought particular independence and vast experience with judicial proceedings into the process. IOM's appeals commission not only relied on the knowledge and experience of its members, but also drew on additional historical expertise that was provided by dedicated staff in IOM's program team and from historians with whom that staff cooperated.

SUMMARY

Processing, reviewing and verifying claims form the substantial part of implementing compensation programs, including the interpretation of eligibility criteria, the establishment of audit committees and finally challenges that local and international partner organizations are faced with when dealing with appeals and legal successor cases.

CHALLENGES AND LESSONS LEARNED

- Given the large number of claims and the standardized and limited compensation available in the forced labor compensation program, the competing goals that needed to be reconciled were providing justice to the individual claimants while at the same time developing and implementing a process that provided compensation to all eligible claimants as quickly and efficiently as feasible.

- The various partner organizations had to deal with different claimant groups and different evidentiary situations, and therefore adopted tailored processing approaches, from the intake of the claims and their registration, to their review, verification, and determination of their eligibility.

---

22 For the steering committee, IOM had asked the largest victims associations in the major claimant countries to agree on a manageable number of representatives.

- In line with the practice of other large claims mechanisms, a relaxed standard of proof was applied, and the forced labor compensation program *actively* assisted claimants in proving their claims, including through presumptions and searches in external archives. As such, the program was not just a purely bureaucratic matter, but claimants also looked for communication, recognition, interaction, and support.

- The extensive use of IT and communications support, including in particular that of databases, was essential to the efficient processing of the claims.

- Of utmost importance are the specific measures taken to ensure the protection of personal claimant data, both within a program and in relation to outside communications.

- Care must be taken to ensure potential beneficiaries are not prevented from filing their claims by "gatekeepers" at the claims reception stage; intake staff needs to be trained and monitored in this respect.

- A particular challenge in the forced labor compensation program was that the interpretation of certain eligibility criteria and historical information was only specified later on in the program. This led to situations where claims were processed only to be rejected afterwards, or that claims had already been rejected when new interpretation guidelines for historical circumstances were disseminated. Thus, clear eligibility criteria and interpretation thereof contribute to an effective claims process.

- The fact that the compensation program relied on a self-contained regime of legal successor eligibility rather than on national inheritance laws contributed greatly to its efficient completion.

- The direct role of the EVZ Foundation throughout the claims processing was a unique feature of the compensation program, compared with other claims mechanisms. It ensured consistency, primarily through providing binding guidance to the partner organizations on eligibility of categories of claims, determination of camps as other places of confinement, and through the auditing and approval of the partner organizations' decisions on the claims; but it also required targeted mechanisms and processes to resolve differences between the partner organizations and the EVZ Foundation.

NORBERT WÜHLER AND DARIUSZ PAWŁOŚ

CHAPTER 7:
CLAIMS PAYMENT

This chapter contains:

— Payment in two installments
— The processes of payment of the claims
— Taxation of compensation payments
— Payment in different currencies
— Setting a deadline for the payment process
— Final accounting and archiving of payment records

INTRODUCTION: FAST, SECURE AND RELIABLE

The payment of the monetary amounts awarded to eligible beneficiaries is the main purpose of a compensation program. It is a crucial stage of the process, both for the beneficiaries and for the program as a whole, and it should be reached as quickly as possible. At the same time, it is also important that the payments are made in a safe and secure way and that the payment system is reliable so that the right beneficiaries receive the correct compensation amount/s and that no fraud or other irregularities occur. As is the case in other phases of a large-scale compensation program, different challenges must thus be balanced at the payment stage as well.

Like the processing and resolution of the claims, in the case of the forced labor compensation program the payment of the awarded compensation was the responsibility of the partner organizations and not the EVZ Foundation. The payment process was a massive task for each of the organizations: together, they paid out 4.34 billion Euros to a total number of 1.66 million eligible beneficiaries.[1] This task was made even more challenging by the fact that the compensation to the beneficiaries was paid out in two installments. This was prescribed by the Foundation Law and was due to the fact that the funds available to each of the partner organizations for the payment of compensation were fixed from the beginning, but the exact number of compensable beneficiaries only became known after completion of the processing of all claims by the respective partner organization.[2] The allocation of funds to the various payment stages was further complicated by the need to keep a reserve for anticipated successful appeals.

All the partner organizations had to deal with certain common issues in the payment process, such as creating an infrastructure for the payments and finding solutions for payments that had been returned. As with the processing of the claims, other aspects of the payment process differed, however, due to the different geographical scope of their work and because of other particularities in the situations of the various partner organizations. Some of the partner organizations used, for instance, the network of a domestic bank, the postal system, or the social security agency for the distribution of the compensation to the beneficiaries. Others worked with an international bank as intermediary to effect the payments to the beneficiaries in a large number of different countries worldwide. Funds were either deposited into the bank, postal office or social security branch for withdrawal by the beneficiary, or checks were issued to the beneficiaries for cashing at the designated bank or its partner institutions.

This chapter describes the most relevant aspects of the payment process for all partner organizations and details the challenges for two of the partner organizations, the FPNP, the Polish partner organization, which issued payments to citizens in Poland, and the IOM, which was responsible for paying out compensations to beneficiaries worldwide.

---

1 These numbers include survivors of forced labor and their eligible legal successors only, and not the other program lines described in Chapter 9.
2 For details concerning estimates of eligible beneficiaries during the negotiations and at the time of the Foundation Law, see Chapter 2.

PAYMENT IN TWO INSTALLMENTS

The payment in installments was necessary because the funds available to each of the partner organizations for the payment of compensation were fixed, but the exact number of beneficiaries only became known after completion of the processing of all claims by the respective partner organization (see Chapter 3). Payments were made in two installments, with different ceilings for the amounts that could be paid out as first installments set by the Foundation Law for the different categories of claims.[3] This payment method had the regrettable, although unavoidable, effect of upsetting many beneficiaries when they did not receive the full amount of their compensation right away. However, a worse option would have been to pay out the full amount only after all claims were processed and decided upon, when the amount available for each eligible claimant would be clearly allocated. This would have meant that the beneficiaries would have waited even longer until they received any payment, and it was thus preferable to at least pay some compensation earlier.[4]

The Polish partner organization FPNP was the only one of the seven partner organizations to initiate preliminary payments even before the EVZ Foundation authorized the first installment. As outlined in Chapters 5 and 6, the Polish Partner organization was able to use existing databases and contacts and was well aware of the claimants' situation. Due to its existing knowledge, the FPNP was ready to begin paying out the first installments shortly after the enactment of the Foundation Law. However, during the international negotiations it was agreed that all claims before US courts had to be withdrawn before the beginning of the payments, and this process took longer than anticipated. There were also other factors that led to an initial delay of the "green light" for partner organizations to start with the payments. In Poland, the FPNP experienced an "atmosphere of waiting" during these months as well as political pressure to begin with the payments.

Eventually, the FPNP decided to issue preliminary payments to the oldest and most vulnerable beneficiaries. This was a group of about 60,000 individuals who were born before January 1921 and who were able to present claim forms and evidence of their eligibility. In March 2001, the FPNP sent out checks to this group who had to sign an agreement that this sum would be deducted from the regular first installment. This decision was taken entirely by the Polish partner organization, as the EVZ Foundation was legally bound by the Foundation Law.

On 18 May 2001, the last lawsuits against German companies in the US were withdrawn or rejected and the German Parliament on 30 May 2001 decided that this amounted to "legal security." In June 2001, about ten months after the enacting of the Foundation Law, the FPNP was finally able to pay out the first regular installment to the beneficiaries.

---

3   The ceiling for the first installment to beneficiaries in Category B was 35 percent, the ceiling for the first installment in Category A was 50 percent. In addition, IOM had to make a (third) "top-up" payment to certain legal successor categories.
4   Taking into account international agreements and other specific regulations, payments in Poland were made up of three segments: payment of a first installment (75 percent of the total amount), a lump sum payment to cover losses that were caused due to unfavorable exchange rates (this is explained in more detail in Chapter 3), and the payment of the second installment (25 percent of the total amount).

THE PROCESSES OF PAYMENT OF THE CLAIMS

The main stages of the payment process were the same for all the partner organizations. They were closely coordinated with the EVZ Foundation and followed a mutually agreed procedure. Payments were made to groups of beneficiaries according to lists (so-called "tranches") of beneficiaries from the partner organizations, which were approved for payment by the EVZ Foundation. First, the funds needed for the payment of such a group (tranche) were transferred from the EVZ Foundation to the respective partner organization. The partner organization then arranged for the actual payout to the individual beneficiaries pursuant to the arrangements it had put in place in its area of responsibility.

In principle, it was decided that the lists of eligible claimants should be transferred to the EVZ Foundation every two months. This timeframe was decided together with all seven partner organizations, which allowed enough time for internal review and data registration in the EVZ Foundation's own database, as well as the provision of financial resources needed to prompt tranche payments and other review activities. Either simultaneously with or prior to the payment, beneficiaries were informed about the decision on their claim, the amount of the compensation awarded to them, and the method of payment.

Setting up the payment infrastructure

The partnership agreements required the partner organizations to make arrangements with banks regarding payment procedures. In choosing banks to cooperate with, factors such as shareholder background, deposit guarantees, and a sufficient branch network with ample cash supply played an important role. The selected banks and respective cooperation agreements needed the approval of the EVZ Foundation. In order to avoid any risks due to instability of banks, the EVZ Foundation and its partner organizations negotiated state guarantees for eventual losses with the respective governments. This was the case in the Ukraine, for example.

To transfer payments to the Polish beneficiaries, the Polish partner organization cooperated with the PKO Bank. Payments made available by the EVZ Foundation took place nationwide via 1,200 PKO bank branch offices. For this, the FPNP concluded a contract with the PKO Bank that stipulated the conditions and principles regarding the disbursement of the compensation payments. The contract also defined the form of the financial accounting on both sides, the principles of controlling, as well as logistical aspects of the payment process.

Like the other partner organizations, the Polish partner organization established a separate Department for Compensation Payments, the main tasks of which were:

- Preparing and sending out payment notices to the beneficiaries;
- Collecting and disseminating information about the paid compensation;

- Cooperation with the implementing bank, e.g., explaining questions raised by the bank employees, confirming payment notices, or correcting personal data;
- Receiving and registering payments that had been carried out; and
- Corresponding with legal successors of persons who had received notices of payment but who could for various reasons not realize them.

When IOM evaluated different options for making worldwide compensation payments, it became clear that a decentralized payment strategy in a large number of countries was complex to implement and required extensive staff involvement. Wholesale bank transfers were very difficult and costly to implement as many claims lacked the necessary banking information in the claim form. Cash payments, on the other hand, were neither practical nor cost effective, as it required all claimants to come to the IOM country offices to collect the funds. Both scenarios involved issues related to logistics and security, as well as significant expense. On balance, IOM decided to pay by check with an international bank as intermediary. Citibank, which was selected through a bidding process, was accessible in most of the countries where IOM needed to make payments; Citibank's IT systems were compatible with the GFLCP database; and the price charged by Citibank was competitive.

Compatibility of IT systems and competitive pricing were also reasons given in the selection of the service provider for the mailing of the letters by which the checks were sent and through which the award and payment information was provided.

Similarly to the FPNP, within IOM's GFLCP program, a separate team was responsible for the payment process. This ensured that dedicated staff members with relevant expertise were working in this area, and staff who were organizationally independent, and who had not been involved in the prior review and verification of the claims, did this work.

Transferring money to the beneficiaries

Once the payment infrastructure was established and the claims were decided, the payments could be transferred to the beneficiaries. In Poland, the procedure of paying out compensation was based on lists of eligible beneficiaries sent by the FPNP to PKO Bank branches electronically. By means of these lists, the banks could make the respective payments. At the same time, beneficiaries received a payment notice by mail, which entitled them to pick up the payment. Exceptions were made for beneficiaries who were very old, bedridden or seriously ill and who had no possibility of visiting a PKO branch themselves. In these cases, a FPNP team visited the respective beneficiary to hand out the money personally.

In the case of IOM, which paid compensation to beneficiaries in some 80 countries, the payments were made through checks mailed to the individual beneficiaries, which the beneficiaries could, in turn, cash in the branches of the designated bank.[5] The checks were generated by the partner bank of IOM, based on data from the GFLCP database that IOM transmitted electronically to that bank. The checks were then mailed by an international service provider to the beneficiaries, together with information on the decision on the claim, the amount of the compensation awarded, and instructions on how to cash the checks. An exception to this procedure was made in Romania, where the majority of the beneficiaries were Sinti and Roma for whom access to the banking system would have been difficult. Here, IOM issued payments through local post offices.

The workflow of IOM's payment process can be summarized as follows. From the GFLCP database, an electronic file was created with all relevant data to be included in the checks that were to be sent to the beneficiaries included in a particular payment tranche. This file was transmitted electronically from IOM to Citibank, based on an agreed technical protocol. Citibank generated a check for each beneficiary in the tranche, in the language of the country of the beneficiary's residence. The checks were transmitted to the selected service provider for inclusion in the notice letters to the beneficiaries. These letters also contained information, drafted by IOM, about the appeals possibility and about the payment in two installments. The service provider then mailed out the letters to the beneficiaries.[6]

A more general aspect, particularly in large reparations programs such as this one, is the question of prioritization, that is, should there be certain beneficiary groups that receive their compensation before others? Again, this depends on the context and purpose of a reparations program, as well as the (technical) possibilities to identify such groups. In this program, it was indeed an important issue as some of the claimants were extremely old and/or vulnerable. It was decided that any priority order of payments was left to the partner organizations themselves, some of which chose to pay out compensation first to those who were born before a certain date, and/or who were in category A (forced labor in concentration camps or similar situations).

Finally, the payment phase of such a program must not be looked at merely from a technical perspective. This is perhaps the most symbolic moment of the process for the beneficiaries of a reparations program, and organizations involved in the process could acknowledge that in several ways. The authors of this book feel that in the forced labor compensation program it was, for example, a missed opportunity that the checks were not accompanied by a direct message from the German side. In fact, it was discussed at one point to include a letter with the payment notification mail or check envelope. A possibility would have been to include a copy of a 1985 speech by former German President Johannes Rau who had apologized for

---

5   For property loss claims, payments of amounts higher than 10,000 Euros were made through transfers into a bank account designated by the beneficiary.
6   Difficulties arose with the mailing of letters to Roma beneficiaries in Romania. Because of the similarity of names and other obstacles for the postal service in identifying the proper recipients, IOM decided to add the birth date of the beneficiary on the envelope by which the notice letter was mailed, and to engage in additional training for the postal service. This increased the reliability of the delivery process considerably.

German war crimes, including forced labor, during a visit to Poland.[7] Including such a message with the checks would certainly have been easy to realize and would possibly have increased the sense of acknowledgment on the part of the beneficiaries.

Receipt of the payments by the beneficiaries

Depending on the different payment system that each of the partner organizations had set up, the way in which the beneficiaries ultimately received the compensation amounts, in hand, differed.

In Poland, the PKO Bank was well prepared for these procedures and very few complaints were filed in this matter. Bank employees received special training about compensation payments and each branch office was informed on disbursements by mail. In addition, the FPNP tested their payment infrastructure. Employees of the Polish partner organization were sent to several PKO Bank branches to check whether the procedure was working properly and reported back positively. Bank employees dealt with beneficiaries in a respectful manner and the latter did not hold back their emotions. Payments were indeed running so smoothly that already on the first day of disbursements one third of all beneficiaries included in the first tranche received their payments.

To better ensure security of the payment process, the FPNP also approached the head of the prevention office at police headquarters to request special assistance by the police. The organization was concerned that beneficiaries who had received their payments in cash were at risk of being robbed. In cooperation with the Polish police it was agreed to increase police presence near banks on payment days. The police received a map of Poland informing about the number of beneficiaries in every district, which helped them to adequately position police officers.

In IOM's case, a beneficiary could cash the check in any Citibank branch in its place of residence, or in the branch of a bank cooperating with Citibank for this purpose in places where Citibank had no branch. Normally, the check was made out in Euros, and the beneficiary received the corresponding amount in Euros.

Frequently, checks were returned to IOM because the notifying letter could not be mailed to the beneficiary or because the check was not cashed at the bank. These instances increased during the payment of the second installment. Typically, the reason was that the claimant had changed address without informing IOM, or he or she was deceased before compensation

---

7   Authers describes that this has actually happened, but he may have observed individual actions by staff members of some partner organizations (John Authers, "Making Good Again: German Compensation for Forced and Slave Laborers," in *The Handbook of Reparations*, ed. Pablo de Greiff (Oxford: Oxford University Press, 2006), 440. The authors of this book are not aware of such practices.

was awarded or received. In the latter case, legal successors had six months to notify IOM of the death of the claimant. However not all legal successors complied with this deadline and some were not aware that their relative had claimed the compensation or even that they had been forced laborers at all. When a check was returned, IOM attempted again to locate the beneficiary. If it did not succeed, the unpaid amount was credited to a future payment tranche.

TAXATION OF COMPENSATION PAYMENTS

In addition to these more technical aspects, several issues have to be considered when paying out compensations. First, financial compensation payments may, inadvertently, be subjected to taxes or count as income for people receiving social welfare. When administering such a program, this possibility has to be kept in mind. In order to ensure that payments remain tax free, for example, the organizations involved in such programs should make clear arrangements with all authorities involved. This is particularly important as taxation is not in the domain of organizations, but has to be coordinated with government authorities and needs government collaboration.

In the case of the forced labor compensation program, it was decided beforehand that amounts received under the Foundation Law should not be taxed in the beneficiary's country or count as social security benefit. Therefore, no amount was to be deducted from any compensation payment. The EVZ Foundation and the partner organizations attempted to ensure compliance with this obligation through understandings with the national authorities concerned. At the same time, the Federal Foreign Office of Germany directly contacted numerous governments to ensure that these conditions were implemented. This is by no means standard procedure — for example, there are no such agreements in the recent German compensation program for former Soviet prisoners of war.[8]

The issue of taxes is again important when reparations programs have clauses for legal successors, as these sums may then be subject to inheritance tax as well, and this may require different agreements with different authorities. In Poland, for example, payments to legal successors were paid nominally and they were exempt from all fees and taxes (including inheritance and gift tax). The Polish parliament issued a law in this regard in 2000.[9]

---

8   This compensation program was decided upon by the German Parliament in 2015. It is carried out by the German Federal Office for Central Services and Unresolved Property Issues (BADV). See www.badv.bund.de/EN/UnresolvedPropertyIssues/PaymentToFormerSovietPrisonersOfWar/start.html (accessed 13 April 2017).
9   Polish Law of 21 September 2000 on tax exemptions of compensation payments for victims of Nazi persecution *(Dz. U. 2000 Nr. 93, Poz. 1028)*.

PAYMENT IN DIFFERENT CURRENCIES

While this may be not relevant for many reparations programs, the issue of different currencies has to be thought about when setting up a payment infrastructure or process. There may be different possibilities depending on the context, and reparations programs may choose certain currencies for particular reasons. The choice of currency of the payment can also be left to the beneficiaries, which in turn requires a certain infrastructure.

In the case of the forced labor compensation program, the situation was rather complex as payments were issued to beneficiaries all over the world. The EVZ Foundation made the funds for the compensation amounts at first available in the German currency Deutsche Mark, and starting from January 2002 in Euros.[10] It was left to each partner organization whether it would make the actual payments in Euros or in the currency of the beneficiary's residence. National organizations, like the FPNP, mostly issued payments in the national currency.

A more fundamental problem arose in the forced labor compensation program due to a currency conversion that happened *before* the actual payments to beneficiaries, namely when the EVZ Foundation exchanged a large lump sum dedicated for the Polish Partner organization from Deutsche Mark into Złoty, the Polish currency. As a result, and a large sum of money was lost during the transaction. This incident is primarily related to financial management and communication and is described in Chapter 3.

SETTING A DEADLINE FOR THE PAYMENT PROCESS

In order to avoid a reparations program from becoming open-ended and to ensure it remains "active" until the last claim is settled and the last beneficiary is paid, a cut-off date for making payments may be a good solution. The drafters of the Foundation Law did not foresee this, but as the sums to be distributed were fixed and eventually it was known how many beneficiaries were eligible, setting an end date for the payments was the most efficient way to conclude the compensation program. It was therefore agreed that payments were no longer to be made available after 31 December 2006, including payments to legal successors. The EVZ Foundation set this date to avoid that large numbers of staff still had to be employed for the processing of very little numbers of cases. This also had to be coordinated with the German Ministry of Finances, and the Foundation Law had to be amended accordingly (Section 14 (4) of the Foundation Law was later supplemented).

For the partner organizations, this meant that they had to actively seek out and inform beneficiaries and legal successors whose cases were still open. While all claims had been processed at the

---

10   European Union countries that opted for the Euro changed to this currency on 1 January 2002.

time, legal successors still had six months to claim their eligibility in case the beneficiary passed away in the meantime, and beneficiaries still had three months to file an appeal. When setting the deadline, these time limits could no longer be offered, so the respective individuals or families had to be adequately informed. Moreover, not all legal successors were aware that they were eligible. For example, the FPNP organized a separate information campaign in Poland and used public records to find potential legal successors. The aim was to pay out as much as possible to the eligible beneficiaries and successors and the organization was able to process more than 6,000 cases in 2006.

Despite the efforts of the partner organizations, certain sums could not be paid out by 2006. Chapter 11 discusses how these so-called "leftover funds" were used to finance humanitarian projects for the benefit of Nazi-era victims.

FINAL ACCOUNTING AND ARCHIVING OF PAYMENT RECORDS

At the end of the payment process, the EVZ Foundation undertook a detailed and comprehensive final accounting with each of the partner organizations. This did not reveal any discrepancies or other issues. The Foundation also performed checks for a random sample of individual beneficiaries of each of the partner organizations to establish whether they had indeed received the amounts awarded to them (this is explained in Chapter 8). Again, no significant problems were found, which was a remarkable result given the total amount paid out (4.34 billion Euros), the number of 1.66 million beneficiaries and their spread over 89 countries.

Each partner organization implemented its own system of archiving and maintaining payment records.[11] IOM, for instance, keeps one set of its payment records on paper, and it also maintains a database of its payment information. Pursuant to an agreement between the Foundation, IOM and Citibank, the latter also maintains its payment information from the program in electronic form and has undertaken to make the respective data available to IOM or the Foundation in the event that there are specific questions concerning an individual payment. The amounts and the beneficiaries paid are also contained in a comprehensive database about its program that IOM made available to the EVZ Foundation and the German Federal Archive upon completion of the program.

SUMMARY

The payment is perhaps the most meaningful and yet a very technical moment of a reparations program. This chapter outlined how the partner organizations of the forced labor compensation program issued payments to beneficiaries and highlighted a number of issues that have to be taken into consideration.

---

11   For details concerning archiving of the files related to the program generally, see Chapter 11.

CHALLENGES AND LESSONS LEARNED

- While unavoidable in the circumstances, the payment in two installments added waiting time for the beneficiaries, as well as cost and administrative and logistical burdens for the partner organizations.

- The problem of "gatekeepers" (such as bank employees, police or even program staff) must also be avoided at the payment stage.

- When compensation payments are made in a currency different from that of the funds originally made available for them, one needs to address the issue of currency conversion and define who bears the risk of fluctuations in the value of the respective currencies.

- Each partner organization was struggling with the consequences when payments could not be made or were returned, for instance because the beneficiaries had moved to a different address or had deceased.

- Provision must be made for the secure storage and preservation of payment data, both within the program and with service providers used in the payment process. Considering the total amount paid out, the number of beneficiaries and their spread over so many countries and locations, the payment systems and controls implemented by the partner organizations and the EVZ Foundation worked very well and no significant discrepancies or other issues arose in the process.

- Compensation payments could have been complemented by a formal apology, given that compensation for historical injustice exceeds well beyond being a merely technical matter. In view of the relatively small payment amount available for each beneficiary, it would have been appropriate to recognize the injustice and the suffering of the victims together with the payment notice.

- The safety of the actual payout was not an issue in the forced labor compensation program. It can be, and has been, a major challenge in other programs, particularly if payments are made in cash.

UTA GERLANT

CHAPTER 8:
CONTROLS AND AUDIT

This chapter contains:

— Establishing control mechanisms
— Legal supervision
— Financial audits
— Controlling the claims processing
— Reporting obligations

INTRODUCTION: CONTROLS AND AUDITS — NECESSARY PARTS OF EACH PROGRAM

Controlling and auditing are necessary processes within any reparations program in order to ensure that funds are spent in accordance with the agreed purposes and eventually reach those entitled to compensation. Moreover, controls and audits are tools to prevent arbitrariness, abuse or fraud of the allocation of funds, including by those who are directly involved in the process. Controls aim at ensuring that in fact only the entitled beneficiaries and nobody else will receive the actual payments. This way, controls and audits can contribute to making a program more transparent and credible particularly for victim parties, and ultimately increase its legitimacy and overall acceptance.

In addition to typical procedures of claims processing such as internal supervision, claims verification, and appeals processes, the compensation program also featured so-called "control teams." This was due to the unique collaboration between the EVZ Foundation and its partner organizations whereby the EVZ Foundation was expected to monitor the work of the partner organizations. Control teams were employees of the EVZ Foundation who inspected the review, verification, and appeals processes of the partner organizations on a random basis. In so doing, the EVZ Foundation performed regular process and result checks. With this it was also guaranteed that the seven partner organizations were developing comparable standards when reviewing claims.

This chapter describes in detail the legal supervision, financial auditing, and process and result controls of the compensation program. It critically evaluates the contribution of controls to the successful implementation of the program.

ESTABLISHING CONTROL MECHANISMS

Generally speaking, control mechanisms are tools to examine data or operations of processes and/or whole institutions. Controls can counteract negligence and restrain dishonest conduct. Announcing the mere possibility of controls may lead employees to work more carefully and perhaps more fair, and may even stimulate good performance. At the same time, an exaggerated use of controls may lead to undesired effects: inappropriately strict decision-making, anxiety to make any decisions at all, or exuberant bureaucracy. A good balance is the key.

When establishing control mechanisms for reparations programs, three principal questions need to be addressed: What shall be controlled, with what objective? Which bodies should perform these controls and which methods should be used? Who decides what to do with the results?

Regarding the first question, the EVZ Foundation drew three conclusions:

- Legal supervision of administrative actions — Objective: maintaining the legal framework within which the program operates;
- Financial auditing of administrative actions — Objective: funds are appropriately, economically, and efficiently spent;
- Process and result controls and reporting obligations — Objective: the objectives of the program are fulfilled.

Controls and audits were already discussed in the process of establishing the EVZ Foundation. The agreement between the governments of the US and Germany (Annex 3) provided "that the Foundation will be audited by the [German] Federal Court of Audit and that all partner organizations will also be audited."[1] Hence, in the beginning there was only a rough understanding of what needs to be audited and which supervisory bodies should be responsible.

Nonetheless, following this rather general wording, the subsequent control mechanisms were established, including the involvement of already existing institutions:

Legal supervision:

- The German Ministry of Finance (BMF) audits the EVZ Foundation

Financial audits:

- The German Federal Court of Audit audits the EVZ Foundation
- The German Federal Office for Central Services and Unresolved Property Issues (BADV) audits the EVZ Foundation
- Public accountants audit partner organizations

Controlling the claims processing:

- Control teams of the EVZ Foundation audit the partner organizations

Reporting obligations:

- The German Government reports to the German Parliament about the work of the EVZ Foundation.

---

1   See Annex 3: US-German Agreement, Annex A (3).

Furthermore, the EVZ Foundation's Board of Trustees also held a supervisory role besides its strategic function in controlling. The Board discussed reports issued by the Board of Directors, the current status of procedures, adopted budgets and approved financial reports.

LEGAL SUPERVISION

Given the organizational structure of the EVZ Foundation as a public law foundation, legal supervision constituted one of the control mechanisms supervising the program. The principal task of legal supervision is to monitor that the formal criteria of the program are fulfilled and to ensure the achievement of the program's objectives. The aim of the legal supervision of the compensation program was thus to monitor that the EVZ Foundation abided by all applicable laws and regulations. This task was assigned to the BMF. The Foundation Law stipulated that the EVZ Foundation would submit its yearly budget to the BMF for approval after the Board of Trustees had passed it.[2]

Over the course of this program, legal supervision particularly dealt with issues that were not clearly defined from the beginning. The experience of the EVZ Foundation illustrates that the clearer regulations are defined the better they can be implemented during the program. At the same time, it is beneficial to leave some leeway for making further decisions which may be needed but which also were unforeseeable at the outset of the program. A certain level of flexibility contributes to making the program a more complete undertaking. Our experiences have also shown, however, that regulations that are only put in place when the program is already running may in fact complicate it (such as the issue of eligibility criteria, as described in Chapter 2).

From time to time, the EVZ Foundation turned to the BMF to clarify questions regarding the legal interpretation of the Foundation Law. One example concerned the regulation that "prisoner of war status does not constitute entitlement to compensation,"[3] which meant that prisoners of war who were used as forced laborers were not eligible for compensation payments. However, it was not always clear who should be categorized as a prisoner of war, and the issue was decided upon in a rather inconsistent way for different claimant groups. The Italian Military Internees (so-called IMIs) were denied the status of war prisoners by the Germans during the Second World War and thus performed forced labor as civilians. Yet, the BMF decided against their eligibility in the compensation program. This was perceived as unfair from the IMI's point of view, especially as other groups received an exemption in this regard (e.g. former Polish prisoners of war who were also forced to work under a civilian status as well as prisoners of war who were incarcerated in concentration camps). This example demonstrates not only how

---

2   See Annex 1: Foundation Law, Section 8 (1) and (2); see also Annex 4: Statutes of the EVZ Foundation, Section 10.
3   See Annex 1, Foundation Law, Section 11 (3).

sensitive eligibility criteria were in the German compensation program, but that such decisions must be taken with great caution, especially when a program is already running — in this case, many of the IMIs had received unclear outreach messages regarding their eligibility status.

FINANCIAL AUDITS

The objective of financial auditing is to ensure that the available funds are spent appropriately, economically, and efficiently. The German Federal Court of Audit and the BADV inspected the EVZ Foundation's use of funds, while public accountants audited the partner organizations.

The Federal Court of Audit only audits every five years, and it conducted an audit of the EVZ Foundation in the year 2005. In its findings, it gave recommendations to improve the EVZ Foundation's administrative actions.

The BADV was tasked with auditing the EVZ Foundation's budgetary and economic administration on a yearly basis. It reviewed the annual financial statements, which were compiled by an external accounting company, and randomly checked expenses. The BADV then submitted its audit report with results and recommendations to the Board of Directors. BADV audits prompted the EVZ Foundation to arrange its expenses clearly and document them in a well-founded and comprehensible way. Chief principles were to allocate funds only for the intended purposes outlined in the law as well as use funds in the most economical and efficient way. The BADV regularly audits public institutions, so the standards applied to the EVZ Foundation were comparable to those applied to other institutions.

To audit administrative costs of the partner organizations the EVZ Foundation commissioned public accountants. The EVZ Foundation's seven partner organizations were responsible for the processing of claims. In order to cover the expenses for staff and material, the EVZ Foundation had agreed to a ratio of between 3.5–15 percent for administrative costs with all partner organizations separately. This large variation can be explained by the fact that two partner organizations had to process claims coming in from all over the world and in a number of languages. Also, typically, salaries are significantly higher in international organizations compared to organizations based in Central and Eastern Europe.

Administrative costs had to be covered by the overall funds allocated to each partner organization, which were not to be exceeded. Partner organizations were obliged to provide transparent bookkeeping and accounting records so that accountants could inspect whether funds were spent appropriately, economically, and efficiently. In addition to this, partner organizations were also controlled by the respective national auditing authorities (and in the case of IOM and JCC, external auditors).

The EVZ Foundation commissioned a public accounting firm, the employees of which were required to have local expertise of the respective countries, to perform yearly audits. Reports of these audits were sent to the EVZ Foundation, which could then require necessary changes from the respective partner organizations. This included, for example, unjustifiably high salaries for managing staff or the excessive use of company cars. These controls served to prevent the improper use of administrative resources and reminded staff to spend available funds responsibly. At the same time, it was crucial that auditors were operating independently and were not receptive to corruption, i.e. that they received reasonable financial compensation and were unimpressionable in the face of threats or enticements.

The EVZ Foundation's financial department received the audit reports and inspected whether the expenses of the partner organizations stayed within the agreed yearly budgets and whether correct exchange rates were used. The department was responsible for transferring quarterly installments of administrative funds according to administrative requirements and the partner organization's actual account balance to prevent partner organizations from unnecessarily accumulating money. The EVZ Foundation also paid attention that at the outset of the program the partner organizations only purchased the most needed supplies and equipment, and that all purchases could later be depreciated (according to its decline in value during the course of its useful economic life). Also, with a decrease of the intensity of claims processing, partner organizations were asked to reduce staff.

Finally, a special case was a management audit of the IOM. At the outset of the program in 2001, the EVZ Foundation approached the German Federal Office of Administration to request this audit for the IOM. The inquiry was prompted by the unusually high budget for administrative costs while the number of claims to be processed by IOM was still uncertain. Moreover, it became apparent early on that IOM would have to reject a much higher percentage of claims than the other partner organizations. After a review of the respective management and the claims processes, the Federal Office of Administration concluded that both IOM's organizational and procedural approaches as well as its budgeting were appropriate for its situation and that it could be expected to perform the task assigned to it in an efficient way. The Federal Office of Administration recommended that the EVZ Foundation should provide IOM as quickly as possible with further guidance concerning the eligibility of those claims where this guidance was not yet available.

All audits were based on a double control principle, including those of the BADV, which were later subject to supervision by the Federal Court of Audit. From the start, it was necessary to have established a balanced system of implementation and audit in order to accurately respond to occurring challenges (for instance, unfavorable exchange rates or inflation rates in the case of international compensation payments).

CONTROLLING THE CLAIMS PROCESSING

One of the unique features of the compensation program was that the EVZ Foundation had assigned the processing, reviewing, and deciding on the claims to its partner organizations. In order to monitor their work and homogenize the procedure across the different partner organizations, the EVZ Foundation established a system of control teams. They regularly visited partner organizations and performed random process and result checks.

The main goal of the control teams was thus to contribute to making compensation available directly and immediately to eligible claimants. They helped ensure that eligible claimants would receive compensation payments for the correct category, and vice versa, that claimants who were not eligible would not receive compensation.

Control teams

The establishment of the control teams was already foreseen in the partnership agreements between the EVZ Foundation and its partner organizations. The agreements specified that the EVZ Foundation would check eligible claimants on lists from the partner organizations within four weeks after their receipt. As part of this process, partner organizations allowed the EVZ Foundation the inspection of their files and documents. If the EVZ Foundation found irregularities, it would put the respective payments on hold. Also, to avoid the risk of funds being misused or lost in risky investment activities, the EVZ Foundation chose not to make blanket transfers of earmarked funds. Instead, it provided the funds for claims only after they were approved (in the so-called "tranches" that could be submitted every two months) following the random checks by the control teams.

There were three control teams of EVZ Foundation: one was responsible for Poland and Ukraine (the countries with the majority of survivors of forced labor), a second one for Belarus and Russia, and a third for the Czech partner organization, the IOM, and the JCC. Later on, another audit team was added, assigned to deal with "other personal injury" claims (see Chapter 9). This team monitored all seven partner organizations with respect to these cases, since this program line had an overall ceiling in place (instead of a separate allocation for each partner organization, as was the case for the forced labor compensation).[4]

Each control team consisted of one manager and two to three staff members who brought with them different forms of expertise, namely language skills, knowledge of the historical background, and intercultural competences. Some of the control team members had already worked as volunteers and could apply their experiences to the program. While control team

---

4   The third program line that dealt with property loss claims had an altogether different system of controls, also described in Chapter 9.

members adapted their work to the concerns of claimants of the respective partner organizations — taking into account historical differences, specific program regulations, such as different opening clauses — they also interacted with the members of the other control teams so that the same benchmarks were applied for all partner organizations. This was done by consulting not only within but also between the control teams and also with EVZ Foundation's lawyers on the results of their inspections.

How were these controls prepared? Every two months, partner organizations could submit a tranche of eligible claimants to the EVZ Foundation. This electronic list contained as many claims as the respective partner organization had managed to process and decide on during this period. The data transfer was encrypted. At the EVZ Foundation office, electronic data processing provided a random but nonetheless targeted sample of claims (normally 1 percent of the list) that was compiled by means of certain parameters.[5] An encrypted list with cases that needed clarification as well as the random sample was then sent back to the partner organization, which was required to provide all related documents for auditing within the next couple of days.

What was the subject matter of the controls? In the beginning, control teams inspected only approved claims, i.e. whether claimants were really entitled to payments and whether they had been assigned to the right category of compensation. Later on, however, they also tested the accuracy of claim rejections in order to prevent the exclusion of eligible claimants from the compensation program. In addition to the control of the claims process, also the appeal process was controlled, both with respect to approved and rejected claims. With the addition of legal successor claims, the lists to be checked doubled in numbers, again comprising of approved and rejected claims and appeals. Separate lists needed to be submitted and handled for the first and second installment payments. Thus, the control process — similarly to the claims review and payment procedures — gradually became more complex.

What did the control process look like? In principle, the control teams acted as if they had to decide on the claims anew and then compared their decisions with those made by the partner organization. This control process took place after the claims were already decided upon by the partner organization, and a random sample of claims was selected for controls. Control team members worked on site in the offices of the partner organizations using their own database that contained all data of the respective claims under inspection. First, they compared personal data with those in the claim forms, and checked identification documents and signatures. This was done to ensure that compensation payments were made to claimants who were actually alive. The control teams also checked whether the waivers had been signed.[6] Second, the

---

5 There were no complete checks because it would have been too laborious and would have resulted in the EVZ Foundation usurping the procedure rather than leaving it up to the partner organizations. Random checks could perhaps not remedy every error, but could help eliminate systematic errors.
6 This refers to the waivers for legal closure, see Chapter 10.

control teams collected the most relevant data from the documents (claim form and documentary or other credible evidence) in order to make a decision on the claim and added the data to their own database as if they had to make a decision themselves. In a third step, they compared their own "decision" with that of the partner organization. The database was designed in such a way that the decision of the partner organization was only visible after the control team had entered its own "decision."

When both decisions were consistent, there were no further matters to discuss. Whenever there were deviations, the control teams would discuss with employees of the partner organization why they decided the way they had. This way, any misunderstandings on the part of the control team could be resolved. Whenever a disagreement remained unresolved, the respective cases were documented in the audit report alongside those where an agreement had been reached. The partner organizations had the opportunity to provide within one week a response to the report. These processes fostered a close communication on the interpretation of the Foundation Law, the need for historical research, and the necessity to introduce further regulations.

When either side realized it had made an error, the respective decision was revised. This mostly referred to individual cases, but at times also concerned more systematic issues, for instance, when the partner organization's decision-making process was generally too rigid. When more time was needed to clarify a case, the claim was taken from the list and resubmitted by the partner organization after the matter was resolved. Occasionally, and in the case of more systematic issues, a group of claims would be taken from the list and their payment put on hold until clarification was reached. Making corrections together helped the EVZ Foundation and the partner organizations develop a common understanding of the Foundation Law and the principles derived from it, which then enabled consistency in the procedures.

After receiving a partner organization's response to the audit report, the EVZ Foundation compiled a list from its database, containing all data on beneficiaries and individual compensation amounts. The list was encrypted and sent to the partner organization while the EVZ Foundation's finance department transferred the corresponding total amount.

With this kind of procedure, the EVZ Foundation avoided the transfer of funds without a thorough checking of the data's validity. This had happened in some reparations programs in the 1990s, where it later appeared that considerable funds were lost (the losses amounted to double digit million Deutsche Mark). At the same time, program staff members at both the EVZ Foundation and the partner organizations attained a better understanding regarding complex historical and country-specific contexts. Over time, they built a trusting cooperation, but nonetheless had to maintain a critical independence. In that sense, it was beneficial that control team members did not make any recommendations for correcting decisions themselves, as this was the responsibility of the Board of Directors. This way, control team members acted rather as messengers and mediators between the EVZ Foundation and the partner organizations, which proved to be an intelligent model of dividing responsibility, and helped preserve independence.

Fraud and special controls

Besides regular control procedures there were also special controls, one of which took place in summer 2001 in Ukraine. The control team of the EVZ Foundation noticed that the signatures on some claim forms for the compensation program appeared conspicuously "young" compared to those on claim forms submitted in an earlier program in the 1990s. The cases were compiled for a sample check and two members of the control team personally visited the claimants concerned. The claimants had to provide their signature again, and often it turned out that their relatives were in fact the ones who had filed the claim, but fortunately with the knowledge of the eligible claimants. Subsequently, partner organizations made sure that claimants personally signed the claims (and not their relatives).

Another special control took place in certain archives, prompted by the use of documentation from earlier claims processes by one partner organization. Here, the control team tried to retrace which evidence from the old files was used to support the approved claims in the compensation program. It turned out that some individual employees used the old documentation in a fraudulent way. They had already falsified evidence during an earlier claims process, and they now used the same falsified evidence again. This illustrates that decisions made in other programs should not be trusted blindly if it is not known in which circumstances the respective evidence was collected or how the review process was designed. Depending on the circumstances it is thus advisable that each compensation program should strive to obtain and inspect its "own" evidence.

Specifically, in this fraud case involving one partner organization, forged documents were re-used from a previous claims program, leading to a substantial loss of funds. During the earlier program, employees of a partner organization collaborated with an unauthorized third party acting as a claimant, who was then granted compensation payments on the basis of forged documents. When these respective documents and positive decisions were included as evidence for the forced labor compensation program, the fraudsters gained again. The partner organization discovered these practices only after the completion of the program and subsequently pressed criminal charges.

Which kind of fraudulent cases did the control teams uncover? At times, claimants attempted to forge evidence. Certificates attesting that claimants were detained as forced laborers were printed on copied documents of the International Tracing Service (ITS) in Bad Arolsen.[7] Given that the ITS had changed their letterhead over time, the falsifications were easily uncovered. Other times it was noticeable that a single document was copied together using several other templates. After inquiring with the ITS and other archives such cases were also

---

[7] The ITS in Bad Arolsen holds around 30 million documents about the fate of victims of Nazi persecution. The ITS index comprises information on 17.5 million people.

resolved quickly. Several fraud cases were uncovered because claimants had submitted falsified German documentation using the letter "B" instead of "ß" and "q" instead of "g" and in some individual cases claimants had forged the legal records of testimonies. The respective partner organizations handed these cases over to the prosecution.

Nonetheless, it is important to remember that the mere attempt to falsify documents did not necessarily mean that a claimant was not entitled to compensation, but rather that he or she may not have had any evidence to prove they were legitimate claimants. In most of these cases, however, claimants were not entitled to compensation payments.

Ex-post surveys

Control teams also conducted surveys after the compensation payments were made to find out whether beneficiaries actually received the money. These inspections focused on whether beneficiaries had received the complete payments and whether this had happened in a timely manner, but they also left space for beneficiaries to voice their opinions about the program. Auditors sent out questionnaires to more than 7,000 beneficiaries worldwide (which equaled about 0.4 percent of all recipients). Partner organizations were informed that inspections of this sort took place but did not know who had been contacted. After a letter campaign reminding those who had not yet answered, the response rate came to overall 90 percent.

The results of these so-called "ex-post" surveys confirmed that compensation payments were disbursed in an orderly manner. Some of the recipients could not remember if they had received any payments. In such cases or in cases of discrepancy, partner organizations were contacted to clarify the matter. After that, the respective beneficiaries were contacted again and asked whether they could confirm the information the respective partner organization had provided. For those who did not answer, confirmations of payments that were stored in the Federal Archives in Berlin were consulted. Ultimately, payments could be confirmed for all cases, something that cannot be taken for granted given the range and extent of the program. Also, there were no irregularities in terms of compensation amounts, payment periods, or the choice of currency. Still, it is important to note, the aforementioned case of false claim approvals resulting from the collaboration of the staff of a partner organization with an unauthorized third party as claimants was not exposed by means of these measures.

REPORTING OBLIGATIONS

The German Government regularly submitted to the parliament a report "On the state of affairs regarding payments and on the cooperation of the Foundation 'Remembrance, Responsibility and Future' with partner organizations," that had in turn been prepared by the EVZ Foundation.[8]

---

8   See Register of the German Parliament, BT-Drs 14/6465, p. 2, available at http://dipbt.bundestag.de/doc/btd/14/064/1406465.pdf (accessed on 13 April 2017).

Between 2001 and 2008, six reports were published and can be found online.[9] The final report gives an overview over the complete program.

SUMMARY

Taking into account the extensive oversight bodies and monitoring procedures concerning compensation for survivors of forced labor, the question arises whether they met the requirements, as outlined at the beginning of the chapter. Although the system of checks and balances was not without gaps, it contributed considerably to making the compensation program more transparent by preventing misuse, with only very few exceptions. The EVZ Foundation and the partner organizations discussed any mistakes and errors together and rectified them where possible, thereby constantly improving and adjusting the overall procedure. Despite occasional tensions between control teams and partner organizations — a fact that can easily be explained by their different roles and perspectives — it can be said that both sides have learned a lot from each other. Inspections did not prevent confidence building but in fact fostered and justified it. Ultimately, controls contributed to the legitimacy of the compensation program in the eyes of beneficiaries as well as the public. For this reason, it can be said that audits met the requirements placed on them.

CHALLENGES AND LESSONS LEARNED

- The clearer regulations, such as on eligibility criteria, are defined in the beginning of the reparations program, the better they can be implemented, and hence controlled. Several times the legal supervision had to clarify how the Foundation Law was to be interpreted, which in turn had direct repercussions on the overall procedure. Once a decision was made on the issue, it needed to be communicated via outreach to all affected people, thus making the procedure more complex for the staff.

- Financial audits can contribute to administrative actions being clear, well founded and comprehensible. Auditors can also give valuable advice on how to optimize the procedures.

---

9   The reports are available in German at the online register of the German Parliament: 27. November 2001: BT-Drs.14/7728, http://dipbt.bundestag.de/doc/btd/14/077/1407728.pdf
19. March 2002: BT-Drs.14/8673, http://dipbt.bundestag.de/doc/btd/14/086/1408673.pdf
30. December 2002: BT-Drs.15/283, http://dipbt.bundestag.de/doc/btd/15/002/1500283.pdf
25. June 2004: BT-Drs.15/3440, http://dipbt.bundestag.de/doc/btd/15/034/1503440.pdf
21. July 2005: BT-Drs.15/5936, http://dipbt.bundestag.de/doc/btd/15/059/1505936.pdf
9. July 2008: BT-Drs.16/9963, http://dipbt.bundestag.de/doc/btd/16/099/1609963.pdf
(all accessed 13 April 2017).

- Auditors can also be contracted as advisors, as was the case with the IOM and the establishing of their processes.

- During the auditing process, certified public accountants were faced with different administrative practices in various countries, some of which were country-specific, but nonetheless plausible. Other times, they encountered "peculiarities" which could not be tolerated, such as the excessive use of company cars. These issues were often solved in negotiations in which it would be determined what it means to spend funds appropriately, economically, and efficiently.

- Random audits conducted by control teams could neither expose all mistakes, nor all systematic errors or fraud attempts. Nonetheless, they contributed to developing overall consistent understanding of the Foundation Law and its regulations between EVZ Foundation and the partner organizations.

- It proved very useful for control teams to discuss their reports together, align the inspection standards and with them the resulting regulations. This kind of exchange also fostered knowledge management processes, from which all persons involved could benefit.

- It proved important to also control rejected claims and appeals to prevent the exclusion of eligible beneficiaries.

- It proved beneficial that the Board of Directors was given the responsibility of the results of the work of the control teams, and not the control teams themselves. This helped to maintain independence of the process.

- Rather than using documents and decisions from previous reparations programs, claims programs should strive to gather their 'own' evidence. In this case, previous frauds were repeated and were only uncovered by a comprehensive internal audit.

- Based on lessons learned from earlier compensation programs in the 1990s — where considerable sums were paid to partner organizations without checking or controlling to whom these payments were paid — it was decided that transfers of payments to partner organizations were made in tranches and calculated according to the actual amount needed for already approved claims contained in the tranche.

- Submitting the lists of approved claims ("tranches") in regular intervals ensured reliability and continuity of the process. The tranches did not require a certain minimum or maximum number of claims, and therefore allowed partner organizations to work according to their capacity.

- Encrypted data transmission was an essential tool for preventing data abuse for criminal purposes.

- Directly contacting and inquiring with beneficiaries whether they had actually received their payments increased the legitimacy of the program.

NORBERT WÜHLER

CHAPTER 9:
ADDITIONAL PROGRAM LINES

This chapter contains:

— Overview of the additional program lines of the forced labor compensation program
— Personal injury
— Property loss
— Humanitarian and social programs

INTRODUCTION: COMPLEMENTARY FEATURES OF THE PROGRAM

As introduced earlier, the main focus of the compensation program was to provide financial compensation to the victims of forced labor. They constituted by far the largest number of claimants, and the majority of the funds were allocated for them. However, the Foundation Law also entailed a number of additional program lines that specified compensation payments for other types of claims.

As agreed in the international negotiations, the Foundation Law included compensation for so-called "other personal injuries," for property losses, and for certain insurance claims. In addition, funds were allocated for humanitarian and social projects for certain Jewish and Sinti and Roma survivors of Nazi persecution. These groups were not required to file claims to receive these additional benefits, but their fate was regarded as sufficiently linked to the circumstances surrounding forced labor and as severe enough to be included in the program.[1]

This chapter provides a description of the most relevant aspects of the additional program lines of the compensation program for forced labor. It focuses on the programs "Other Personal Injury," "Property Loss," and "Humanitarian Programs" in order to provide a comprehensive picture of the activities of the EVZ Foundation and its partner organizations.

ADDITIONAL PROGRAM LINES

The additional program lines were created in the Foundation Law partly because class action lawsuits against German companies before US courts also referred to other crimes perpetrated by the Nazi regime. These program lines were thus included to achieve legal closure on all US lawsuits against German companies. In addition, there was a particular interest on the side of the JCC to cover certain property losses. While these were not directly related to forced labor, they thus became part of the overall "package."

---

1   This is a similar feature as the *cy pres* compensation awarded to certain victims in the Swiss Banks Holocaust Settlement. *Cy pres* is a feature of US class action settlements which allows the distribution of settlement funds in circumstances in which direct payment to individual class members is not economically feasible, or where funds remain after class members have been given a full opportunity to make a claim.

Overview of all program lines and funding

Program line	Fund (in million Euros)
Compensation for Forced Labor	4,535
Compensation for Other Personal Injuries	54
Compensation for Property Loss	102
Compensation for Insurance Claims	102
Humanitarian and Social Programs	153
Humanitarian Programs of the ICHEIC	179
Funds of the EVZ Foundation	102
Remembrance and Future Fund	358

Table 3: Overview of all program lines and funding. Note: All numbers are rounded. In addition to the amounts allocated by the Foundation Law, these numbers include additional income from accrued interest and donations received during the course of the program.

PERSONAL INJURY

Like survivors of forced labor, many individuals who suffered serious physical and emotional harm had not received compensation. Harsh treatment by authorities of the Nazi regime caused all kinds of serious health damages and personal injuries to the persons affected. Two situations were included in the compensation program since they were more closely related to forced labor or to captivity in a concentration camp. The Foundation Law referred to these in the following way:

> The funds […] shall be awarded in cases of medical experiments or in the event of the death of or severe damage to the health of a child lodged in a home for children of forced laborers; in cases of other personal injuries they may be awarded. (Section 11 (1)

The first category included victims who were detained mostly in concentration camps and were subjected to so-called medical experiments. A broad range of such pseudo-medical experiments were performed that had no medical merit but were mostly serving military purposes, for instance to assess the chances for surviving in cold water, under particularly low pressure, or without drinking water. These cruel and extremely painful experiments, often also involved high doses of adrenaline and potassium cyanide, resulting in long-lasting health damage or death.

The second category was related to the children of forced laborers. During the early years of the war, women who became pregnant after being deported to Germany to perform forced labor were sent back to their home countries. Later, as the Nazi authorities became suspicious that women were becoming pregnant intentionally in order to escape from Germany, this approach was changed. Pregnancies were either forcefully terminated, or the women were forced to give birth in designated places. From there, babies of "inferior racial stock" born to Polish or Soviet forced laborers were taken away from their mothers and put into special children's homes *(Kinderheime)*. Intentional under-nutrition in these homes led to mortality rates between 25 and 50 percent, in some cases up to 90 percent. Those who survived suffered severe health damage and were often traumatized for life.

Eligibility

As stated in the Foundation Law, to determine which other personal injuries were eligible for compensation was left to the implementation phase of the program. Yet, it soon became clear that the limited funds allocated to this category of claims would only be sufficient to pay survivors of medical experiments, and survivors of children's homes or the parents of children who died in such homes, whose compensation the Foundation Law explicitly mentioned. The Foundation Law foresaw that eligible claimants in these groups could receive up to 7,670 Euros.

In comparison to the main forced labor compensation program, the eligibility criteria for these groups were relatively clear. Still, it was difficult to identify which children's homes were covered, as at the time there was no clear distinction between "normal" foster homes and the abusive homes designated for children of forced laborers. Therefore, the distinction between "normal" foster homes and homes for the children of forced laborers was left to the implementation stage of the program. Also, regrettably, victims of forced medical treatments were not eligible. It was argued that when the medical "treatment" received by a victim was not a "pseudo-medical experiment" but rather an inappropriate physical treatment without experimental character, the claim was not eligible even though these cases also included extreme atrocities. An example was the forced sterilization of Sinti and Roma.

Processing and resolution of the claims

Claims for other personal injuries were processed by the partner organizations along the same lines of responsibility and according to a similar procedure as the forced labor claims (see Chapter 6). Applicants had to submit a written form explaining their fate.[2] After claims had been decided by the partner organization, the positive decisions were put into an electronic list for approval by the EVZ Foundation, which would check a sample of decisions for their accuracy. Appeals against negative decisions could be brought before the appeals bodies established by the various partner organizations.

The biggest challenge in the verification of the claims was the significantly different levels of detail in the information provided by the claimants. In particular victims of medical experiments often found that they were not able to talk or write about any detail of their painful experiences. To make up for this, IOM, for instance, compared their claims with the personal statements of others, with historical records and with claims and knowledge available from other partner organizations, and aimed at identifying patterns that could match the claims of "mute" victims.

To ensure consistency, the partner organizations and the EVZ Foundation discussed rules, regulations, guidelines, and jurisprudence under the Foundation Law and their application on a regular basis. Based on historical facts and additional research, including by experts of the JCC, the EVZ Foundation compiled and shared with the partner organizations a list of more than 100 medical experiments carried out in different concentration camps that served to support the eligibility of many claims. Similarly, due to the lack of historical knowledge and inconsistency in the information available in the claims, additional research was needed and carried out to support the eligibility of the *Kinderheim* claims. Also, a designated EVZ control team was responsible for the controls of these claims.

Limited funds

A major difference in this program line was that there was a closed fund for all partner organizations together, rather than a separate fund per partner organization. The Foundation Law foresaw that persons who had suffered personal injuries could receive a maximum amount of approximately 7,670 Euros. Even though it was stocked up during the program, the relatively small amount of 54 million Euros allocated for the claims for personal injuries — for all partner organizations together — resulted in two limitations. First, no claimant outside the two priority groups could be given any compensation. And second, this allocation did not

---

2   While most of the partner organizations used a separate claim form for personal injury claims, IOM incorporated the personal injury category into its forced labor claim form. It thereby simplified the claims submission for the claimants and reduced the time needed for the registration and processing of the claims.

allow for paying the maximum amount even to the priority categories of eligible claimants. This was problematic in view of the cruelty of the atrocities that were inflicted on the victims. By supplementing the allocation with interest earned on the Foundation's capital, the EVZ Foundation achieved that each eligible claimant could initially be paid at least 4,240 Euros. At the time of the final distribution of the interest accrued by the program, the EVZ Foundation was able to increase this amount by an additional 2,450 Euros for all surviving eligible victims in the priority categories. If they had also submitted a claim and were awarded compensation for forced labor, that compensation amount was not deducted. The same applied to compensation for property losses.

PROPERTY LOSS

The property loss program addressed persons who suffered property losses as a consequence of persecution or other Nazi injustices, with the essential and harm-causing participation of German businesses. Victims suffered these losses in connection with the economic policies enforced in the German-occupied territories of mostly Central and Eastern Europe. Persons who had already been eligible for compensation under previous post-war German legislation could not file claims under this program line.

From the total funds of the EVZ Foundation, an overall amount of approximately 500 million Euros was allocated for various property losses. This amount was divided according to specific purposes.[3] Some 102 million Euros were allocated for payment of individual claims for property losses. These claims and their processing are dealt with here.

Eligibility

In a very complex provision, the Foundation Law set out the criteria for the compensation of property losses suffered during the Nazi period as a consequence of racial persecution or as a result of other Nazi injustices if German companies caused these losses.[4] Accordingly, two sub-categories were established, one for persecution-related losses, and one for non-persecution-related losses. In both cases, there had to be "essential, direct, and harm-causing collaboration of German businesses"[5] with respect to the loss concerned. In addition to this specific requirement, the criteria contained a second narrowing factor: payments were reserved to cases that did not

---

[3] In addition to the amount for individual claims for property losses dealt with in this chapter, another sub-fund of 102 million Euros was established for the payment of claims against German insurance companies; this sub-fund was administered by the International Commission on Holocaust Era Insurance Claims (ICHEIC). The ICHEIC was in addition allocated 179 million Euros for humanitarian purposes.

[4] See Annex 1, Foundation Law, Section 11 (1), Sentence 1, Number 3 and Sentence 4.

[5] Ibid.

qualify for other German post-war programs for the compensation of property losses. As a result of these limitations, this compensation program only covered a fraction of the actual property losses caused by Nazi Germany.

Processing and resolution of the claims: IOM and the Property Claims Commission

IOM was responsible for the collection and processing of all property loss claims worldwide, including claims from Central and Eastern Europe. Property claims filed with other partner organizations were transferred to IOM. Like for the forced labor claims, IOM applied similar procedures relying on its global network of country offices once again for claims intake. In addition, it performed targeted outreach, developed a separate claim form in seven languages and created a special database for the property loss claims. The registration of the claims and their review was performed by a dedicated team of specialized staff at IOM's headquarters in Geneva. This team of some 30 staff also supported the Property Claims Commission in its resolution of the claims.

The Property Claims Commission was an independent body composed of three members: two members appointed by the German and the US governments respectively, and a chairman chosen by these two members. At the beginning of its work, the Property Claims Commission drafted its own rules of procedure to provide a framework for itself and guidance to the claimants (Supplemental Principles and Rules of Procedure of the Property Claims Commission). These rules dealt with key questions of claims processing and resolution, such as definitions, eligibility, waivers, evidentiary standards, and basic principles to be applied. The Commission held regular meetings at IOM's headquarters for which the IOM team provided legal and administrative support.

In order to resolve the high number of property loss claims (which reached almost 35,000 — many more than expected when the program was set up) in an efficient and consistent manner, the Property Claims Commission decided early on to use mass claims techniques.[6] It first reviewed a sample of some five percent of the claims to identify and determine the main factual, legal and valuation issues represented in the claims as a whole. This sample had been extracted by the IOM team from the database of the property loss claims pursuant to criteria provided by the Commission. The Commission issued specific guidance on these issues and drafted the corresponding determinations to be used in its decisions on the claims. The Commission then delegated the review of the individual claims to the IOM team that applied the Commission's

---

6   The pressure to complete the resolution of the claims as quickly as possible also came from the fact that no successful claimants could be paid until all property loss claims were finally decided (Section 9 (10), Foundation Law).

rulings to each similarly situated claim in the remainder of the claims population. The IOM team recorded the Commission determinations in an internal "Conclusion Index of Jurisprudence" which was reviewed and approved by the Commission at each meeting.

The Commission adopted or revised the IOM team's claim determinations and issued its corresponding decisions during its regular meetings in Geneva. These decisions were drafted with the help of standardized text components that the IOM team had built into the database for the various claims types pursuant to detailed instructions from the Commission. The text of a decision was generated from that database in English and one of six other languages most suited for the claimant.

The key question in most cases was whether the loss of property occurred in connection with the involvement of a German enterprise.[7] This so-called German enterprise requirement turned out to be the most critical one in separating compensable claims from non-compensable ones. Nazi economic policy and actual expropriations and confiscations were exercised in different ways in different parts of occupied Europe, but individual claimants rarely were able to submit evidence on this issue. The Commission therefore adopted a relaxed standard of proof.[8] Based on extensive historical research performed by the IOM team, the Property Claims Commission established clusters of historical situations that occurred in certain geographical areas during certain periods of time, and used these clusters to arrive at a number of presumptions. The most important distinction it developed was that the causation of the property loss was presumed if the respective German enterprise benefited from this loss within a year after it had been suffered. For example, if a company or small enterprise was expropriated by the Nazi authorities or occupying forces, the involvement of the German enterprise in the property loss was presumed if the subsequent takeover by that enterprise took place within a year's time.

The Foundation Law did not set a fixed or maximum amount for the compensation of property losses. It was thus the task of the Property Claims Commission to award a certain amount for a particular loss. The Commission realized that it could not provide a unique valuation specific to every compensable loss because the vast majority of claimants were not able to provide the information necessary to do so. It therefore created a "valuation matrix" in which it categorized

---

7   The Property Claims Commission defined property in Section 1 of its Supplemental Principles and Rules of Procedure comprehensively as "any and all immoveable and moveable, tangible and intangible assets," (unpublished document on file with the author).

8   As stated in Section 22.1 of its Supplemental Principles and Rules of Procedure, "the Commission's decisions on compensability shall be based on relaxed standards of proof taking into account the lapse of time between the date the loss occurred and the date the claim was made; the circumstances in which the specific loss or types of losses occurred; the information available from other cases; and the background information available to the Commission regarding the circumstances prevailing during the National Socialist era and the Second World War and the participation of German enterprises in the commitment of National Socialist wrongs," (unpublished document on file with the author).

the loss within a table of standardized values. Nearly 70 such property classifications were drawn up, with the most common relating to farms, small- and medium-sized businesses, professional practices, and bank accounts. The Commission chose the amounts of the standardized values based on a number of factors, including

   (1) the values used in prior German compensation programs;
   (2) historical research;
   (3) information found in the claims, particularly those in the sample of claims that had high-quality evidence; and
   (4) other sources.

The first was the most influential factor, and the Commission decided to use the pre-established, fixed tax or repurchase values of an earlier German compensation legislation, the *Bundesentschädigungsgesetz* (BEG), as a guide. In order to weigh the categories appropriately in relation to each other, a point system was used for each property type and a value of 145 Euros was assigned to each point.[9] This standardized methodology also contributed to consistency in the treatment of the claims, particularly given the limited funds available for property losses.

Closed fund

The Property Claims Commission first issued decisions on the compensable claims (varying between twelve and one million Euros) in favor of more than 15,000 claimants in over 30 countries without making payments. In its decisions, the Commission noted that the standardized values in its matrix (and in the decisions) did not represent current market values or repurchase values, and that given the limited funds available for property loss claims, it was likely that at the time of payment the awarded amounts would need to be reduced even further. To use current market or repurchase values would have meant to grant awards that would have vastly exceeded the funds allocated to pay property loss claimants, ensuring a *pro rata* reduction of up to 90 percent. The Commission instead aimed at limiting the *pro rata* reduction to approximately ten percent.

Appeals against these decisions were possible, but were limited to a reconsideration based on a manifest error or new evidence not taken into account in the first decision, and only if claimants could show that the omission in the first instance was not their own fault. The Property Claims Commission itself carried out the reconsideration. Only a small number of reconsideration requests were successful; the most common ground was the submission of new evidence.

---

9   Alternative methods were used for calculating the awards for real property and bank account losses.

The successful claimants received compensation payments after all claims were finally resolved, i.e., after the last reconsideration request was decided upon. In the end, the reductions at the payment stage were about 13 percent for persecution-related losses and 32 percent for non-persecution-related losses.

Final Report of the Property Claims Commission

Further details on the property loss part of the compensation program and the procedures and methods used in the processing, valuation, and resolution of these claims are contained in a comprehensive final report that the Property Claims Commission submitted to the Board of Trustees and in the EVZ Foundation's final report.[10]

HUMANITARIAN AND SOCIAL PROGRAMS

So-called humanitarian programs were foreseen in the Foundation Law, as it was felt that the fate of certain survivors of Nazi persecution was sufficiently linked to forced labor, but that these groups did not have any means to show a qualification for claims, or individual payments to them were not economically feasible.

The Foundation Law allocated certain sums for humanitarian projects: The JCC received 141 million Euros for the benefit of Jewish Holocaust survivors, and IOM was allocated 12 million Euros for projects benefiting Sinti and Roma who were persecuted by the Nazi regime. These two programs are briefly summarized below. A third humanitarian program with an amount of 179 million Euros administered by ICHEIC concentrated on home care and assistance to Jewish survivors and two Holocaust education projects.[11]

The great majority of the assistance under the JCC program was provided to Jewish survivors through partner organizations in Israel, the United States, and countries of the former Soviet Union. In Israel, these supported neighborhood assistance for elderly survivors, day care centers, home care, and geriatric and nursing homes. In the United States, the emphasis was on home care. In Central and Eastern Europe, home care, meal deliveries, heating, winter clothing, medical aids, and medicines were made available.

---

10 See Michael Jansen and Günter Saathoff, eds., *"A Mutual Responsibility and a Moral Obligation": The Final Report on Germany's Compensation Programs for Forced Labor and Other Personal Injuries* (New York: Palgrave Macmillan, 2009).

11 For the mandate of the ICHEIC to deal with insurance claims see footnote 3. For more information on the humanitarian and social programs see Michael Jansen and Günter Saathoff, eds., *"A Mutual Responsibility and a Moral Obligation,"* 136–139.

The program for Sinti and Roma administered by IOM is well-documented in a final report on its humanitarian projects.[12] The implementation of this program was extremely challenging in particular for two reasons: first, the difficult living conditions of the Roma communities in Eastern Europe, which were characterized by social discrimination and deep-seated rivalries within the various communities; and second, the lack of reliable information at the start of the program as to how many persons would be eligible to benefit from it. With the collaboration of a specialized search firm and local partners including Roma organizations, IOM eventually identified and supported 70,000 beneficiaries in 13 Central and Eastern European countries.

IOM originally hoped that the humanitarian assistance would contribute to a more fundamental improvement in the living conditions of the Roma survivors in their communities. In practice, this objective was not achievable. In places where no social framework existed, attempting to build sustainable structures would have required so much time that the results of such efforts would likely have only benefited the descendants of the survivors, and not the survivors themselves. While development aid normally focuses on promoting long-term skills and integration among the younger generations, in the circumstances IOM had to concentrate on getting direct assistance as quickly as possible to the most needy, elderly Roma, including basic relief goods such as food, clothing, and heating fuel. By reaching 70,000 individuals, this humanitarian assistance also served to build confidence and pave the way for counseling and so-called "encounter projects" that continued beyond the compensation program and were later funded by other sources (see Chapter 12).

SUMMARY

The additional program lines for personal injury and property losses and the humanitarian assistance programs, while benefiting deserving victims of Nazi persecution, did not fit neatly within the overall program's focus on forced labor. Their inclusion at a late stage of the negotiations raised questions about the wisdom of integrating them into the much larger forced labor compensation program. The challenges arising from this were compounded by the fact that the first two of these program lines were severely underfunded compared to the number of eligible claimants, and that the number of these beneficiaries was only known when all the respective claims had been processed. Difficult choices about prioritization of claims and levels of compensation had to be made, and frustration and disappointment by the claimants were the result.

---

12   See International Organization for Migration, *Humanitarian and Social Programs: Final Report on Assistance to Needy, Elderly Survivors of Nazi Persecution* (Geneva: IOM, 2006), www.swissbankclaims.com/Documents/DOC_74.1_hsp_1.pdf (accessed 28 April 2017). This report also covers the similar projects that IOM administered under the Swiss Banks Settlement.

CHALLENGES AND LESSONS LEARNED

- The additional program lines for other damages each required the design and application of *special features* and mechanisms, thus adding to the complexity of the overall program.

- In the case of personal injury claims, the allocated funds that were agreed in the negotiations turned out to be much too limited to fully compensate all eligible claimants. Therefore, difficult decisions on *prioritization* between in principle compensable claims and on the maximum payout per claimant had to be taken in the course of program implementation.

- Supported by a secretariat experienced in mass claims methods and processes, the Property Claims Commission of IOM applied several *key techniques* to achieve an efficient and consistent resolution of large numbers of claims in a short period of time. These were, in particular, the use of a sample of claims to identify and decide representative factual, legal and valuation issues; and the reliance on relevant research and the corresponding grouping of claims to apply presumptions and arrive at consistent legal determinations.

- Sampling and grouping of claims have proved useful in other compensation programs as well. They need, however, an *experienced secretariat to be applied in a consistent and efficient way.*

- The limited funding available for the compensation of eligible property loss claims led the Property Claims Commission to the development of a *"valuation matrix"* that assigned values to loss types not based on calculations of actual losses, but in amounts as close as possible to the eventual awards.

- Since the number of eligible claimants was not known and, in contrast to the forced labor program, no fixed sums or ceilings had been set for property losses, payments could only start once *all the claims had been processed and finally resolved.*

- The fact that the initial awards first notified to the successful claimants prior to payment still had to be reduced *pro rata* at the payment stage led to further disappointment of property loss claimants. This could only have been avoided if the awarded claimants had been notified after the resolution of *all* the claims. However, this would have frustrated the claimants equally, if not more so.

- The humanitarian assistance program for Sinti and Roma survivors in Central and Eastern Europe, albeit limited in scope, served to increase awareness of the great need for the most basic relief which, until then, was largely unnoticed.

ROLAND BANK

CHAPTER 10: LEGAL CLOSURE

This chapter contains:

— Why was legal closure so important?
— Measures adopted to ensure legal closure
— Was legal closure achieved?

INTRODUCTION: PAINFUL, BUT UNAVOIDABLE

"Legal closure" is about settling, for good, potential or actual claims arising from a specific historical injustice through a designated claims program and thereby preventing future claims or legal action. In general, this can relate to resolving claims and counter-claims. In the context of a compensation program for serious human rights violations, it will usually be focused on protecting those responsible for human rights violations and eventually funding the program against future lawsuits. This may be considered particularly problematic in the case of programs that do not provide for full compensation, as it conflicts with the expectations — and, depending on the actual circumstances, also with the material rights — of the victims of the human rights violations. However, in cases where the money for a reparations program comes from the side of those responsible for the human rights violations, legal closure usually constitutes a necessary component of the negotiated solution without which there would be no such solution. Finally, it may be understandable that stakeholders of those responsible for violations would not agree to pay for the same violations again in the future. It is important to underline, however, that this legal closure does not relate to aspects of criminal responsibility of individuals for the crimes committed.

In the case of the forced labor compensation program, legal closure was a major interest of the German side, both for the government and for German companies. The commitment on the part of the German side to establish the EVZ Foundation and pay significant amounts of money into the Foundation's funds had been motivated, at least partly, by the expectation to settle for good the lawsuits pending against the German State and German enterprises before courts elsewhere (particularly in the US) and to ensure protection from future lawsuits. It was decided already during the negotiations that every claimant of the compensation program would have to waive any claims outside the program against German companies in any matter connected to Nazi-era injustice and against the German State for forced labor and property damage. It was also agreed that all cases pending before US courts would be withdrawn and terminated before the program would start. None of the provisions on legal closure related to eventual criminal responsibility of individuals involved.

This chapter explains the motivations of the German State and companies for seeking legal closure and how this was implemented in the program. It also discusses to what extent legal closure has in fact been achieved.

WHY WAS LEGAL CLOSURE SO IMPORTANT?

Even though legal closure is a frequent component in compensation programs, it may seem surprising that this was still so important in the case of forced labor such a long time after the crimes took place. Indeed, for several decades, no legal action that had been initiated in Germany against the German State or German companies concerning forced labor had been successful. However, when the so-called class action lawsuits were launched in US courts in the 1990s, the legal situation was less clear. Also, the sheer number of these lawsuits in the United States created an economic and political pressure irrespective of the actual prospect for success of the lawsuits. By participating in the negotiations for a compensation program, German companies sought to settle these cases. Moreover, both the respective companies as well as the German State sought protection against lawsuits that concerned Nazi injustice addressed under the program in any future proceedings.

There were many reasons why lawsuits for compensation of forced labor had remained unsuccessful in German courts until the end of the 1990s:

- Lawsuits were turned down by German courts with the argument that they came too late, citing a three-year deadline under German law for claiming compensation of damages caused by a violation of certain personal rights.

- Some victims of forced labor lacked an addressee of a claim if the company in question no longer existed.

- In the opinion of some courts, there was no contract between companies and forced laborers; consequently, a claim a company could not be based on the violation of a contract or on a contractual obligation to pay wages.

- Claims against the German State were refused for the reason that state immunity shields states from being sued before courts of other states.

- Finally, there were problems of proving in a lawsuit the fact of having carried out forced labor in cases in which former victims did not avail of any documentary evidence.

However, in the US, the legal situation was more difficult to assess. First, it was argued that for certain violations, such as crimes against humanity, there should be no time limitation under civil or public law. Also, rules on state immunity had started eroding with respect to atrocities such as torture or crimes against humanity, at least in the criminal law sphere. And, regarding the lack of documentary evidence, courts were potentially willing to accept personal statements as sufficient proof.

Perhaps more important than the legal risks for German companies, the class action proceedings in the US developed their potential for creating significant public pressure irrespective of the prospect for success of the claims. Coverage in the media on companies fighting with sophisticated legal arguments against legal responsibility for atrocities in which they had clearly been involved impacted negatively on their reputation and amounted to an economic threat. At the same time, high fees for lawyers constituted a relevant economic consideration given that defense in class actions is very costly.

These factors not only contributed to the readiness of German companies, and ultimately the German State, to take financial responsibility and negotiate for a compensation program, but underlined their interest in "legal closure"— namely the protection from all future claims in these and similar matters.

MEASURES ADOPTED TO ENSURE LEGAL CLOSURE

A number of measures were adopted to ensure protection from future lawsuits. Given the fact that the US had been the forum of the class action lawsuits (i.e. a court system where respective legal action was admissible in the courts), some of the measures pursuing legal closure were directly related to this forum. Other measures aimed at legal closure in Germany, and yet others were designed to avoid the possibility of legal action anywhere in the world.

Measures related to the forum of the United States of America

With respect to legal actions in the United States, three elements had to be distinguished: the stated position of the US regarding reparation claims; the protection of Germany and respective companies against legal action brought by individuals in US courts; and the settlement of claims pending before US courts at the time of the negotiations.

Regarding the first element, in the "US-German Agreement" the US affirms that "(t)he United States will not raise any reparations claims against the Federal Republic of Germany." This statement contains a binding waiver of any eventual reparations claims by the United States. The wording of the rest of the intergovernmental agreement does not give rise to any doubts in this respect.

With a view to the second element — legal action brought by individuals in US courts — the US Government offered to "take appropriate steps to oppose any challenge to the sovereign immunity" in cases where such a matter would be brought before US courts. This was a statement of the legal position of the US that Germany is entitled to immunity before US courts with regard to acts committed during the Second World War. In addition, the US Government undertook to issue a Statement of Interest in any case in a US court involving claims against Germany, Austria, or German or Austrian companies that involved or related to the subjects covered under the respective compensation programs. A Statement of Interest would then make the following points:

- The respective compensation program was designated as the exclusive forum which provided for a fair and equitable resolution for all issues addressed under the program; and

- The dismissal of the lawsuit would be in the foreign policy interests of the US and therefore was recommended on any valid legal ground.[1]

That said, a Statement of Interest does not provide an absolute protection against future legal action in its field of application since it does not constitute an independent legal basis for the dismissal of the respective lawsuit.[2]

As a third element, in order to secure protection against the class action lawsuits that were pending before US courts at the time of the negotiations, it was agreed that the US Government would urge the courts to dismiss these cases. This dismissal would then be the condition for the financial contribution of German companies as well as the beginning of payments.

The point in time when the contribution on part of the German companies was due was regulated by the following provision made in the "Joint Statement":

> Assuming the request for a transfer referred to in paragraph (e) is granted, the DM 5 billion contribution of German companies shall be due and payable to the Foundation and payments from the Foundation shall begin once all lawsuits against German companies arising out of the National Socialist era and World War II pending in U.S. courts including those listed in Annex C and D are finally dismissed with prejudice by the courts. (Joint Statement, Section 4.d)

Another point mentioned in the quoted subsection of the Joint Statement was to begin payments only once legal closure in the US had been established. To this end, the Foundation Law set out the establishment of "sufficient legal peace for German companies" as a legal requirement before the first monies could be transferred to partner organizations for payments to eligible

---

1 See Annex 3: US-German Agreement, Annex B; see also Agreement between the United States of America and Austria, Federal Ministry of Foreign Affairs of the Republic of Austria, No 2140.02/0044e-BdSB/2001, Annex B, Wien, 23 January 2001. With regard to the latter, it remained somewhat unclear whether based on the reference made to the intergovernmental agreement on forced labor it could be expected that the US Government would issue a Statement of Interest in the respective cases.

2 This would have only been possible on the basis of an amendment of US federal law or on the basis of a bilateral treaty under international law by inserting a compulsory reason for inadmissibility in such cases. There were hardly any prospects for obtaining the necessary approval in this respect given the fact that this would have required a two-thirds majority in the US Senate.

victims.[3] A certain political flexibility was maintained by empowering the German Federal Parliament (Bundestag) to establish whether "sufficient legal peace" had been achieved. Therefore, it remained possible to declare a situation of "sufficient legal peace" and start with payments even if not all of the lawsuits pending in US courts had been dismissed. Arguably, this was only possible leaving aside the agreement reached in the Joint Statement according to which the beginning of payments would depend on the dismissal of all pending claims listed in the annexes of the Joint Statement.

In any event, the room for political maneuver was limited. The contribution of the German companies was still dependent upon the dismissal of all lawsuits. Moreover, the entire project had been achieved in a joint effort by German political bodies and German companies. It was therefore regarded as relevant criterion that the "Foundation Initiative of the German Industry," which represented the interests of German companies during the negotiations, would agree that "sufficient legal closure" had been established. Consequently, the German Parliament only made its statement on legal closure once this agreement had been given by the "Foundation Initiative of the German Industry".

A deadlock arose after a judge, in one of the lawsuits pending before US courts, refused dismissal of the case as long as the EVZ Foundation had not been fully funded, while German companies argued that they would only transfer their money to the EVZ Foundation once all lawsuits were dismissed. The way out of this deadlock was that leading German companies publicly issued a guarantee for any eventually lacking amount towards the share of the Foundation Initiative of the German Industry of approximately 2.6 billion Euros that needed to be raised. However, the responsible judge still refused to dismiss the case. She also was left unimpressed with the — non-binding — Statement of Interest that had been issued by the US Government, and the obstacle constitute by this case still pending was only removed by a decision of the Court of Appeals. This delayed the start of the compensation payments from January to June 2001.

This situation demonstrates that relying on a legally weak instrument such as a Statement of Interest may cause unwarranted delays. If legal closure is part of the deal — which will often be the case in compensation programs — clear-cut legal rules and binding instruments may be more desirable to avoid subsequent disputes and delays to the detriment of all concerned. In the case of the EVZ Foundation, the delays described could have been avoided if the US side had agreed to introduce a legally binding reason for the dismissal of lawsuits concerning claims covered by the Foundation Law. At the same time, a legally binding obligation of specific German companies with respect to the financial contribution due on part of the Foundation Initiative of the German Industry also would have served to avoid controversies and delays in the process.

---

3   See Annex 1: Foundation Law, Section 17 (2).

Measures related to the forum of Germany: Designation of the compensation program as the exclusive forum for forced labor claims

Within the reach of German jurisdiction, the German legislator established clear rules to exclude future lawsuits. Accordingly, the protection of public bodies and German companies was further reinforced in the German Foundation Law by making the compensation program the exclusive remedy and forum for claims relating to Nazi injustice apart from already existing norms granting compensation in specific legislation.[4] Before the Foundation Law had entered into force, it had been unlikely that any legal action stood a chance of success, but full certainty had not been achieved. In view of a number of legal actions pending before German courts it was considered necessary by the German legislator to exclude any claims based on forced labor from other fora.[5]

A legal problem could have been found in this context in view of the protection of private property under the German Constitution (Section 14 of the German Basic Law). This protection could have been seen to include the right to receive compensation for forced labor the pursuit of which could not have been excluded. In an earlier case, the Federal Constitutional Court had endorsed the transfer of legal claims under private law into legal claims against an adequately financed fund in a judgment concerning a foundation for children who had been born with a handicap caused by a certain medicine.[6] The reasoning of this judgment was considered all the more valid in the case of forced laborers since only their aspirations and unconfirmed legal claims were addressed in the Foundation Law rather than existing and enforceable legal claims. The German Federal Constitutional Court confirmed the compatibility of the Foundation Law with the German Constitution in 2004.[7] In particular, the "social function" of the EVZ Foundation was emphasized which made claims independent from the continued existence of the company for which the forced labor had been performed.[8]

---

4   See Annex 1: Foundation Law, Section 16 (1).
5   See explanations on Section 16 (1) of the draft of the Foundation Law, Register of the German Parliament, BT-Drs 14/3206, http://dipbt.bundestag.de/doc/btd/14/032/1403206.pdf (accessed 13 March 2017).
6   See court decision on the "Law on the Creation of a Foundation 'Hilfswerk für behinderte Kinder'" (German Federal Law Gazette, Year 1971, Part I, no 131, page 2018) of the German Federal Constitutional Court, BVerfGE 42, 263, 295 et seqq., 8 July 1976).
7   See court decision on the "Constitutionality of the Exclusion of Claims by the Foundation Law" of the German Federal Constitutional Court, BVerfGE 112, 93–117, 7 December 2004.
8   See BVerfGE 112, 93–117; see also the Explanatory Report of the Foundation Law, Register of the German Parliament, BT-Drs 14/3206, explanation on Section 16 (1).

Using similar arguments in assessing a violation of the right to property under the European Convention of Human Rights and its First Protocol, the European Court of Human Rights found in its negative admissibility decision in the case *Poznanski v Germany* that the EVZ Foundation scheme did not upset the fair balance to be struck between the protection of individual property and the "substantial public [interest] in setting up the Foundation Law to deal with all compensation claims for forced labour".[9]

Measures related to any forum in the world: Collection of waivers

On the level of the individual claimants, legal closure was achieved with the requirement to sign a waiver of any additional claims as a condition for payment. Such a waiver could be used as a defense by companies who were sued anywhere in the world: whenever and wherever legal action would be initiated by a claimant in the German program who had signed a waiver *and* who had received a payment, this waiver could be used to seek the rejection of a claim based on forced labor through such a legal action. While such a rejection would not be guaranteed but depended on the acceptance of the waiver by the respective court, it would make the rejection by the court very likely.

When filing a claim, applicants had to sign a statement that, with the receipt of a compensation payment, they renounced irrevocably any future claims outside the forum of the German compensation program. The Foundation Law (Section 16 (2)) specified that in the case of German companies the waiver was effective for any forms of compensation related to the Second World War, while against the German State, it only concerned claims related to forced labor and to property damages. The waiver only became effective upon receipt of the compensation payment and thereby did not apply to persons who were not found eligible. The Foundation Law did not limit the waiver to the types of damages addressed under the law but spoke more generally about waiving all claims against German companies arising "in connection with National Socialist injustice" and concerning forced labor and property damages against the German State.[10]

The definition of "German companies" in the respective laws was rather broad. Since the waiver excluded any claims against such companies it was crucial how these companies were defined if any protection outside Germany was to be achieved. Therefore, the term "German company" was not limited to those companies that had their seat within the borders of the German Reich of 1937 or that are now registered in the Federal Republic of Germany, but also included so-called "mother" companies, whether in Germany or abroad. Moreover, it also covered those companies abroad, where a stakeholder with shares of at least 25 percent had its seat or was registered in Germany.[11]

---

9   *Poznanski and Others v. Germany.* Judgment, European Court of Human Rights, HUDOC 25101/05, 3 July 2007; see also Matti Pellonpää, "Due Process in Mass Claims Proceedings and Article 6 of the ECHR," in *The Protection of Human Rights at the Beginning of the 21st Century,* ed. Jürgen Bröhmer (Baden-Baden: Nomos, 2012), 91–122.
10 See Annex 1, Foundation Law, Section 16 (2).
11 Ibid., Section 12 (2).

The administration of the waivers caused considerable organizational efforts. In particular, waivers had to be collected by the partner organizations together with the claim forms and transferred to Germany for archiving. In the claims process, this had to take place before the second installment payment was effected in order to secure proper administration of the waivers. The waiver documents first kept in the German Federal Archive and later with a private firm, so that they can be identified and presented in case of any new lawsuit being initiated. Finally, a separate report was issued for the German parliament that detailed the status of legal closure.[12]

Signing a waiver as part of application claim often caused very negative reactions on part of the applicants since they had to declare a forfeiture of what they considered their legitimate entitlement when they did not even know what they would get in return.

WAS LEGAL CLOSURE ACHIEVED?

The US court cases listed in the Annexes to the Joint Statement on the EVZ Foundation were finally dismissed. The consent to the withdrawal of the lawsuits was conditional on the full funding of the EVZ Foundation, a condition that was fulfilled some time after its establishment.

Also, with regard to claims covered by the Foundation Law, legal protection against further claims appears to be effective. There is no case known where a payment under the Foundation Law was not considered "sufficient," and where a court granted additional payments.

However, there is no guarantee of comprehensive protection against parallel or future litigation. In particular, cases concerning Nazi injustices that were not covered by the Foundation Law kept being litigated. Moreover, state immunity for cases involving serious human rights violations or grave breaches of international humanitarian law is eroding in state practice. In Italy, Germany was denied immunity against such litigation for compensation in the *Ferrini Case,* by the Italian Corte di Cassazione in 2004, concerning a former forced laborer (a so-called IMI) who was not eligible under the program criteria[13], and in subsequent decisions by Italian courts in 2008. In the resulting case brought by Germany against Italy before the International Court of Justice, the latter held that jurisdictional immunity of Germany was

---

12 See "11th Report of the Federal Government of Germany on the Status of Legal Closure for German Companies in the Context of the Foundation "Remembrance, Responsibility and Future," Register of the German Parliament, BT-Drs 17/1398, http://dipbt.bundestag.de/dip21/btd/17/013/1701398.pdf (accessed 13 March 2017).
13 *Ferrini c. Republica Federale di Germania.* Judgement, Italian Supreme Court of Cassation (Riv. Dir. Int. 87 (2004) 539), 11 March 2004.

to prevail.[14] Also, litigation in Greece showed that protection against claims related to the Second World War may not necessarily be provided by the provisions for legal closure of the Foundation Law. In a case concerning a massacre by German troops in the village of Distomo, the Greek courts, including the Supreme Court, decided that Germany owed an overall amount of more than 28 million Euros to the descendants of the victims. A massacre by German armed forces was not an act falling under a waiver under the compensation program. Moreover, the Greek Supreme Court denied state immunity to Germany. However, enforcement was only possible with the consent of the Greek Minister of Justice, which was refused several times.

SUMMARY

The German Foundation scheme relied on multiple layers for securing legal closure. While some of these layers proved to be watertight, others were less reliable. In particular, the obligation of the US Government to issue a Statement of Interest in individual court proceedings in order to exclude the United States providing a forum for claims against German companies resulted in producing delays in the start of payments because of its non-binding character. Apart from these caveats, the measures adopted with a view to legal closure seem to have worked by and large. Of course, legal action related to situations not covered by the Foundation Law could not be argued against with the help of the instruments on legal closure. Some legal action was faced by Germany in Italy and Greece related to situations not covered by the Foundation Law and thereby beyond the reach of a waiver.

Without providing for mechanisms aimed at legal closure, it would probably have been impossible to motivate the German State and German companies to establish the EVZ Foundation and commit to granting the respective funds. This will be similar in other situations as well. The central question is whether legal closure is acceptable in a situation where a reparations program addresses atrocities of the severity and scope such as those under the Foundation Law. Taking into account the uncertainties regarding the existence of individual rights to compensation as well as the prospect of ever realizing any such rights, the Foundation scheme may indeed seem "acceptable." Also, the large number of victims of forced labor which was reached through the program in contrast to probably a much more limited number of claimants potentially benefitting from any successful court proceedings speaks in favor of acceptability of the EVZ Foundation scheme in return for legal closure. A "fair" balance, however, may be difficult to find, given the seriousness of atrocities covered and the time which had elapsed since their commission.

---

14 *Jurisdictional Immunities of the State (Germany v. Italy: Greece intervening)*. Judgement, I.C.J. Reports 2012, pg. 99 para. 107, 3 February 2012. http://www.icj-cij.org/docket/files/143/16883.pdf (accessed 21 March 2017).

LESSONS LEARNED

- It is important to realize that without legal closure, German companies (and the German State) would not have paid for the compensation program.

- Ideally, legal closure provisions should balance the interests of victims in the payment of compensation and of those responsible for human rights violations and potentially funding a program in protection against future monetary law suits. While victims may have an interest in being able to pursue all options of litigation with the aim of achieving comprehensive compensation also beyond a designated program, the funding side has an interest in excluding additional claims and further court action.

- Legal closure must not be equated with moral closure and thereby with a notion that atrocities committed in the past were made good by the payment program and cannot be a matter of a moral debt anymore. Legal closure on compensation claims also does not affect criminal responsibility for the crimes involved.

- The farther a reparations program is away from comprehensive compensation or restoration of victims' rights, the more critical the fairness of legal closure has to be assessed.

- The waiver as an instrument of legal closure should not go beyond the scope of situations covered by the reparations program. For situations not covered in the respective program, claimants cannot be expected to waive their right to legal action.

- Legal closure should not be granted in situations where there is no guarantee for full funding. In turn, funding should not be granted before potentially agreed guarantees for legal closure reliably can become effective.

- Asking applicants to waive their rights before knowing about their eligibility and the respective amount imposes a high burden and has highly emotional components. This has been balanced out to a certain extent by partner organizations in their direct dialogue with applicants when submitting their applications in person. In a huge program like that of the forced labor compensation program, this has limitations in view of the sheer number of applicants.

UTA GERLANT

CHAPTER 11:
ENDING THE PROGRAM

This chapter contains:

— Practical implications of a temporary program
— Use of leftover funds for humanitarian projects
— Archiving records of the compensation program
— Continuing tasks
— Transferring program-related knowledge

INTRODUCTION: KEEPING THE END IN MIND FROM THE BEGINNING

The completion of a compensation program should be kept in mind from its inception. The final phase of such a program usually involves many processes that can already be anticipated during the implementation phase, such as:

- Which cut-off dates and deadlines are necessary for the program?
- How should employment contracts be formulated?
- What should be done with leftover funds?
- How should documents be maintained: is there a need for contractual agreements regarding their storage and how should they be kept for future use?
- Which tasks need to be taken care of during the completion phase and what kind of employees and other resources will be needed for this?
- Are there any continuing tasks after the formal termination of the program?
- Will organizations involved in the process still exist after the program is completed?
- After the completion, to whom can concerned parties turn with their questions?
- How will the knowledge that was generated be preserved and/or made available to the public?

In the case of the forced labor compensation program, what needed to be done towards the end of the program only became gradually clear during the implementation phase. For instance, this is why only during the course of the program was a passage added to the Foundation Law determining an endpoint for the program rather than keeping it open-ended for an indefinite period of time (Section 14 (4) of the Foundation Law). Unlike in other compensation programs, some staff remained employed by the EVZ Foundation even after all the payments had been completed, as the organization continued with the administration of the "Remembrance and Future" Fund (Chapter 12). Therefore the infrastructure of the EVZ Foundation was maintained and funds needed to complete the final tasks were also available.

This chapter describes a number of practical issues that are related to "ending" the compensation program, such as the setting cut-off dates, downsizing organizational structures, the role of archives, and continuing tasks. The chapter further illustrates with some examples how leftover funds were used in a meaningful way.

PRACTICAL IMPLICATIONS OF A TEMPORARY PROGRAM

The forced labor compensation program was temporary in nature. The program paid out fixed amounts and did not provide for periodic benefits (e.g. pensions). Given the substantial administrative costs for which there were no long-term funds available, it was crucial to observe a tight time perspective. All partner agreements concluded between the EVZ Foundation and the seven partner organizations foresaw as the final stage the completion of the payments.

On 11 June 2007, the Board of Directors submitted its final report to the Board of Trustees, which then declared the completion of the compensation program. On 12 June 2007, a ceremonial act hosted by the German Federal President and attended by the German Chancellor officially concluded the compensation program.

Figure 8: Festive act of the EVZ Foundation in 2007. German President, Horst Köhler, and Chancellor Angela Merkel hold the final report of the compensation program. Source: Bundesregierung/Sandra Steins

Cut-off dates and deadlines

As described in Chapter 3, there were mainly two reasons for designing the compensation program as a temporary program. First, the financial resources were a fixed amount to be distributed as fast as possible. Second, and consequently, it would have been practically impossible to keep the program running for an indefinite period of time. This required the imposition of a number of deadlines. Some of these dates were determined right from the start, such as those for submitting claims and appeals (some of these were extended during the running period of the program, for instance for the submission of claims). Others were introduced only in the course of the program (e.g. deadlines for legal successors, the end of the claims processing period, and the period until which compensation awarded could be received).

Putting a time limitation on the temporary compensation program was closely related to the historical circumstances of the program. The crimes took place a long time ago and survivors were very old, so they needed to be reached fast. As there was a significant number of staff needed in both the EVZ Foundation and the partner organizations, time limitation also had a practical advantage. Financing for a limited and foreseeable period of time kept the administrative expense to disbursed funds ratio at a manageable level.

Even when the program drew to a close, there were still a number of open claims due to a combination of different deadlines and ongoing processes. In order to avoid lengthy processing time and to keep costs under control, the German Parliament, with consideration of all partner organizations, issued a general completion date of 30 September 2006 (and 31 December 2006 for certain exceptional cases). Even after these dates, the validity periods of some checks were still running for a limited time.

Implications for the organizational structure

From the outset of the compensation program, the employees of the EVZ Foundation and the partner organizations knew that their positions were only temporary. Employees received fixed-term contracts that were renewed until the program was concluded. While it was not known at the beginning how long the process would take, plans needed to be developed based on assumptions and targets had to be set and resources allocated, including deadlines and budgets. What did this entail in practice?

When the workload started to decrease towards the end of the program, staff had to be reduced, as was to be expected. This mostly affected employees of the partner organizations who received claims, advised claimants and dealt with the processing of claims and appeals. Supporting departments such as administration, accounting, IT, and legal advice also underwent job cuts. At the EVZ Foundation, the jobs of most employees ended upon the completion of the compensation program; this mostly concerned the control teams and the department in charge of databases. The departments that were still needed after the completion of the compensation program, such as the finance department, IT, and legal advice, were downsized. A few staff members of the control teams remained with the EVZ Foundation to administer and monitor leftover funds that were used for humanitarian programs.

After the completion of the compensation program, the situation of the various organizations involved differed considerably. The EVZ Foundation remained in place because besides the temporary responsibility of carrying out the program, it was also entrusted with the permanent task to administer the "Remembrance and Future" Fund, which was sponsored by the revenues of its own assets and was used to promote respective projects.

Four of the partner organizations continued in existence after the compensation program. The German-Czech Future Fund and the JCC continued to operate, mainly as they had taken on the implementation of the forced labor compensation program as an additional task on top of their already existing work. The IOM, of course, already existed before taking part in the compensation program and continued to perform its many other projects after the completion of the claims process. In terms of its financial volume, the forced labor compensation program was its largest project to date; yet it was only one of several hundred programs administered by IOM, which has thousands of employees. As introduced previously, the Polish partner organization FPNP was founded in 1992 to oversee the distribution of an earlier compensation program to victims of Nazi persecution, and it therefore had several times implemented collective, humanitarian programs dealing with Nazi victims. It expanded its scope of activities, which now includes projects in the field of history education.

The three other partner organizations ceased to exist. The foundations "Understanding and Reconciliation" in Belarus and Ukraine were transformed from state-run to "civil" foundations (International Public Organization "Understanding" in Belarus, and the International Foundation "Mutual Understanding and Tolerance" in Ukraine). Thus, in both countries there are still contact points for the concerns of Nazi victims, despite the fact that they are not located within the same institutions as before. In Russia, the government closed the Foundation "Understanding and Reconciliation" in 2011 without providing a substitute body.

Today, the organizations are no longer official partner organizations of the EVZ Foundation, as they are no longer operating under the partnership agreements of the forced labor compensation program. They are, however, still partners in the sense that they can, just as any other institution, apply for project funding under the "Remembrance and Future" Fund or share common activities.

USE OF LEFTOVER FUNDS FOR HUMANITARIAN PROJECTS

Whenever a compensation program is designed in such a way that it operates with a predetermined fixed amount, it will eventually reach the point when leftover funds can no longer be spent effectively (comparing the administrative effort and the actual payment amounts). Since the compensation program provided a fixed fund for each partner organization, leftover funds were generated in all seven partner organizations from the program funds as well as the "other damages" program line. In addition, the EVZ Foundation accumulated leftover funds from saving on its administrative budget, accrued interest, and additional donations. In total, these funds — after the completion of the individual payments — amounted to more than 46 million euros.

In such a situation, there are different possibilities: for example, to return the leftover funds to the donors, or to spend them in other ways for the benefit of the intended beneficiaries. Regarding the forced labor compensation program, the Board of Trustees chose the second option and allowed the leftover funds to be used for humanitarian projects for vulnerable survivors, as well as for the safeguarding of acquired knowledge, research and education.

The EVZ Foundation's Board of Directors authorized humanitarian projects on the basis of proposals by the partner organizations.[1] Target groups were those especially needy or ill survivors and those with particularly difficult histories of persecution. When necessary, assistance was prioritized based on social situation, health needs, and history of persecution. The assistance included orthopedic and eye surgeries, home care, health treatments, the establishment of social meeting points, and provided supplies of medical drugs, medical devices and medical aids, as well as food, material support, and legal advice. All these projects required that the partner organizations continue employing staff beyond the completion of the compensation program. In total, more than 108,000 survivors of Nazi persecution benefited from these humanitarian projects.

ARCHIVING RECORDS OF THE COMPENSATION PROGRAM

During the course of a compensation program, a considerable amount of claim forms and other documents are produced and databases are created. From the beginning, it should be regulated who will keep these documents after the completion of the program and how they will be stored. Moreover, it needs to be considered according to what kind of archive

---

1   To clarify, this description concerns only humanitarian projects financed by leftover funds from the forced labor compensation funds. According to the Foundation Law, certain humanitarian programs were planned from the beginning of the program (153 million Euros for humanitarian and social programs and 179 million Euros out of the ICHEIC humanitarian fund, see Chapter 9). In addition, some of the EVZ Foundation's permanent project funds from the "Remembrance and Future" Fund were also dedicated to humanitarian projects for forced labor survivors (see Chapter 12).

regulations the records should be stored (e.g. according to national archiving regulations) to ensure their safekeeping in terms of data protection and preservation for further use. It should also be determined who has access to these archives and how the storage will be financed.

In the case of the EVZ Foundation, all its own files as well as the database on all the compensation payments remained in-house. The legal closure waivers, which were transferred to the EVZ offices in Berlin from each partner organization, were temporarily handed over to the German Federal Archives. Claim forms and documents, as well as other records and databases of the partner organizations remained mostly in the latter's possession.

After the completion of the program the partner organizations had to decide which long-term archiving solution would be appropriate for these records, taking into consideration, where necessary, national legal provisions. For instance, the JCC kept its files and the database, not least because they had previously implemented compensation programs for the same clientele and continued to do so. An electronic version of all files and the database compiled by the IOM was transferred to the German Federal Archives. In Russia, Ukraine and Belarus, state archives kept files and records. In Ukraine and Belarus, databases were given to the respective non-governmental organizations that were founded after the completion of the program as successors of the partner organizations. In Poland and the Czech Republic, documents and databases remained within the partner organizations, which continued their work beyond the compensation program.

For access to and use of the documents that are now stored in state archives, the respective national archival rules and regulations apply. In this context, it should be kept in mind that it is possible that not all documents were taken on and stored as a whole. Another important question is how long files should be stored and whether/when they will be accessible to the public, and under which conditions they will be accessible sooner to individuals who have a legitimate interest to gain access (e.g. family members or researchers).

CONTINUING TASKS

From the outset consideration needs to be given to the number of tasks that need to be carried out after the completion of the program. When an organization ceases its work entirely, it needs to consider which entity can take on continuing tasks. This applies to three specific fields:

- Lawsuits concerning the program, which require legal expertise;
- Queries from affected persons, which require knowledge of the completed program and which possibly need to be answered with a certain amount of historical expertise; and
- Storage and retrieval of respective documents in those cases where reparations programs need to prove legal closure (i.e. the waivers).

Lawsuits after the completion of the program

A number of lawsuits were filed after the completion of the program in several countries. In case these concerned the work of the EVZ Foundation, the judicial department had to submit statements. Claimants raised objections regarding decisions by partner organizations that dismissed the claims due to lack of eligibility (under the Foundation Law) or due to failures to meet the submission deadline. The respective courts rejected all lawsuits because, as laid down in the Foundation Law and described in Chapter 10, there was no direct legal relationship between claimants and the EVZ Foundation that would have justified an entitlement to compensation payments. Simply put, the Foundation Law did not give claimants a legal right to compensation (see discussion in the concluding chapter). In isolated cases, partner organizations were also sued after the end of the program. As far as is known, courts either dismissed these lawsuits as inadmissible or they rejected them on the merits, given that plaintiffs had no legal entitlement to compensation payments.

Queries

Despite the various deadlines and a fixed completion date of the program, queries still arose after its completion. Claimants and their relatives who still wanted to send in applications or who had questions regarding past procedures continued to submit queries. The remaining staff at the EVZ Foundation, while engaged in ongoing tasks, dealt with these queries in their respective languages. These employees needed to be well informed regarding the completed compensation program, have good historical expertise, and, ideally, possess intercultural competences. Reusable response template texts were drawn up to address typical and recurring questions, while other requests needed to be dealt with on an individual level. In some individual cases, where former partner organizations and their successor organizations were still in place, the EVZ Foundation was able to consult with them in order to produce more informed responses.

Legal closure waivers

For purposes of legal closure, it was important that the waivers which the claimants had signed together with their claims, as well as the acknowledgements of having received payments (through which the waivers came into force), could easily be traced and assigned to a particular claim. While Chapter 10 describes in detail the enforcement of legal security, it needs to be pointed out here that there are also practical aspects to be taken into account. Such documents have to be kept permanently and stored in a way that they can be made available upon request. This was ensured by the partner organizations handing over all waivers to the EVZ Foundation, which passed them on to the Federal Archives.

Again, depending on the size of the program, transporting and storing such documentation requires considerable organization and cost planning. The IOM had to organize several trucks to physically transport the waivers to the EVZ Foundation offices in Berlin. Several dozens of running meters of documents were made available in the German Federal Archive. In 2016, the documents were transferred to a private firm for storage because the Federal Archive could only temporarily provide the necessary space. Also, such storage arrangements incur considerable costs. Ultimately, it was crucial that the paper documents were linked to an electronic database in such a way that the waivers were easily and quickly traceable. Given that in the case of the forced labor compensation program this encompassed 1.66 million claimants (at times involving several legal successors), this presented quite a challenge. It was important to design the database, which is kept in the premises of the EVZ Foundation, as self-explanatory as possible, and that employees knowledgeable about the use of the database are kept on staff.

TRANSFERRING PROGRAM-RELATED KNOWLEDGE

Transferring the knowledge gained during the implementation of a compensation program, both with respect to the historical context as well as the process itself, makes reparations more complete and serves to guarantee non-repetition, even though it may not be pivotal to the specific compensation program. Prerequisites for knowledge transfer are political will, financial resources, and committed employees. In the case of the forced labor compensation program, the undertaking was for the most part financed by funds that the EVZ Foundation had saved from its administrative budget.

Securing and disseminating program materials

During the course of the program, substantial knowledge and experience was gathered, secured, and made available to the public. For example, a list of Jewish citizens residing in Germany between 1933 and 1945 was drawn up, as part of an agreement to compensate insurance policies that were never disbursed to Jewish policyholders due to their persecution (the so-called ICHEIC Agreement, see Chapter 9). The Federal Archives compiled the list and the EVZ Foundation handed it over to the German Government, which then shared it with the memorial site Yad Vashem in Jerusalem and the United States Holocaust Memorial Museum in Washington, D.C..

The EVZ Foundation also drew up a register comprising of around 3,800 camps and detention sites identified and determined as particularly severe places of confinement and which formed the basis for payments in a higher claims category.[2]

---

2   The register can be found online on the website of the Federal Archives, www.bundesarchiv.de/zwangsarbeit/haftstaetten/index.php (accessed 29 April 2017).

Education and remembrance projects

After the completion of the program, a number of other projects were implemented that made use of the topic of Nazi-era forced labor for remembrance and education purposes. The EVZ Foundation financed a large international travelling exhibition called *"Zwangsarbeit. Die Deutschen, die Zwangsarbeiter und der Krieg"* ("Forced Labor. Germans, Forced Laborers and the War") with the aim to create and maintain public awareness of Nazi-era forced labor and commemorate its victims. The exhibition opened in Berlin in September 2010 and travelled to Moscow, Dortmund, Warsaw, Prague, Hamburg, and Steyr. The exhibition was designed by the Foundation "Gedenkstätten Buchenwald und Mittelbau-Dora."[3]

The Internet portal *"Mit Stempel und Unterschrift"* ("with stamp and signatures") emerged from the direct work with evidence that was attached to the claims. On this portal, pupils and students can inform themselves on the topic of Nazi-era forced labor on the basis of 30 selected documents and can practice their interpretation of original sources. Each document comes with commentaries and teaching material in order to stimulate explorative learning. The documents provided are of different origins and all of them were submitted in the context of compensation claims.[4]

Also, the EVZ Foundation published the life stories of thirty-five people whom it had come to know during the compensation program to give a voice to the survivors.[5]

Research activities

During the program implementation, it became apparent that despite the vast amount of research on the Nazi history, there were still blatant research gaps. For this reason, the EVZ Foundation commissioned a research program to finance research projects, particularly on forced labor of non-deported individuals who remained in areas occupied by Germany, on forced labor of minors and on the terrible fate of forced laborers who were repatriated to the Soviet Union. The results were published in 2013 under the title *"Zwangsarbeit in Hitlers Europa: Besatzung, Arbeit, Folgen"* ("Forced Labor in Hitler's Europe: Occupation, Labor and its Consequences").[6]

---

3 See www.ausstellung-zwangsarbeit.org (accessed 22 May 2017).
4 See www.mit-stempel-und-unterschrift.de (accessed 29 April 2017). Another important online portal was established with funds from the "Remembrance and Future" Fund to portray around 600 biographical interviews which had been transcribed, indexed and equipped with didactic tools: www.zwangsarbeit-archiv.de (see Chapter 12).
5 Stiftung "Erinnerung, Verantwortung und Zukunft," ed., *Geraubte Leben. Zwangsarbeiter berichten*, compiled by Kathrin Janka (Cologne, Weimar, Vienna: Böhlau, 2008).
6 Dieter Pohl and Tanja Sebta, eds., *Zwangsarbeit in Hitlers Europa: Besatzung, Arbeit, Folgen* (Berlin: Metropol, 2013).

After the completion of the compensation program, the EVZ Foundation authorized a group of independent historians to examine the respective work of the EVZ Foundation and its partner organizations. All organizations granted the historians access to their archives and allowed them to interview their staff. The result of this research is a publication consisting of four volumes with the title *"Die Entschädigung von NS-Zwangsarbeit am Anfang des 21. Jahrhunderts"* ("Compensation of NS Forced Labor at the Beginning of the 21st century").[7]

SUMMARY

The EVZ Foundation did not have the program's end in sight from the outset. Of course, the organization knew that at some point the program would be concluded, but it did not fully anticipate what the termination would look like, what it would entail legally and practically, and when exactly the conclusion would come about. The EVZ Foundation could not orientate its worldwide program on other examples, but rather had to run it "on sight," sometimes on a trial and error basis, and, if needed, make adjustments accordingly. Only in hindsight it became apparent:

- Which tasks were needed to be done in order to conclude the program formally and with legal certainty;
- That there would be leftover funds that could be allocated to special purposes (e.g. social projects, education and research);
- Which documents and databases had to be archived; and
- Which tasks needed to be done even after the program was completed (appeals, queries by claimants, ensuring access to legal security waivers).

Finally, the chapter described how the legacy of this program could be secured and made available to the public.

CHALLENGES AND LESSONS LEARNED

- During the course of the forced labor compensation program it became evident that a temporary program not only needed deadlines for submitting claims and appeals, but also for the submission of claims by legal successors.

---

7   Constantin Goschler et al., eds., *Die Entschädigung von NS-Zwangsarbeit am Anfang des 21. Jahrhunderts: Die Stiftung „Erinnerung, Verantwortung und Zukunft" und ihre Partnerorganisationen* (Göttingen: Wallstein-Verlag, 2012).

- The actual end of the claims processing for each of the partner organizations and the setting of an overall completion date for all pending or unresolved claims could only be determined once the program was already running. Thus, the end date of the program could neither be determined theoretically nor in advance, and required a separate legal assessment.

- It proved very useful that some former partner organizations continued to exist beyond the completion of the program, and that the knowledge gained was passed on to other organizations dealing with queries from claimants, researchers, and other people committed to the topic. Former partner organizations are also important in terms of pooling the interests of affected persons and in implementing projects for their benefit nowadays and in future.

- When a total compensation amount is fixed at the start of a program, but it can only be estimated how many claimants will be entitled to receive compensation, it can be expected that some leftover funds will remain. Such leftover funds can be used to fund humanitarian projects for the benefit of affected people or to finance projects in the fields of education and research that are in the interest of survivors to whom raising public awareness can be of major concern, thereby complementing the compensation program.

- It is important from the outset of such a program that agreements be made to ensure a long-term storage of documents, particularly with regard to legal closure.

- Competent staff may be needed even after the completion of a program to respond to queries coming from affected persons or their relatives.

- Additional resources may be required to defend lawsuits submitted after the completion of a compensation program — either by keeping a legal department or by contracting external lawyers.

- One option to preserve and transfer knowledge and experience gathered throughout a compensation program can be to materials available to the public.

RALF POSSEKEL

CHAPTER 12:
THE "REMEMBRANCE AND FUTURE" FUND

This chapter contains:

— A compensation program as a one-time engagement or long-term mandate
— Opportunities and risks of managing an endowment fund
— Operationalization of the EVZ Foundation's mission statement
— Overview of funding programs and project examples

INTRODUCTION: A PERMANENT TASK OF THE EVZ FOUNDATION

While one of the aims of the Foundation Law — the result of the international negotiations that took place at the end of the 1990s — was to bring about legal closure, it was not meant to constitute moral closure. Material compensation, no matter how much, cannot be sufficient to "make amends" for historical crimes committed. Thus, the negotiators also formulated political objectives to ensure that some consequences for the future would also be drawn from dealing with the criminal past. It was thus decided that a part of the sum for the EVZ Foundation would be put aside for a so-called "Remembrance and Future" Fund. This fund should design the future of the EVZ Foundation as a permanent grant maker, with the purpose of the latter funding projects of a collective nature, different from the individual compensation payments described thus far in this book.

This chapter describes the processes involved in formulating the purpose of the Foundation Law that in turn paved the way for project funding as well as how projects were identified according to the Law. It outlines major decisions that operationalized a general political goal, presents examples of selected project formats, and evaluates the experiences made in retrospect.

ONE-TIME ENGAGEMENT OR LONG-TERM MANDATE

Determining a second field of activity — beyond providing the compensation payments to individual beneficiaries — was the result of a compromise between the international negotiators for the program. Initially brought forth by the US Government this idea was later supported by representatives of the German companies as well as a number of German parliamentarians who also strongly promoted the funding of forward-looking activities.[1] They supported the notion of a "Future Fund" and intended, at the outset, to equip it with 50 percent of the financial resources. However, victim representatives and the majority of the German parliamentarians pointed out that this would mean that a significant amount of the fund would not flow into individual compensation payments. In turn, the representatives of the German companies tried to strengthen its position by stating that they would only be able to gather the funds required for the program among German companies if it also included "future-oriented activities" (this was not further specified). Only under this condition, they argued, could those companies be approached to participate in the fund-raising that had not been involved in any Nazi crimes or those which had not yet existed during the time of the Third Reich, such as software companies. Conversely, the term "Future Fund" gave rise to a significant amount of distrust among victim representatives, civil society groups, and political stakeholders committed to dealing with the past of National Socialism — such words brought to mind the all-to-familiar strategies of wiping the slate clean and doing away with 'dealing with the past' once and for all.

---

1 Susanne-Sophia Spiliotis, *Verantwortung und Rechtsfrieden – Die Stiftungsinitiative der deutschen Wirtschaft* (Frankfurt am Main: Fischer, 2003), 62.

Within the framework of international negotiations, both sides were able to compromise. Victim representatives prevailed in determining that the largest part of the EVZ Foundation's total capital would be invested in providing individual compensation payments that would be paid out in a one-off payment. In the end, only seven percent of the overall funds went into the permanently remaining "Remembrance and Future" Fund. Moreover, the Fund was expected to also serve survivors and their descendants. The representatives of the German companies agreed to the expansion of the Fund's purpose and to the reduction of its financial resources, while the "comprehensive package" still allowed them to accommodate their interests.

On a symbolic level, the "Remembrance and Future" Fund as well as the financial resources made available for it could on one hand be understood as a dedication to all victims of Nazi persecution who were no longer alive to see the establishment of the EVZ Foundation 55 years after the end of the war and therefore did not receive any compensation payments. All parties involved were aware of the fact that it was practically impossible to really reach all descendants or heirs of former forced laborers. Thus, the "Remembrance and Future" Fund was coupled with the expectation that it would promote projects *in the interest* of descendants.

The political compromise eventually resulted in the following formulation stipulated in the law establishing the EVZ Foundation:

> A "Remembrance and Future" Fund will be established within the Foundation. Its continuing task is ... to foster projects that serve the purposes of better understanding among peoples, the interests of survivors of the National Socialist régime, youth exchange, social justice, remembrance of the threat posed by totalitarian systems and despotism, and international cooperation in humanitarian endeavors. In commemoration and respect of those victims of National Socialist injustice who did not survive, it is also intended to further projects in the interest of their heirs. (Section 2 (2) Foundation Law)

The lawfully stated second "purpose" of the EVZ Foundation, namely covering long-term funding activities, contains *seven general purposes*. In hindsight, this decision proved to be a stroke of luck for victims' associations as well: beyond one-off payments, it was possible to create long-term projects that dealt with the past of National Socialism, as well as fund social projects for the benefit of survivors.

OPPORTUNITIES AND RISKS OF MANAGING AN ENDOWMENT FUND

With the end of the compensation payments in 2007, the first purpose of the EVZ Foundation was completed and administering the "Remembrance and Future" Fund became the sole activity of the Foundation. Since 2007 the EVZ Foundation and the Fund are identical. At its inception, the Fund was equipped with an endowment of 358 million Euros (seven percent of the total sum of the program). The intention was to fund projects and administrative costs through revenues, which were to be accrued in the capital market through an investment strategy. This way, it was neither necessary nor provided for that there was any kind of permanent financing from the state budget or by contributions from companies.

Therefore, the EVZ Foundation remains financially independent, especially in terms of potential political changes regarding the topics with which it deals. Even when there are no longer any contemporary witnesses and should the memory of the history of forced labor fade, the EVZ Foundation can resort to its own resources to keep this memory alive. In other words, it does not depend on political majorities in the legislative to continue its work.

Funding of the "Remembrance and Future" Fund

	Total assets	**5,585 million Euros**
of which	**Compensation program** (all program lines)	**5,227 million Euros**
	"Remembrance and Future" Fund	**358 million Euros**

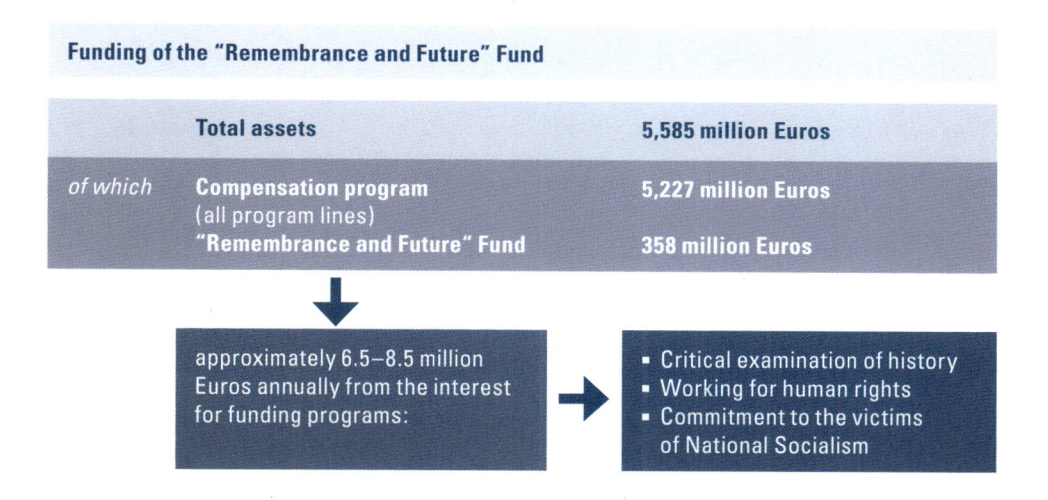

approximately 6.5–8.5 million Euros annually from the interest for funding programs:
- Critical examination of history
- Working for human rights
- Commitment to the victims of National Socialism

Figure 9: Funding of the "Remembrance and Future" Fund out of the overall funds of the program. Note: In addition to the amounts allocated by the Foundation Law, these numbers include additional income from accrued interest and donations received during the course of the program.

However, the dependence on the financial market, especially in times of crisis, may prompt organizations like the EVZ Foundation to look for other sources that can help finance their projects. Could private donors be convinced? Despite the fact that the notion of the "Remembrance and Future" Fund finds wide social approval, it remains difficult to convey to citizens why a state organization with a significant endowment fund should need additional private donations. Thus, the advantage of having a large endowment fund can be a disadvantage when collecting donations.

Another possibility to obtain additional funding are partnerships with other organizations or implementing temporary state-funded programs. For example, in cooperation with a private foundation in 2015, the EVZ Foundation instituted a funding program for combatting the discrimination of people based on their sexual orientation — a program that would have been unthinkable at the time of the establishment of the Foundation in 2000. Also, against the backdrop of Russian attempts to destabilize Ukraine since 2014, the EVZ Foundation succeeded in receiving funds by the Federal Foreign Office of Germany for the implementation of German-Ukrainian and German-Ukrainian-Russian youth exchange programs.

In hindsight, equipping the EVZ Foundation with an endowment fund for its continuing tasks was a stroke of luck that was owed to a special historical constellation. But despite a smart management of fixed assets, constellations may arise that call for the need to acquire additional funding in order to being able to carry out the Foundation's objectives.

OPERATIONALIZATION OF THE EVZ FOUNDATION'S MANDATE

After securing the preservation of substance and deducting administrative costs, the EVZ Foundation was able to provide 6.5–8.5 million Euros yearly and which could be invested in the funding of projects. In the Foundation Law there was no regulation on how these funds had to be spent; neither on what should be the geographical reach of the funding activities, nor on the precise purposes. Thus, an operationalization of the Foundation's mandate was absolutely necessary. This kind of constellation meant that the Board of Trustees and the Board of Directors had a considerable leeway at hand to define how funding purposes should be implemented in funding programs and projects.

The issue of which countries should be the focus of funding programs was more or less defined by the composition of the Board of Trustees, i.e. with the nations that were represented therein: Germany, Poland, Czech Republic, Ukraine, Belarus, Russia, Israel and the US. Given the less obvious constellation of countries, it was argued that these were the countries in Central and Eastern Europe that had suffered most under German occupation while Israel and the US had received and accommodated particularly high numbers of Holocaust survivors. This led to the perpetuation of the specific international make-up of the negotiation round at the end of the 1990s: The Baltic States, Serbia and, to some extent, Greece, Hungary, and Slovakia remained largely unconsidered in this list of preferable countries of funding.

The content-related operationalization of the funding mandate was defined in several phases. In the beginning, a clear strategy was still missing. On the one hand, rather pragmatically, projects were approved that were submitted to the EVZ Foundation by known partners. Victims' associations and civil society groups, for example, already submitted a number of projects to provide social and psychological support to elderly victims of Nazi persecution, independent of the compensation payments. On the other hand, there was a self-understanding among the Board of Trustees of how the mandate could be operationalized. For example, all parties quickly agreed that transnational encounters between victims of the Nazi regime and German pupils would be eligible for funding because they would contribute to intercultural understanding.

The EVZ Foundation has funded projects of this sort since 2001. Furthermore, a large international travelling exhibition on the history of Nazi-era forced labor was met with unanimous approval. The Buchenwald Memorial organized the exhibition which was already on display in Berlin, Moscow, Warsaw, Prague, Dortmund, Hamburg, and in Austria.

By way of such ad-hoc approvals, however, funding activities were at risk of increasingly deviating from the original intentions of its initiators. It became clear that a systematic program development was needed. This took place in two steps: at first, all pronounced and implicit expectations of negotiating partners were collected and published in a memorandum (guiding principles, adopted by the EVZ Foundation's Board of Trustees on 20 January 2005). Out of the seven provisions detailed in the Foundation Law, a four-page document was compiled, comprising around 30 "objectives and concerns." These broad expectations, however, exceeded the EVZ Foundation's factual possibilities by far. Among those suggestions were also a number of basic statements on the future focus of foundational activities, for instance transnational support of civil society. It was left to the Board of Directors to develop a proposal that would find a majority vote among the Board of Trustees and that could also be operationalized in practice.

Eventually, *three major fields of activity were proposed*, with clearly defined *objectives*, for the achievement of which precise *funding programs* would have to be developed:

FIELD OF ACTIVITY 1: A CRITICAL EXAMINATION OF HISTORY

- Permanently anchoring the history of Nazi-era forced labor in Europe's collective memory and conveying the experiences of victims

- Promoting an understanding of the diversity of historical perspectives within Europe

- Strengthening awareness for the Jewish share of and contribution to European history

FIELD OF ACTIVITY 2: WORKING FOR HUMAN RIGHTS

- Reinforcing commitment to democracy and human rights by means of historical learning

- International projects against right-wing extremism, antisemitism and modern forms of forced labor, as well as providing for victim protection

- Supporting descendants of minority groups who fell victim to Nazi persecution

FIELD OF ACTIVITY 3: COMMITMENT TO THE VICTIMS OF NATIONAL SOCIALISM

- Contributing with humanitarian programs and in an exemplary manner to ensure that *victims of Nazi persecution* in old age can lead self-determined and dignified lives which will notably increase their concrete livelihood conditions

- Promoting civil society *stakeholders* who campaign for more readiness to help and who foster practical solidarity with victims of Nazi persecution

- Encouraging committment in German and European politics and society to take on more responsibility to increase the social conditions of victims of Nazi persecution

It has become evident that the interpretation of the EVZ Foundation's mission statement and its objectives, listed here, need to be reexamined and balanced out from time to time. For example, while the field of German-Jewish history has grown and developed over the past 15 years and a a number of new stakeholders are active in the field, other, more fundamental issues have come to the fore, such as dealing with the implications of a migration society when it comes to the memory of National Socialism. While at first human rights education was still somewhat unchartered territory, urgent questions have surfaced in the context of racism, antisemitism, and antigypsyism.

During the time of compensation payments and in the following years, there was a consensus that there should be an equal balance between the three major fields of activity. However, it became apparent that there was a continuous need for the social support of victims of Nazi persecution, despite the fact that their absolute numbers were decreasing. The notion to demonstrate practical solidarity with survivors does not necessarily lose any of its importance given the growing distance of historical events. Perhaps the opposite is actually the case: the more societal attention decreases, the more important the issue became for the EVZ Foundation. This, for one, has to do with the fact that affected people become more indigent with increasing age. On the other hand, this group increasingly turns to the EVZ Foundation with their expectations, especially at times when societal attention for historical events wane.

In 2012, these circumstances led to another strategic debate which resulted in the reallocation of funds by reducing funds for the so-called field of activity "Working for Human Rights," redirecting them for several years and for the benefit of the third field of activity "Commitment to the Victims of National Socialism." At the same time, the objectives of the first and second field of activity have been readjusted:

In the first field, namely "A Critical Examination of History," the topic of Nazi-era forced labor was emphasized even more by establishing a particular funding program for international projects dealing with forced labor and scarcely remembered victim groups (e.g. victims of the 'euthanasia' crimes). The EVZ Foundation increasingly focussed on the challenge of bringing testimonies into formal and nonformal education. Finally, it seeks to provide innovative impulses to the German culture of memory, particularly with view to the increasing number of migrants in the country, many of whom have different historical backgrounds. In the second field, "Working for Human Rights," the focus on tackling human rights and historical learning was replaced by a stronger focus on antisemitism and antigypsiism. In hindsight, it therefore became apparent that the concrete interpretation of the EVZ Foundation's mission statement cannot be determined once and for all.

FUNDING PROGRAMS AND PROJECTS

How can the objectives of the EVZ Foundation be best achieved: by implementing its own projects or by promoting projects of other stakeholders? Aside from a few exceptions, rather than instituting its own projects, the EVZ Foundation decided to predominantly fund projects on the basis of clearly and well-defined grant programs for suitable organizations. These, in turn, will carry out the project in accordance with the organization's own set and approved objectives. This way, the EVZ Foundation can fulfill its purpose in society and at the same time strengthen civil society actors. However, it also hands over the responsibility for the project's implementation and outcome to the funded parties. As a donor, the EVZ Foundation thus largely remains in the background; it facilitates, but does not implement. The challenge is to stimulate good projects on the basis of well-targeted funding programs and to identify and select the most promising among a large number of incoming project proposals. For this reason, the EVZ Foundation cannot take full responsibility in terms of implementation, quality, and possible political implications for these projects. Some examples of selected funding programs and projects are briefly presented as follows.

Example 1: Biographical interviews with victims of Nazi persecution

Given the objective to permanently establish the history of Nazi-era forced labor in European collective memory and convey the personal experiences of victims, the EVZ Foundation set up a program, in 2003, dedicated to documenting the life stories of former forced laborers. This was partly inspired by Steven Spielberg's large-scale initiative between 1994 and 1999 to interview more than 52,000 Holocaust survivors and those who were politically persecuted during the National Socialist regime. The Foundation also followed in the footsteps of various oral history projects in Germany. It was found that the compilation of interviews is only a first step in a number of activities to follow; steps which are necessary to ensure that these interviews can be put to use in educational work and — in this particular case — in explorative learning projects.

Which individuals should be chosen as interlocutors and victims of National Socialism? Should the same inclusion/exclusion criteria used for the compensation program apply? Quickly it was realized that the project offered a big opportunity to leave the limitations and hierarchies of the compensation program behind and potentially give all victims of National Socialism a voice. In practice, this would also mean to include Italian military detainees and Soviet prisoners of war into the remembrance project.

Conducting interviews

In 2005, more than 30 initiatives in 27 countries received EVZ Foundation funds and were assigned with the task of conducting interviews with former forced laborers. One particular challenge was to bring together 32 projects with a total of 75 employees and have them work using the same methodical approach and homogenized technical standards. This was ensured by a team from the Fernuniversität Hagen under the guidance of Professor Alexander von Plato who developed standardized parameters and conducted methodological workshops. As a result, 1,900 hours of interviews, spread over 390 audio and 192 video interviews were compiled.

At the center of the interviews was the interviewee's life story. In other words, they were given the opportunity to not only speak about their persecution, but also speak freely about their life as a whole, without being interrupted or led by the interviewer. This way, the interviewee's narrative interpretation of his or her life story could be documented. In the second part of the interview, the interviewer asked follow-up questions for a better understanding or in order to get more details on historical events on the basis of a checklist. The average length of such interviews were about three hours and 20 minutes. Additionally, for each interviewee, the following data was also gathered:

- A questionnaire including biographical details, collected for a database;
- Brief minutes to document the interview setting, especially with regard to how the interview came about and how the interviewee had been found, as well as some details on the interviewer etc.;
- A short biography of the interviewee to provide future users with a quick overview; and
- A written consent for non-commercial use of the interviews.

A number of interviewers made use of this unique opportunity to also document letters, photos, and other historical documents which were in possession of the interviewees. More than 4,600 photographs could be documented this way. All projects were granted rights of use for the interviews they had conducted.[2]

---

2   See Alexander von Plato, Almut Leh and Christoph Thonfeld, eds., *Hitler's Slaves. Life Stories of Forced Labourers in Nazi-Occupied Europe* (New York, Oxford: Berghahn, 2010).

(Digital) archiving

In 2006, the Center for Digital Systems (CeDiS) at the Freie Universität Berlin digitalized all materials and established the internet portal *"Zwangsarbeit 1939–1945: Erinnerungen und Geschichte"* ("Forced Labor 1939–1945: Memory and History"). This way, a total of 400 interviews could be made available to registered users — researchers and private persons who were looking for family members.

Pedagogical Use

In hindsight, it became apparent that the mere collecting of interviews was not sufficient, because the material needed to be prepared for future use as well. At the outset of the interviews, the promise was made that the interviewee's personal experiences would be passed on to future generations. This pledge entails sustained efforts, which remains an ongoing challenge in an ever more rapidly changing world.

In this case, in order to encourage students to work with the historical material autonomously, more projects needed to be facilitated. The Freie Universität Berlin developed a CD-ROM with a small number of interviews or interview excerpts, contextualizing historical information and work tasks. More than 8,000 copies were distributed in cooperation with the Federal Agency for Civic Education. Technical progress takes its toll, however: CD-ROMs have become less important as a medium — now the challenge is to make the pedagogical material available in a web-based, interactive environment. In addition to the digital archive, a web-based learning environment is also being developed. This way, new opportunities arise to provide these learning activities for users outside of Germany as well, including interviews in their respective original languages, such as Russian, Polish, and Czech, and equip these sources with contextualizing historical information.

Will the project goals be achieved this way? It is likely that more effort is needed: teachers need to be recruited to ensure that the issue of Nazi-era forced labor and the respective interviews will not only be integrated into the syllabus but also into project work. This can only be achieved, however, if the importance of these reports for the present is convincingly argued and demonstrated.

Example 2: Human rights education by means of historical learning

The Foundation Law does not explicitly mention human rights. Nonetheless, the Board of Trustees recognized that the 1948 Universal Declaration of Human Rights was an internationally agreed consequence of the history of the Second World War and that it therefore was relevant to the work of the EVZ Foundation. With that, the EVZ Foundation entered a highly important field and began focusing its work on human rights education. A particular challenge was to prepare the issues of historical education in terms of National Socialism, the Holocaust, and the Second World War to make them relevant for human rights education. When the EVZ Foundation started its funding program in 2003, this approach was still largely disputed in Germany.

Figure 10: Humanity in Action Polen, Jan Karski Educational Foundation, conference and workshop in the Sejm (Polish parliament), 29 November 2014. Source: Stiftung EVZ/Mateusz Gołąb

The EVZ Foundation was involved in this field for more than ten years. During its first funding program "History and Human Rights," it funded about 170 projects. In 2007, an external evaluation assessed strengths and weaknesses of the program and its funded projects and made recommendations for future funding. Essentially, they recommended going beyond mere financial funding and expand the scope toward including networking, exchange, and qualification offers. As a result, in 2008, the funding program was readjusted under its new title "Teaching Human Rights" and continued to operate until 2014. During this period, more than 50 projects were funded. In addition, in 2008, the EVZ Foundation organized a major international expert conference in Nuremberg, the results of which were documented and published.[3] The EVZ Foundation also developed an International Academy "Remembrance and Human Rights" which brought together project leaders from various countries who were active in the fields of human rights and history education, and which took place three times in 2009, 2010, and 2011.[4]

---

3   See Rainer Huhle, ed., *Human Rights and History: A Challenge for Education* (Berlin: Stiftung "Erinnerung, Verantwortung und Zukunft," 2010).
4   For an overview of all projects in the field of human rights education, see Foundation "Remembrance, Responsibility and Future," *Teaching Human Rights: Funding Programme for Human Rights Education Through History Learning: Information and Selected Projects*. (Berlin: Stiftung EVZ, 2013), www.stiftung-evz.de/fileadmin/user_upload/EVZ_Uploads/Handlungsfelder/Handeln_fuer_Menschenrechte/Menschen_Rechte_Bilden/20130820_EVZ_Broschuere_MRB_en.pdf (accessed 25 May 2017).

The connection between human rights education and historical learning has become a well-developed field within and outside of Germany, in which a number of stakeholders are active who pursue various approaches. For this reason, the Foundation decided to end the program. At the conclusion, a publication was funded that reflects on the outcomes of the completed projects and prepared these for specific learning environments.[5]

It has become evident that solely providing financial resources is not sufficient to achieve pre-defined project goals. Only when other necessary forms of support are taken into consideration at the inception of such programs and are funded accordingly can one expect to create sustainable impact. As other foundational activities have shown as well, a term of ten years for such programs is not uncommon.

The human rights issue had a specific dimension: the Board of Trustees agreed that the EVZ Foundation's commitment to human rights was anchored in and based on the experiences of National Socialist persecution. Human rights, however, are *per se* universal rights. Therefore, it is only natural that they claim validity in a number of contexts. This also entailed that projects which were funded by the Foundation raised concerns about issues such as the discrimination of Jews, Sinti and Roma, LGBTI[6], and refugees in focus countries and main operational areas of the EVZ Foundation. Other concerns were equal educational opportunities, modern forms of slavery and human trafficking, the right to seek asylum etc. The transfer into other contexts which were no longer directly related to the original aspiration of the Foundation's mandate led to processes of newly redefining and reconceptualizing of the Foundation's self-image. The central question for the EVZ Foundation was which areas of today's human rights issues should the organization involve itself in and where can it make a significant contribution?

In retrospect, it shows that it was easier for the EVZ Foundation to define its commitment by focusing on specific issues such as ongoing forms of racism, antisemitism, antiziganism, homophobia, and the forms of discrimination and hate crimes resulting from these issues, rather than through the universal human rights. In 2015, the program "Teaching Human Rights" was therefore replaced by another program that deals with these specific issues.

Example 3: Commitment to survivors: Dialogue programs

At the outset of the funding activities, the EVZ Foundation had a number of proposals at hand, outlining how survivors should be supported in addition to and beyond compensation payments. Given limited funds, the biggest challenge was to make the best choice.

---

5   See Martin Lücke, Felisa Tibbitts, Else Engel and Lea Fenner, eds., *Change – Handbook for History Learning and Human Rights Education for Educators in Formal, Non-formal and Higher Education* (Berlin: Wochenschau-Verlag, 2016).
6   Lesbian, Gay, Bisexual, Transsexual and Intersex.

There was general agreement that the funding of humanitarian projects offered the chance to overcome the boundaries, limitations, and hierarchies of the compensation program. Former Soviet prisoners of war, victims of the Siege of Leningrad and of burned villages, and also individuals who had not been deported but nonetheless had to work as forced laborers in occupied territories were also considered eligible beneficiaries. However, some questions remained, such as whether it was legitimate to predicate access to humanitarian projects on circumstances that lie in the distant past alone? Here, some argued that all individuals who had experienced war and occupation and who were in need of assistance due to their old age should be considered a potential target group. However, such a wide interpretation of the Foundation's mandate of "international cooperation in humanitarian endeavors" was in the end not accepted.

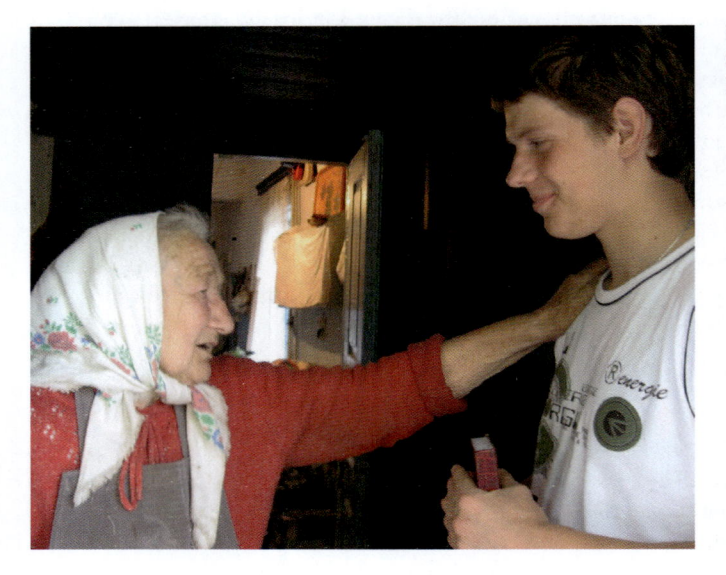

Figure 11: Encounter program. Source: Stiftung EVZ/ Iwan Woshdaenko

The EVZ Foundation dissolved these tensions in a pragmatic manner: funded projects needed to ensure that at least one third/one half of the people to receive support were victims of Nazi persecution, at least in a broader sense. Moreover, the EVZ Foundation expected that implementing partners would actively seek out and contact such individuals. This approach was of a legitimatory nature: it must be ensured that individuals whose persecution gave rise to the formation of the EVZ Foundation would not, for whatever reason, be denied access to the funded projects. All funded projects take part in target group monitoring at regular intervals to ensure the operational implementation. In 2014, through funded humanitarian projects, the EVZ Foundation reached a total of 28,000 victims of National Socialism, as defined in the aforementioned broader sense of the term, as well as 4,000 elderly without them having an explicit persecution background. Also, some 5,600 volunteers served in these projects.

The Dialogue programs also detach themselves from the inner logic of the compensation program in terms of distributing funds. They do not directly address survivors, but rather turn to civil society in their respective countries: all organizations who seek to implement projects for the benefit of survivors can apply for funding. On this level, a fair distribution of funds is assured, given that the scale of available funds is more or less consistent with the number of organizations which are able to implement such projects in a professional manner. Funds have been tendered publicly in Belarus, the Russian Federation, and Ukraine. In their respective countries, expert juries conducted comparative assessments and, ultimately, every second or third project proposal actually received funding. This way, not only survivors receive effective support, but potentials are unlocked and neighborly solidarity stimulated in their home countries as well. Furthermore, the EVZ Foundation contributes to strengthening the civil society in these countries, which will in turn make state institutions realize the importance of a vibrant civil society, ideally prompting them to seek collaborations with such projects.

It is clear that humanitarian project funding cannot simply follow the logic of compensation payment programs. Instead, other approaches need to be developed which can nonetheless be employed on a project-bound and temporary basis. The immediate addressees no longer are the survivors but social stakeholders who are relevant for the implementation of such projects. However, breaking with the logic of how support was previously given calls for explanation to a range of stakeholders. It was the subject of many debates in the Foundation's committees, among victims' associations, and the general public and it took several years for this new approach to be recognized and accepted.

SUMMARY

Since the beginning of its work, the "Remembrance and Future" Fund has funded 3,900 projects with a budget of 99 million Euros (as of 2016). The projects fostered a number of multifaceted relations between people and project partners in Germany, Central and Eastern Europe, Israel, and the US. The EVZ Foundation commemorates the victims of National Socialist persecution and annihilation of people between 1939–1945. It is a somewhat 'living memorial' that has to be reinterpreted time and again and that makes itself available to constantly being reexamined. Whenever the design of the foundational mission moves too far away from its historical motive, its work risks becoming too arbitrary. Conversely, when it clings too narrowly to its original cause, it risks losing its social relevance in the present. Its relative indetermination — or the openness of the design — of the EVZ Foundation's mandate is just as much a strength as is the diversity of perspectives represented by the Board of Trustees. Being equipped with its own capital resources presents itself as a great opportunity.

CHALLENGES AND LESSONS LEARNED

- Since reparations programs rarely address all matters in a concluding manner, it can be beneficial to consider and plan continuing activities from the outset of such programs.

- It is important to consider that material, symbolic (and also geographic) limitations and hierarchies that are often part of reparations programs can and should be overcome in an appropriate manner by way of such continuing programs, instead of being reinforced.

- Lessons for the future are not formulated once and for all; rather, they are being negotiated in political processes and need to be reexamined and reinterpreted at regular intervals, in the interest of maintaining their relevance.

- In the planning phase of project funding, attention should be paid to the institutional setting, because institutional dynamics may have a considerable influence on the operationalization of programmatic concerns.

- Instead of handing project funding to already exiting state agencies for social services it is recommended to establish a special organization, that is visible and approachable at all times, and that gathers experiences systematically in the field and is able to face newly arising challenges.

- In cases where the historical motive is linked to large assets and profits, a possibility is to invest a part of these resources in a unique endowment fund. Out of this fund, revenues can be used to finance activities on a sustained and independent basis. Should this not be possible, at least a legal obligation (or otherwise) should be aspired to ensure the permanent state funding of such activities. Additional fundraising activities remain unaffected by this, since most have only poor prospects of success without a sound basic funding.

- Given limited resources, it is the responsibility of any organization's board to continuously review activities in light of its relevance.

GÜNTER SAATHOFF AND FRIEDERIKE MIETH

CONCLUSION

This chapter contains:

— Moral and political aspects of the forced labor compensation program
— Did the program deliver "a measure of justice"?
— Impact of the compensation program

INTRODUCTION: ASSESSING THE OUTCOME AND IMPACT OF THE FORCED LABOR COMPENSATION PROGRAM

The EVZ Foundation has been viewed by many as a *modern* answer to the question of Germany's dealing with the past. The key feature of this compensation program was the so-called "foundation model," which differed from previous German attempts to (financially) deal with injustice perpetrated by the Nazi regime. It was not simply legislation that entitled certain victim groups to receive a certain sum of money. For the first time, the victims' side was included in the negotiations that eventually led to the formulation of a law on the compensation program. Moreover, representatives of victims and relevant governments sat on the Board of Trustees of the very foundation that was tasked with administering the compensation payments, thus having continued oversight over the program.

In many ways, this program differed from previous German compensation legislations:

- International negotiations determined most of the provisions, such as eligibility, the allocation of funds, etc.;
- Claims were not received, processed, and decided by a German administration, but by international partner organizations that were chosen by the respective governments or by the German Parliament;
- Claimants were no longer divided into "Jewish" and "non-Jewish," but treated equally when they endured the same suffering, e.g. when held in the same camps.

Such features made the program more thorough and comprehensive than previous compensation legislations.

Still, can it be said that the program's outcome was successful? In June 2007, the Board of Trustees of the EVZ Foundation officially announced that the compensation payments had been "successfully completed." An extensive summary of all the figures was drawn up by the EVZ Foundation and the German Government, allowing the German Parliament and the public to review the accounts.[1] The report indicates that 1.66 million beneficiaries in 89 countries received payments of a total amount of 4.34 billion Euros under the forced labor compensation program.

Yet the success and impact of such a program, which is first and foremost political and symbolic in character, must be scrutinized on broader levels. A range of questions arise in this context:

---

1 See "Sechster und abschließender Bericht der Bundesregierung über den Abschluss der Auszahlungen und die Zusammenarbeit der Stiftung 'Erinnerung, Verantwortung und Zukunft' mit den Partnerorganisationen", Nr. 16/9963 available at http://dipbt.bundestag.de/dip21/btd/16/099/1609963.pdf (accessed 8 May 2017).

Did the program design adhere to guiding principles of reparations, and did it — by provisions in the law or by implementation — fulfill these principles?[2] Did the program provide a "measure of justice" for the atrocities it sought to redress, as stipulated in the preamble of the Foundation Law? How did its intended beneficiaries, as well as the wider public in the many involved states, receive the compensation program? What were the political implications of the process?

To answer these questions, a number of perspectives must be taken into consideration. The chapters of this book discuss the practice and experiences of establishing and implementing the program from the "implementer's" point of view. In reality, however, there are many other perspectives that are relevant when evaluating the success and/or impact of the compensation program, including:

- The intended beneficiaries;
- The "donors," i.e. the German State and German companies;
- The legal representatives of claimants (particularly those who brought the class action lawsuits before US courts, a decisive development in bringing about the negotiations);
- Victims' representatives and associations, which participated directly or indirectly in the negotiations or liaised with partner organizations;
- The Board of Trustees, which in its set-up was largely a representation of the stakeholders involved in the negotiations;
- The organizations that implemented the program;
- The general public in Germany and abroad; and
- Politicians and governments of all involved states.

Taking these various perspectives into account, this chapter is structured into three parts. It first presents a discussion on how the focus on Germany's "moral obligation" has led to an increased acknowledgment of the suffering of victims of Nazi persecution; secondly, the question of whether this program really contributed to a "measure of justice" is considered; and third, which effects the program had on the broader political and societal level are examined.

A "MORAL OBLIGATION"

In some key aspects, the forced labor compensation program is an example of a *moralization of German politics*. The EVZ Foundation was set up to administer both a compensation program

---

2   See United Nations, *Basic Principles and Guidelines on the Right to a Remedy and Reparation for Victims of Gross Violations of International Human Rights Law and Serious Violations of International Humanitarian Law,* General Assembly Resolution 60/147, 21 March 2006, available at www.un.org/ruleoflaw/files/BASICP~1.PDF (accessed 8 May 2017). However, these principles were published in 2006, after the establishment of the forced labor compensation program, and were therefore not available to the negotiators of the program.

and a permanent funding organization after the conclusion initial payments. As a funder, the EVZ Foundation encourages programs and projects that deal with historical injustice, acknowledge the victims of Nazi persecution, and work towards preventing future injustice. With the establishment of such a foundation, the German State demonstrated its commitment to acknowledge the harm done and keep the memory of the injustice alive, as well as its willingness to adhere to the so-called principle of non-recurrence.

Focus on responsibility

The political approach of the program did not center on the question of "historical guilt" but on "responsibility for the victims." This can be seen in the context of the time that passed since the crimes took place, the gradual replacement of old elites and thus a changing political landscape with Germany becoming more and more willing to face its history and to promote a culture of dealing with the past. The preamble of the law establishing the program reads:

> Recognizing that the National Socialist State inflicted severe injustice on slave laborers and forced laborers, through deportation, internment, exploitation which in some cases extended to destruction through labor, and through a large number of other human rights violations, that German enterprises which participated in the National Socialist injustice bear a historic responsibility and must accept it,
>
> that the enterprises which have come together in the Foundation Initiative of German Industry have acknowledged this responsibility, that the injustice committed and the human suffering it caused cannot be truly compensated by financial payments,
>
> that the Law comes too late for those who lost their lives as victims of the National Socialist régime or have died in the meantime, the German Bundestag acknowledges political and moral responsibility for the victims of National Socialism. The Bundestag intends to keep alive the memory of the injustice inflicted on the victims for coming generations as well.

From a practical point of view, the shift towards "responsibility" made it easier to fundraise for the program, as half of the funds were to be collected from German companies whose contribution would be entirely voluntary. It allowed companies to be involved in the program without signaling that they are automatically guilty of the crimes. In some instances, this also convinced some companies that did not even exist during the Third Reich to give funds to the program, presumably because they realized a common responsibility of Germans towards the past.

It was also important to emphasize responsibility, as in the decades before many German courts decided that in the case of forced labor, claims against German companies — and therefore their guilt and resulting obligation to compensate — could not be based on German law. Furthermore, a conceptualization of the program that focused on guilt would have possibly implied determining the 'level of guilt' of each participating company.

Acknowledgement

Considering that any amount of compensation would be insufficient to "repair" the initial crime, it is imperative to understand that reparations cannot merely be material, but that they must be accompanied by a display of atonement and remorse.[3] This is particularly so when such programs take place in a politically sensitive context. The messages and public acknowledgement of past wrongs that are announced before and during such programs impact directly on how meaningful these measures become for survivors and the general public. Simply put, the success of reparations programs can depend to a great extent on measures that take place outside of it.

In the case of the forced labor compensation program, the public apology by German President Johannes Rau in the year 2000 was a decisive event. He declared that Nazi forced labor "meant being carried off, stripped of a homeland and rights, and having one's human dignity brutally violated. It often intentionally served the purpose of working people to death". He then added: "in the name of the German people, [I] beg forgiveness."[4] This was particularly significant as until that point Germany had not officially recognized its responsibility for the systematic crime of forced labor.

The compensation program also had a second level of political acknowledgement, as particularly in the former Soviet Union, forced laborers were looked at with suspicion when they were repatriated after the Second World War. Many were thought to have collaborated with the Germans, were stigmatized in society or even sent to "corrective" forced labor camps. Thus, by participating in this compensation program, governments of countries where partner organizations were located also offered a form of acknowledgement the suffering of compensation claimants.

Acknowledgement of past wrongs is not only a matter of political gestures. It should be imbued in every step of the design and implementation process of the reparation program. The

---

3 Naomi Roht-Arriaza, "Reparations Decisions and Dilemmas," *Hastings Int'l & Comp. L. Rev. 27*, 157–220 (2004), 159.
4 Jansen, Michael and Saathoff, Günter, eds., *"A Mutual Responsibility and a Moral Obligation": The Final Report on Germany's Compensation Programs for Forced Labor and Other Personal Injuries*. (New York: Palgrave MacMillan, 2009), 173. For a discussion of how public apologies illustrate Germany's move towards accepting responsibility for the crimes of the Third Reich, see Stefan Engert "Germany-Israel: A prototypical political apology and reconciliation process," in *Apology and Reconciliation in International Relations: The Importance of Being Sorry*, ed. Christopher Daase et al. (Abingdon: Routledge, 2016).

manner in which a program is announced, how careful it is designed, as well as how respectful and responsive its implementers communicate all impact claimants' feelings of whether their suffering is really acknowledged. Thus, a fair and victim-friendly design of the program contributes greatly to a sense of acknowledgement.

The need for the design of the compensation program to adhere to these principles was reflected in the Statutes of the EVZ Foundation which stipulated that the compensation payments had to be administered in a *quick, fair,* and *victim-friendly* way. These criteria were a result of the interest of all negotiation parties that the compensation should be paid out in as fast and unbureaucratic a manner as possible since many of the beneficiaries were already very old. Many decisions were taken during the negotiation phase already in order to reach this goal, such as the decision to provide one-time lump sums.

During the implementation process, acknowledgment can be expressed in the communication with claimants and beneficiaries. As described in Chapter 5, the way in which potential beneficiaries were approached and dealt with had a direct effect on their well-being. It was thus important that employees of the EVZ Foundation, but even more so of the partner organizations, treated potential beneficiaries with as much dignity as possible. As the experiences of the Polish partner organization show, many survivors of forced labor welcomed the opportunity of the application process to talk about their stories and the events that had long been neglected in the public realm both in Poland and in Germany.

To ensure that the claims processing was victim-friendly, several decisions were made to avoid burdening the claimants. As detailed in Chapter 6, the claim process required only few documents. As it was difficult for many claimants to produce any documentary evidence, the partner organizations and the EVZ Foundation actively supported searches in archives, and oral testimonies by other former forced laborers were accepted as evidence. The EVZ Foundation also encouraged the practice to evaluate ambiguous evidence as much as possible in favor of the claimants, and to accept statements that were credible in their context.

At the same time, some aspects of the compensation program were not victim-friendly and may have impacted negatively on the intention to express acknowledgement of the past offences. An aspect that was criticized by beneficiaries was the fact that the payments were not distributed at once, but in two installments. For many of the recipients, the two installments were confusing and they did not understand why they had to wait for a second payment, especially since the program itself came so late and they were very old. Also, claimants found it impertinent that they had to sign a legal security waiver, and because of this a few claimants chose not go further with their claims.

Many of these difficulties could have been avoided if the program fund had been an unlimited open fund, which would have allowed the organizations to pay out the full compensation amounts at once. Chapter 3 explains the reasons why this was, in practice, not possible in the case of the German compensation program. The point illustrates, however, why it is so important to think about the consequences of different kinds of funding when establishing a reparations program. Where politically possible, an open ended funding (or at least the possibility of a replenishing of funds during implementation) should be considered.

A "MEASURE OF JUSTICE"?

The preamble of the Foundation Law states that the payments were meant as a "measure of justice" — probably signaling the awareness of the negotiation partners that the payments can only be of symbolic dimension. Yet, such wording does not render the discussion of justice irrelevant. What kind of justice could this compensation program achieve?

Appropriateness of the compensation

In many ways, the forced labor compensation payments were symbolic. In truth, as stated in the preamble to the Law, no amount of money can compensate for unmeasurable suffering that results from dehumanization, torture, and loss of family members or psychological harm. The payments were also symbolic in that the actual suffering was not taken into account but rather broadly categorized. Also, the reach of the program was not complete because it only concerned living former forced laborers and did not compensate descendants or family members of forced laborers who had already passed away.

So far, no international 'measure' has been found, neither for the extent (what exactly should be compensated?) nor for the amount of compensation payments for victims of systematic or mass human rights violations. This is even the case in many national regulations. Rather, compensations are always political settlements which a legislator, government, or negotiations partners have agreed upon, in some cases also courts. Against this background, whether a compensation amount is individually "appropriate" or not becomes essentially a political question and is therefore always "symbolic." At the same time, the result of negotiations could also be amnesty or no compensation at all. However, this was not an acceptable way to deal with the past of the injustice perpetrated by the National Socialist regime.

What would have been the alternative to a 'symbolic' payment? This would have entailed a precise assignment of "value" and evaluation of each individual fate, i.e. the length of the forced labor, the circumstances in different camps — thus a process that could have taken so long that it could not have been completed within the lifetime of the remaining survivors. Besides, who would have decided these issues, and how would consistency in the treatment of the different individual cases been ensured? Here, symbolic payments were thus oriented not primarily by the criterion of individual justice, but by the 'justice of the large number' and for the victims as a whole.

Yet it is important and necessary to not lose sight of the actual crimes. Thus, one possible dimension to evaluate whether the program was "just" is to consider whether it was *appropriate*, i.e. whether the amount of payment was proportional to both the crime and the situation of the perpetrator side. The UN Basic Principles and Guidelines on reparations state that reparations should be "as appropriate and proportional to the gravity of the violation and the circumstances of each case."[5]

To assess such appropriateness, it needs to be clear what was actually to be "compensated"? This is certainly not an easy question to answer in the case of the forced labor compensation program. There were several aspects of the crime: One is the actual human right violation, that of forcing innocent civilians to work in inhumane circumstances, and under the threat and/or actual use of violence. The magnitude and scope of the forced labor system during the Nazi era makes it all the more brutal. Second, there is an economic dimension of the crime. The forced laborers were either not paid at all or paid very inadequately for their work, so that they would actually be entitled to the outstanding salary. This point is all the more important because the companies profited from forced labor. Not only did the German war economy depend on forced labor, but also many German companies were able to grow into large, multi-national corporations during and after the war, a growth that was in part also based on their profits from forced labor.

In a report conducted during the time of the negotiations, Thomas Kuczynski calculated that the withheld salaries for forced laborers alone would amount to about 180 billion Deutsche Mark (roughly 90 billion Euros), which he later corrected to 228 billion Deutsche Mark (roughly 114 billion Euros).[6] This does not account for the (presumably illegal) profits made by German companies, let alone any compensation for the suffering and rights violations that the forced laborers endured. This was a radical opinion which was seen as controversial not only by scholars and was not even brought forth by the victims' representatives during the negotiations. Yet such calculations can help to illustrate the sheer magnitude of the crime and that the Foundation Law could never "compensate" for the damage done. Considering the sum that was eventually distributed to individuals — 4.34 billion Euros — the program was named by some as the "final insult" to survivors of forced labor.[7]

Thus, the payments were not compensation for the actual work that individual forced laborers performed. Rather, the entire suffering was categorized: the forceful deportation to Germany or its occupied territories, the exploitation through labor, and, as a prior criteria, the confinement in egregious circumstances.

---

5   United Nations, *Basic Principles and Guidelines*, 7.
6   Thomas Kuczynski, *Brosamen vom Herrentisch: Hintergründe der Entschädigungszahlungen an die im Zweiten Weltkrieg nach Deutschland verschleppten Zwangsarbeitskräfte* (Berlin: Verbrecher Verlag, 2004).
7   Gruppe offene Rechnungen, ed, *The Final Insult. Das Diktat gegen die Überlebenden. Deutsche Erinnerungsabwehr und Nichtentschädigung der NS-Sklavenarbeit* (Münster: Unrast, 2003), see also discussion in Kuczynski, *Brosamen vom Herrentisch*, 154.

What did recipients think? Indeed, many beneficiaries found the compensation amount paid to them not appropriate or that it came too late. In a small survey, to which about 7000 beneficiaries responded, the EVZ Foundation sought to find out whether beneficiaries received the compensation payments and what their thoughts were of the process.[8] It is telling that, while the responses revealed a balanced mix of positive and negative opinions, many of the negative perceptions focused on the small compensation amount:

> *It is very painful that one chose to give such little value to my*
> *hard work in Germany.*
> *(Ukraine, after first installment)*
>
> *I think that I would have deserved a higher compensation amount,*
> *considering the length of my forced labor (five years and three months)*
> *and my destroyed spine.*
> *(IOM beneficiary, after first installment)*
>
> *A small compensation for our destroyed childhood, humiliation, and*
> *fear in our youth, and also in later life we had to hide from those who*
> *weren't deported.*
> *(Russia, after first installment)*
>
> *I think that, for so many years of slave labor, hard work, and continuous*
> *fear of death, this sum is ridiculously low. So much hassle for me,*
> *because I had to drive to the bank, didn't receive the money at home.*
> *(Poland, after first installment)*

The aforementioned aspects underline that the questions of individual justice and the appropriateness of the amounts are among the most difficult to address in mass claims programs. The awareness of the gravity of the crimes can and should at the very least inform an attitude of utter humbleness on the side of the designers and implementers of such programs. It also highlights the role of expressing acknowledgement in various ways, as discussed earlier.[9]

---

8   The unpublished report of the so-called "Ex-post" survey is on file with the EVZ Foundation. It is only available in German; translation of the following excerpts by the authors.
9   It should be noted, though, that not from an individual perception, but from an overall appropriateness point of view, by having a fixed overall budget the compensation program only had a limited leeway in deciding on the amount of the payments. Each increase of an amount in one place would inevitably have led to a decrease elsewhere, or to the exclusion of certain victim groups. It would have been possible, for example, to increase the individual amounts for survivors by excluding legal successors from the program, or by limiting the opening clause. Yet this would have caused criticism from other sides.

"Right" vs. "eligibility"

Some have criticized that this compensation program was designed in such a way as to serve the interests of the German State and companies. Even though the preamble of the Foundation Law speaks of *violation of rights* of the victims, this statement was not meant to constitute recognition of a legal obligation of Germany to provide financial compensation. Any acceptance of legal responsibility ('guilt') was strictly avoided before, during, and after the program. Moreover, by stating that the human suffering involved could not possibly be compensated by financial payments, the character of a symbolic gesture of the payments was underlined. The approach of avoiding any impression of a right to compensation is also maintained in the wording of the Foundation Act: it speaks of a *Leistungsberechtigung* ("eligibility to a payment") rather than of a clear *Recht* ("right"). Given the unlikely chances of success in pending lawsuits, which also goes back to the question of whether there is an individual right to compensation for victims of armed conflict, the negotiation partners accepted this approach of not endowing former victims with a clear right.[10]

This issue brings up the question of justice not only from a legal viewpoint but also the beneficiary's perspective. Signing a document in which the future recipients of compensation waived any further claims against German companies perhaps appeared as a legal necessity to the claimants, but it was also a personal imposition. This waiver was only explicable (and in that sense justifiable) by the fact that the companies would not have contributed to the program without this measure of legal security.

While leaving claimants and observers with an uneasy feeling, legal closure is often without an alternative. As described in Chapter 10, legal closure is a typical element of compensation programs, particularly when the 'perpetrator' side finances them. From a practical perspective, this underlines once more the importance of expressing public acknowledgement of victims' suffering and a careful and considerate treatment of the claimants. The least that an implementing organization can do in this situation is to ensure that the necessity of legal closure is explained to potential claimants.

"Relative" justice

Often, reparation programs only address a specific form of human rights violations, or are designed to redress violations of a particular victim group and take place in a landscape where other reparation programs exist. Thus, whether a particular compensation amount is perceived

---

10   See Christoph J. M. Safferling and Peer Zumbansen, "Iura novit curia: Rechtsanspruch auf Entschädigung für Zwangsarbeit im Nationalsozialismus," in *Zwangsarbeit im Dritten Reich. Erinnerung und Verantwortung = NS Forced Labor: Remembrance and Responsibility. Juristische und zeithistorische Betrachtungen,* ed. Peer Zumbansen (Baden-Baden: Nomos, 2002), 233–246.

as appropriate cannot only be seen in relation to the crime, but also in relation *to other mechanisms for redress*. After all, even when a compensation program is in itself perceived as fair, but not so when compared to other programs, it may become less acceptable or even meaningless.

In the case of the forced labor compensation program, there was no systematic integration with already existing compensation programs — neither with those that sought to redress Nazi injustice nor other forms of compensation for victims of wrongful conduct in Germany. In hindsight, this could have been discussed in more detail during the negotiations.

In this case, particularly from the beneficiary's point of view, a comparison with other compensation programs could become a very painful exercise. An example is the so-called "ghetto pension" legislation, established by another law in 2002 by Germany. During the Second World War, "ghettos" were cordoned off sections in cities to which the Nazi regime forcibly relocated persons, particularly Jews. Often, the relocation to ghettos was a waystation before the deportation to death camps. The 2002 legislation provided that those who performed voluntary work in the ghettos were eligible for pension under the ordinary German pension system. Also, descendants of these eligible persons could apply for the pensions. Thus, those who were incarcerated in ghettos and worked "voluntarily" eventually received more money than those who received the one-time symbolic compensation for forced labor, even when the latter were forced to work in the same ghetto.

In sum, for a compensation amount to be meaningful and appropriate, not only the actual crimes have to be considered, but as well other mechanisms of monetary redress. The discrepancies show that in order to avoid creating disadvantages for certain victims groups, and to prevent fault lines between victim groups, more thought could go into integrating different systems of compensation. This is particularly grave in this case, as Germany alone has the responsibility for the different victim groups of the Nazi regime. This said, the amounts of the forced labor compensation program were the result of a lengthy negotiation process, in which the victim groups also participated. For this program, there may have been no other solution.

Completeness

A related aspect is the fact that not all survivors of forced labor received compensation under this program, and the question of whether the program contributed to a measure of "justice" would also have to be considered from the perspective of its completeness. *Completeness* is one of the UN principles of reparations drafted by the UN in 2005, which recommends that reparation programs should be designed to reach all of the victims of the crime in question.

The involved stakeholders attempted to create solutions to make the program as inclusive as possible: by approving many so-called "other places of confinement," large numbers of claimants who were not held in concentration camps could be included in the program. The opening clause, an optional compensation category mostly at the discretion of the partner organizations, was an element that made available compensation for people who did not fit the eligibility criteria but were nevertheless victims of forced labor. Finally, the humanitarian programs and programs created from the leftover funds are examples of how to make reparations available for a larger group of beneficiaries, who may not all fit the eligibility criteria but suffered a similar fate.

In a narrow interpretation, the forced labor compensation program was not complete, however. It was never foreseen during the negotiations to compensate for the loss of life, nor for the families/descendants of those former forced laborers who had already died. Among other reasons, this was done to increase the amount available for those still alive. Moreover, the program was only politically possible at a time when most of the former forced laborers had already passed away. Based on existing research, it was estimated that of the up to 12 million deported forced laborers during the Second World War, only about 2.2 million were still alive in mid-2000.[11]

On the other hand, there were people who were subjected to forced labor during the Second World War and were still alive but were not eligible according to the Foundation Law. This concerned prisoners of war who were excluded *a priori* from the program, and survivors of forced labor who were not subjected to racial discrimination or not imprisoned under harsh conditions (this mostly concerned survivors of forced labor from Western European countries). Also, the interpretation of the Foundation Law was not always in favor of all groups of claimants, such as in the case of the so-called IMI's (see Chapter 2).

The reasons why these victim groups were not included in the compensation program were almost all of a political nature, illustrated by the tense negotiations for each aspect of the program. The case highlights once more the responsibility of those who decide about eligibility criteria. Every time a criterion for eligibility is set, those who do not fulfill it are excluded from compensation, which is an unavoidable fact in each program. At the same time, it also emphasizes the important role of independent appeal committees that can, in a credible way, review the rightfulness of denied claims.

IMPACT OF THE COMPENSATION PROGRAM

It is necessary to start again with a basic question: what can be the overall meaning of a compensation program and its relation to the dimension of an acknowledgement of historical injustice? Historian Lutz Niethammer illustrates the ambivalence of this constellation:

---

11   Mark Spoerer and Jochen Fleischhacker, "Forced Laborers in Nazi Germany. Categories, Numbers, and Survivors," in *Journal of Interdisciplinary History 33, 2 (2002): 202.*

> Observers of collective human rights abuses in the 20th century have become increasingly aware that in this neoliberal globalized world we have no other language than that of money to symbolically and convincingly express acknowledgement. As it is almost inevitably unjust, this language must be spoken as well as overcome. The outcome of this is not the material settlement of what happened, but the possibility of a cultural exchange over past injustice, which memory can free from its monetarization.[12]

Given its immense scope and the severity of the crimes it sought to redress, the forced labor compensation program signified much more than a mere distribution of payments to victims of Nazi persecution; it had symbolic significance and a notable political impact on national and international levels.

Acceptance

In her book, "How to accept German reparations," Susan Slyomovics discusses how such a program can be perceived differently from the victims' side.[13] Both her grandmother and mother were eligible for German compensation payments and Slyomovics describes their differing opinions as to whether this money was even acceptable. While Slyomovics' grandmother claimed compensation payments under the 1953 BEG compensation legislation, her mother, incarcerated and forced to work in a concentration camp by the Nazis, initially did not want to accept payments from Germany.

The discussion whether reparations are "acceptable" is important as it highlights the agony that victims of such crimes experience, often for a lifetime. A case in point is the debate after Germany's first compensation legislation in which victims of Nazi persecution, as they had seen it, were appalled by being offered "blood money" from Germany, asking whether this was a way to buy their silence or relativize their suffering. This discussion was most vivid shortly after the war. However, this changed over the years and in some instances, the same people, who blamed Germany for paying this money, asked for more. Why was that so? One theory is that shortly after the war victims of Nazi persecution were of all ages, and particularly younger people voiced their opposition to the "blood money" — many of them with no families or pensions to worry about. As they grew old, however, their situation changed, and they viewed compensation payments more pragmatically, for example because they needed the money. "Acceptance" of reparation payments thus depends very much on the personal situation of the recipient.

---

12 Lutz Niethammer, "Beschädigte Gerechtigkeit," in *Zwangsarbeit im Dritten Reich. Erinnerung und Verantwortung = NS Forced Labor: Remembrance and Responsibility. Juristische und zeithistorische Betrachtungen,* ed. Peer Zumbansen (Baden-Baden: Nomos, 2002), 258. Translated from German by the authors.

13 See Susan Slyomovics, *How to Accept German Reparations* (Philadelphia: University of Pennsylvania Press, 2014), 48.

What can make a difference — albeit a small one — is the way in which such programs are handled and the messages they spread. Compensation payments have to be understood by all sides as an *acknowledgement* of the suffering experienced by survivors. It should be an expression of the perpetrator's side and/or the public of the knowledge and awareness of the victims' struggles. In this way, the message that Germany sent out shortly after the war was not helpful: basically, the German Government made clear during the first compensation legislation set up in 1953 that this would be a one-time option to claim compensation and there would be no future payments in this matter. In the decades after the war, lawsuits by former forced laborers were repeatedly rejected or compensation denied with often egregious explanations.[14] Rightly so, this made many victim groups doubt the sincerity of the German Government.

It was of great importance for this compensation program that the moral and political acknowledgement of the injustice — as shown in the apology by the German president cited above — but also the long-term engagement of the EVZ Foundation in the field of dealing with the past would emphasize moral credibility more than previous compensation legislation. From the perspective of the survivors these earlier attempts at compensation were often seen as a way to 'get rid' of the past.

Seen in comparison, thus, the overall 'language' of the forced labor compensation program was more careful. One anecdote is illustrative (but not representative): During a public event on the compensation program in the Ukraine, one of the directors of the EVZ Foundation was questioned by a survivor. In quite a rough tone, the survivor asked whether the director thought that the compensation payments were enough, and whether he was satisfied with the program. The director answered that the payments can merely be a gesture that survivors can accept or not, but that he would feel satisfied in case the questioner had accepted the money. In that instance, the director found the right tone; the survivor gave him his autobiography afterwards. Similarly illustrating the importance of individual actions in such contexts, Slyomovics' mother changed her mind about accepting compensation payments in 1999. The reason was a chance encounter with German president Richard von Weizsäcker who apologized to her personally and asked her, "Promise me you will apply."[15]

Still, from the perspective of the authors of this book, more could have been done to show acknowledgement and sympathy. One idea was to include a (translated) copy of the apology speech by President Rau together with the payment notification sent to the recipients. This was discussed within the EVZ Foundation but eventually discarded. It would have been a minimal effort to implement this, and would perhaps have given the notifications a more personalized gesture. Finally, some of the authors of this book would have wished that more stakeholders had internalized the awareness that this was probably the last chance to express acknowledgment for these crimes.

---

14 See Klaus Körner, "*Der Antrag ist abzulehnen*," *14 Vorwände gegen die Entschädigung von Zwangsarbeitern: Eine deutsche Skandalgeschichte 1945–2000* (Hamburg: Konkret Literatur Verlag, 2001).
15 Slyomovics, *How to Accept German Reparations*, 13.

The concept of *complexity* can also be helpful in this regard. According to Pablo de Greiff, complexity refers to the diversity of benefits that a reparations program can offer.[16] By being more complex, such as offering not only financial payments, but accompanying them with public apologies, medical services, and commemoration initiatives, a reparation program can respond better to the victims' needs. From this perspective, the forced labor compensation program had a high complexity. It did not only distribute the compensation payments, but included humanitarian programs that focused on needy victims and sometimes also in their communities. As described in more detail in Chapters 9 and 11, these programs entailed medical and psychological services, as well as other practical help.

Particularly, the ongoing efforts of the EVZ Foundation in funding programs under the "Remembrance and Future" Fund (described in Chapter 12) increase the complexity of the initial compensation program. Many of the diverse projects that are funded now by the EVZ Foundation address medical, psychological, and material needs of survivors of forced labor and other victims of the Nazi regime.

Future-oriented measures

A crosscutting theme that should also be discussed here is whether the German compensation program could contribute to non-repetition. "Satisfaction" and "Guarantees of non-repetition" are distinct forms of reparation mentioned in the UN Principles on reparations that include measures to preserve the memory of the crimes and contribute to preventing the occurrence of similar crimes in the future.

Generally, the establishment of the compensation program provided the ground for dialogue on many levels. First of all, the negotiations brought the crime of forced labor back to the public realm in all affected countries. At the same time, the program led to more dialogue on the community and even the family level. For instance, the Polish partner organization reported that in some families, the descendants or legal successors only learned through the compensation program that their parents had to work as forced laborers during the Second World War.

As discussed earlier, establishing a permanent "Remembrance and Future" Fund together with the compensation program was at the time a modern answer to the question of dealing with the past in Germany. Its broad mandate allows the EVZ Foundation to keep the remembrance of forced labor alive and to provide services to those persecuted by the Nazi regime, but also to have the flexibility to stimulate new projects. Many of these ongoing programs increase greater societal dialogue about the crimes perpetrated during the Second World War and

---

16 Pablo de Greiff, "Introduction: Repairing the Past: Compensation for Victims of Human Rights Violations," in *The Handbook of Reparations,* ed. Pablo de Greiff (Oxford: Oxford University Press, 2006), 10.

encourage youth in many countries to learn from the past of the Second World War. They may increase the impact of the compensation program by addressing the dissatisfaction many beneficiaries and claimants expressed in relation to the process.

Reconciliation and understanding between peoples

After the end of the compensation program, a member of the Board of Directors was told by a survivor during a trip to Poland: "Now we finally don't have to hate you [the Germans] anymore, we hated you for so long." This shows, on an individual level, that the program — in sometimes unexpected ways — also contributed to a better relationship between Germany and its neighbors. If we look back to the international negotiations, several representatives of the involved states had called on Germany that without taking up responsibility for Nazi-era forced labor a reconciliation process with neighboring states would not be possible. Indeed, many commentators and representatives of victims' associations agree that one of the program's main achievements was its contribution towards "national reconciliation."

The notion of "reconciliation" is a difficult one when it comes to relations between states, and it is outside the scope of this publication to discuss the many dimensions of this concept in depth. Moreover, reparations programs do not automatically lead to "reconciliation," but may do so within a wider, more holistic framework with a goal of acceptance. Therefore, "reconciliation" is typically not a direct goal of a reparations program. Yet, in the case of the forced labor compensation program, reconciliation between the former enemies was a very cautious hope of some at the beginning of the negotiations. It is also interesting to note that "reconciliation" is included in the names of some partner organizations, which dates back to earlier compensation programs, such as the Polish "Foundation of Polish-German Reconciliation" or the Belarusian, Russian, and Ukrainian foundations that were called "Understanding and Reconciliation" in their national languages.

Given the difficult history between Germany and its neighbors, the compensation program was a significant symbolic gesture by Germany to acknowledge the crimes it perpetrated during the Second World War, particularly to the peoples of Eastern Europe. Here, it was crucial that Germany not only admitted its responsibility for Nazi forced labor, but also took concrete steps to realize this international project. It was equally important that it did so with the partner organizations in an equal partnership, and that representatives from relevant countries as well as victim representatives had a seat on the Board of Trustees and oversaw the work of the EVZ Foundation. Some see in the program a contribution to an improvement of the relationship between Germany and Poland. This has mainly been attributed to the moral and emotional aspects of the program that made it possible for the Polish side to consider reconciliation with its former aggressor Germany.

Also, in their responses to the survey, some beneficiaries of the program linked the work of the EVZ Foundation and partner organizations to the project of national reconciliation:

> *I thank the German-Czech Future Fund for the compensation due to my forced labor during the Reich at the time of the occupation of the Czech Republic. I'm happy that I can witness this moral compensation for the slave-like forced labor, which has damaged me for the rest of my life. The Prague branch helped me fill in the claims, and I'm grateful for that. I wish your organization much success in their activity to improve the relationship between our nations.*
> (Czech Republic, after second installment)

> *I'm happy that the German society tries to at least partially compensate the material and moral damage done. It's a pity that my parents are not able to witness this gratification. I thank all who have contributed to the reconciliation between our peoples.*
> (Poland, after first installment)

Yet 'national reconciliation' is not measurable and furthermore subject to political frameworks. A once reached consensus of 'belonging together,' or even reconciliation, can easily be put in danger again by emerging conflicts, which can be observed in the European Union today. The same is true for the commitment to responsibly face the crimes of the past.

CONCLUDING THOUGHTS

At the conclusion of the protracted international negotiation rounds in the year 2000, one of the German negotiators, Otto Graf Lambsdorff, stated that they had ended the negotiations with a feeling of "mild dissatisfaction" on all sides. In 2007, after the compensation payments were concluded, the representative of the Polish Government, Prof. Jerzy Kranz, referred to this comment. In a speech he stated that he hoped the end of the compensation payments leaves all involved stakeholders with a feeling of "mild satisfaction." In the opinion of the authors of this book, this is an appropriate summary of the impact of the compensation program.

The forced labor compensation program was a highly complex and politically sensitive program, the full significance of which will only become visible in the years to come. This book is not meant to provide a final evaluation of the program but to preserve the institutional knowledge of the implementers, ten years after the conclusion of the program. Moreover, this book only represents the perspective of some actors of the program, but lacks that of many others. Because of this, the authors of this book hope that their contributions will be debated, evaluated and reflected, and that through this more information will become available, particularly from perspectives not portrayed here.

ANNEXES 1—9

ANNEX 1

THE LAW ON THE CREATION OF A FOUNDATION "REMEMBRANCE, RESPONSIBILITY AND FUTURE"

of August 2, 2000, which entered into force on August 12, 2000 (Federal Law Gazette I 1263), last amended by the Law of 1 September 2008, which came into force on 9 September 2008 (Federal Law Gazette I 1797)

PREAMBLE

Recognizing that the National Socialist State inflicted severe injustice on slave laborers and forced laborers, through deportation, internment, exploitation which in some cases extended to destruction through labor, and through a large number of other human rights violations, that German enterprises which participated in the National Socialist injustice bear a historic responsibility and must accept it,

that the enterprises which have come together in the Foundation Initiative of German Industry have acknowledged this responsibility, that the injustice committed and the human suffering it caused cannot be truly compensated by financial payments,

that the Law comes too late for those who lost their lives as victims of the National Socialist régime or have died in the meantime, the German Bundestag acknowledges political and moral responsibility for the victims of National Socialism. The Bundestag intends to keep alive the memory of the injustice inflicted on the victims for coming generations as well.

The German Bundestag presumes that this Law, the German-U.S. intergovernmental agreement, the accompanying statements of the U.S. Government as well as the Joint Declaration by all parties to the negotiations provide adequate legal security for German enterprises and the Federal Republic of Germany, especially in the United States of America. With the concurrence of the Bundesrat, the Bundestag has passed the following Law:

SECTION 1: ESTABLISHMENT AND HEADQUARTERS

(1) A legally recognized foundation with the name "Remembrance, Responsibility and Future" shall be established under public law. The Foundation comes into being as of the entry into force of this legislation.

(2) The headquarters of the Foundation shall be in Berlin.

SECTION 2: PURPOSE OF THE FOUNDATION

(1) The purpose of the Foundation is to make financial compensation available through partner organizations to former forced laborers and to those affected by other injustices from the National Socialist period.

(2) A "Remembrance and Future" fund will be established within the Foundation. Its continuing task is to use the income primarily produced by the means allocated to it from Foundation monies to foster projects that serve the purposes of better understanding among peoples, the interests of survivors of the National Socialist régime, youth exchange, social justice, remembrance of the threat posed by totalitarian systems and despotism, and international cooperation in humanitarian endeavors. In commemoration and respect of those victims of National Socialist injustice who did not survive, it is also intended to further projects in the interest of their heirs.

SECTION 3: DONORS AND THE FOUNDATION'S CAPITAL ASSETS

(1) Contributors to the Foundation's capital fund shall be the companies joined together in the Foundation Initiative of German Industry, and the Federal Government.

(2) The Foundation shall be endowed with a capital fund consisting of the following:

1. Five billion deutschmarks that the companies joined together in the Foundation Initiative of German Industry have agreed to make available, including the payments that German insurance companies have provided to the International Commission on Holocaust Era Insurance Claims or will provide in the future.

2. Five billion deutschmarks that the German Federal Government is making available in the year 2000. The contribution of the Federal Government includes the contributions of enterprises of which the Federal Government is sole owner or in which it has a majority interest.

(3) There is no obligation for the donors to make supplementary payments.

(4) The Foundation is authorized to accept contributions from third parties. It shall endeavor to obtain additional contributions. The contributions are exempt from inheritance tax and gift tax.

(5) Income from the Foundation's capital fund and other income is to be used only for the purposes of the Foundation.

SECTION 4: THE BODIES OF THE FOUNDATION

The bodies of the Foundation are:
1. the Board of Trustees.
2. the Board of Directors.

SECTION 5: THE BOARD OF TRUSTEES

(1) The Board of Trustees is made up of 27 members, namely:
1. the chairman, to be named by the German Chancellor;
2. four members to be named by the companies joined together in the Foundation Initiative of German Industry;
3. five members to be named by the German Bundestag and two by the Bundesrat;
4. one representative of the Federal Ministry of Finance;
5. one representative of the Federal Ministry for Foreign Affairs;
6. one member to be named by the Conference on Jewish Material Claims against Germany;
7. one member to be named by the Central Council of German Sinti and Roma, the Alliance of German Sinti, and the International Romani Union;
8. one member to be named by the Government of the State of Israel;
9. one member to be named by the Government of the United States of America;
10. one member to be named by the Government of the Republic of Poland;
11. one member to be named by the Government of the Russian Federation;
12. one member to be named by the Government of Ukraine;
13. one member to be named by the Government of the Republic of Belarus;
14. one member to be named by the Government of the Czech Republic;
15. one lawyer to be named by the Government of the United States of America;
16. one member to be named by the United Nations High Commissioner for Refugees;
17. one member to be named by the International Organization for Migration in accordance with Section 9, Paragraph 2, Number 6; and
18. one member to be named by the Federal Information and Counseling Association for Victims of National Socialism e. V. [Registered Association].

The sending body may designate a substitute for each member of the Board.
A different composition of the Board of Trustees may be decided by a unanimous decision of the Board of Trustees.

(2) The term of office for members of the Board of Trustees shall be four years. If a member should resign before the end of his term, a successor may be appointed for the remainder of the term. The members of the Board of Trustees can be recalled by the sending body at any time.

(3) The Board of Trustees shall establish its own rules of procedure.

(4) The presence of half the membership of the Board of Trustees plus one shall constitute a quorum. The board shall make decisions on the basis of a simple majority. In case of a tie, the vote of the chairman shall determine the outcome. Decisions can also be made in writing unless one third or more of the members of the Board of Trustees object to such procedure in an individual case. Such a decision requires the accordance of the majority of the members of the Board of Trustees. The sentences 4 and 5 do not apply to the election of the members of the Board of Directors of the Foundation (Para. 6.2).

(5) The Board of Trustees has the right to decide on all fundamental matters that have to do with the tasks of the Foundation, specifically with regard to budgetary plans, the annual report, and the existence of the specific characteristics referred to in Section 12, Paragraph 1. It monitors the performance of the Board of Directors.

(6) The Board of Trustees makes decisions regarding the projects of the "Remembrance and Future" Fund based on proposals by the Board of Directors.

(7) The Board of Trustees establishes guidelines for the use of resources insofar as their use is not already specified in this Law. In this connection, it shall particularly endeavor to see to it that the partner organizations are able to draw in fair shares upon the eligibilities for payment referred to in Section 11, Paragraph 1, Sentence 1, Numbers 1 and 2.

(8) Members of the Board of Trustees serve in a "pro bono" capacity; necessary expenses will be reimbursed.

SECTION 6: THE BOARD OF DIRECTORS OF THE FOUNDATION

(1) The Board of Directors shall consist of the chairman and one additional member. Members of the Board of Trustees may not at the same time belong to the Board of Directors.

(2) The members of the Board of Directors will be named by the Board of Trustees.

(3) The Board of Directors of the Foundation shall direct the day-to-day business of the Foundation and shall implement the decisions of the Board of Trustees. It shall decide, up to a maximum amount determined by the Board of Trustees, on funding measures and oversee the purposeful and prudent expenditure of the Foundation's funds. The Board of Directors shall represent the Foundation, both in judicial and extrajudicial matters.

(4) If a unanimous decision is not reached by the Board of Directors, the chairman shall decide.

(5) The details shall be determined by the by-laws.

SECTION 7: THE BY-LAWS

The Board of Trustees shall adopt a set of by-laws by a two-thirds majority vote. If a set of by-laws has still not been adopted within three months of the initial meeting of the Board of Trustees, the chairman shall propose a set of by-laws that will be passed by a simple majority. The Board of Trustees may amend the by-laws on the basis of a two-thirds majority.

SECTION 8: OVERSIGHT, BUDGET, AUDITING

(1) The Foundation is subject to legal oversight by the Federal Ministry of Finance.

(2) The Foundation shall prepare a budget in timely fashion before the start of each fiscal year. The budget shall require the approval of the Federal Ministry of Finance.

(3) The Foundation shall be subject to being audited by the Federal Court of Audit. Without prejudice hereto, the Foundation's accounts and the management of its budget and finances are to be audited by the Federal Office for Central Services and Unresolved Property Issues.

SECTION 9: USE OF FOUNDATION RESOURCES

(1) Resources of the Foundation that serve the purpose of the Foundation referred to in Section 2, Paragraph 1, will be allocated to partner organizations. They are to be used for one-time payments to persons eligible pursuant to Section 11, as well as for covering the personnel and non-personnel expenses of the partner organizations. Persons eligible under Section 11, Paragraph 1, Sentence 1, Number 1 or Sentence 5 can receive up to 15,000 deutschmarks, and persons eligible under Section 11, Paragraph 1, Sentence 1, Number 2, or Sentence 2 can receive up to 5,000 deutschmarks. Receiving a payment under Section 11, Paragraph 1, Sentence 1, Number 1 or 2 does not preclude receiving a payment under Section 11, Paragraph 1, Sentence 1, Number 3 or Sentence 4 or 5.

(2) The partner organizations shall have available 8.1 billion deutschmarks including 50 million deutschmarks in accrued interest for payments to persons who suffered personal damage as referred to in Section 11, Paragraph 1, Sentence 1, Numbers 1 and 2, and Section 11, Paragraph 1, Sentence 2, insofar as [the payments are] intended for compensation for forced labor. The total amounts shall be divided into the following maximum amounts:

1. for the partner organization responsible for the Republic of Poland, 1,812 million deutschmarks;

2. for the partner organization responsible for Ukraine and the Republic of Moldova, 1,724 million deutschmarks;

3. for the partner organization responsible for the Russian Federation and the Republic of Latvia and the Republic of Lithuania, 835 million deutschmarks;

4. for the partner organization responsible for the Republic of Belarus and the Republic of Estonia, 694 million deutschmarks;

5. for the partner organization responsible for the Czech Republic, 423 million deutschmarks;

6. for the partner organization responsible for the non-Jewish claimants outside the states referred to in Numbers 1 through 5 (the International Organization for Migration), 800 million deutschmarks; the partner organization must pay over up to 260 million deutschmarks of this amount to the Conference on Jewish Material Claims against Germany;

7. for the partner organization responsible for the Jewish claimants outside the states referred to in Numbers 1 through 5 (the Conference on Jewish Material Claims against Germany), 1,812 million deutschmarks.

The partner organizations must use these monies to make the stipulated payments for all persons who on February 16, 1999, had their principal domicile in their [the organizations'] individual regional areas of responsibility and on that date belonged to their material sphere of responsibility. The partner organizations referred to in Numbers 2, 3, and 4 are also responsible for those persons who on February 16, 1999, had their principal domicile in other states, which were republics of the former USSR; in each case that partner organization is responsible from whose area the claimant was deported.

(3) 50 million deutschmarks are intended for compensation of other personal injuries in connection with National Socialist injustice. Claims are to be addressed to the partner organizations referred to in Paragraph 2. These organizations shall determine the merits and amount of the damage claimed. The amount of the compensation payments shall be determined by the Commission referred to in Paragraph 6, Sentence 2, in accordance with the ratio between the totality of the damages recognized by the partner organizations and the total amount of the monies referred to in Sentence 1, with due consideration given to Section 11, Paragraph 1, Sentence 5. The partner organizations may request the Commission referred to in Sentence 4 to assign the determinations referred to in Sentence 3 to an independent arbitrator. A partner organization that prefers not to make the determinations referred to in Sentence 3 itself must bear the costs of the arbitrator.

(4) The sum of one billion deutschmarks of the Foundation's monies is intended for payments to persons who suffered property loss. This amount is divided into the following maximum amounts:

1. 150 million deutschmarks for property losses resulting from persecution within the meaning of Section 11, Paragraph 1, Sentence 1, Number 3;

2. 50 million deutschmarks for other property losses within the meaning of Section 11, Paragraph 1, Sentence 4;

3. 150 million deutschmarks for the International Commission on Holocaust Era Insurance Claims to compensate unpaid or revoked and not otherwise compensated insurance policies of German insurance enterprises, including the costs incurred in this connection;

4. 300 million deutschmarks for social purposes to the benefit of Holocaust survivors through the Conference on Jewish Material Claims against Germany; 24 million deutschmarks of this shall be paid over to the partner organization referred to in Paragraph 2, Number 6, which shall use it for social purposes vis à-vis the similarly persecuted Sinti and Roma;

5. 350 million deutschmarks for the humanitarian fund of the International Commission on Holocaust Era Insurance Claims.

(5) If additional interest is earned from the monies made available to the Foundation except for the monies intended for the Future Fund, up to 50 million deutschmarks of this shall be made available to the International Commission on Holocaust Era Insurance Claims to compensate insurance losses within the meaning of Paragraph 4, Sentence 2, Number 3, for foreign subsidiaries of German insurance enterprises and for costs incurred in this connection, as soon as the monies are available. Monies referred to in Sentence 1 and Paragraph 4, Sentence 2, Number 3, may also be used for the other purpose in each case.

(6) Claims for payments from the monies envisaged in Paragraph 4, Sentence 2, Numbers 1 and 2, are to be addressed to the partner organization referred to in Paragraph 2, Number 6, regardless of the claimant's residence. Determinations concerning these payments shall be made by a commission to be formed under this partner organization. The commission shall consist of one member each to be named by the Federal Ministry of Finance and the Department of State of the United States of America and a chairperson to be chosen by those two members. The commission shall establish supplemental principles concerning the content and procedure of its determinations, insofar as these are not already established under this Law or the by laws. The commission shall rule on the submitted applications within a year after expiration of the application deadline. The Property Claims Commission shall rule on appeals against its initial determination subsequent to renewed consultation as the appeals organ within the meaning of Section 19. The costs of the commission, the appeals organ, and the partner organization are to be covered pro rata from the total amount referred to in Paragraph 4, Sentence 2, Numbers 1 and 2. If the amount of damages recognized by the commission exceeds the monies available under Paragraph 4, Sentence 2, Number 1 or 2, the payments to be made are to be reduced in proportion to the available monies.

(7) 700 million deutschmarks including the interest accruing thereto are to be used for projects of the "Remembrance and Future" Fund. Of this amount, 100 million deutschmarks may be made available for other than its intended purpose, if well-founded requests are filed based on insurance claims that could not be met under Paragraph 4, Sentence 2, Number 3, and Paragraph 5.

(8) In concert with the Board of Trustees, the partner organizations may subdivide the category of forced laborers, within its quota, in accordance with Section 11, Paragraph 1, Sentence 1, Number 1, insofar as this involves persons interned in other places of confinement, as well as affected persons within the meaning of Section 11, Paragraph 1, Sentence 1, Number 2, into subcategories depending on the severity of their fate and may set correspondingly gradated maximum amounts. This shall also apply to the eligibility of legal successors.

(9) The maximum amounts under Paragraph 1 may only be paid out for the time being in the amount of 50% for claimants under Section 11, Paragraph 1, Sentence 1, Number 1, and 35% for claimants under Section 11, Paragraph 1, Sentence 1, Number 2 or Sentence 2. Another payment of up to 50% of the amounts mentioned in Paragraph 1 for claimants under Section 11, Paragraph 1, Sentence 1, Number 1 and up to 65% of the amounts mentioned in Paragraph 1 for claimants under Section 11, Paragraph 1, Sentence 1, Number 2 or Sentence 2 shall be paid out after conclusion of the processing of all applications pending before the respective partner organization, to the extent possible within the framework of the available means. The partner organizations may set up a financial reserve for appeals under Section 19, in the amount of up to 5% of the monies allocated. To the extent the reserve has been set up, payment of the second installment under Sentence 2 may be made before the conclusion of the appeal proceedings. The Board of Trustees has the right, at the request of individual partner organizations, to allow an increase in the installment payments laid down under Sentence 1, insofar as it is assured that the monies allocated in Paragraph 2 are not exceeded.

(10) Payments under Section 11, Paragraph 1, Sentence 1, Number 3, with the exception of the payments of the International Commission on Holocaust Era Insurance Claims and payments under Section 11, Paragraph 1, Sentence 4 or 5 can take place only after all applications pending before the competent commission have been processed.

(11) Monies allocated under Paragraph 2 but not completely depleted are to be used for persons entitled to payments under Section 11, Paragraph 1, Sentence 1, Numbers 1 and 2. Should the funds provided under Paragraphs 2 and 3 not be completely depleted in spite of payment of the maximum amounts under Paragraph 1, Sentence 3, the Board of Trustees shall decide how they shall be used. Just as in the case of the use of additional monies, the Board must compensate, in particular, any shortage incurred by individual partner organizations in making payments under Section 11, Paragraph 1, Sentence 1, Numbers 1 and 2. The Board will decide on the other use of monies allocated under Paragraphs 2 and 3, which will be available due to a discontinuation of eligibility under Section 14 Paragraph 4. Sentence 4 shall also refer to monies under Paragraph 2, which can no longer be used for payment procedures by the respective

partner organization following the decision on the allocation of the second installment to be paid to eligible persons. Monies referred to in Paragraph 4, Sentence 2, Numbers 1 and 2, which are not drawn down shall go to the Conference on Jewish Material Claims against Germany; those referred to in Paragraph 4, Sentence 2, Number 3, to the International Commission on Holocaust Era Insurance Claims. The Board of Trustees may allow the maximum amounts under Paragraph 1, Sentence 3 to be exceeded if all partner organizations have been able to make payments in the amounts of these maximum amounts.

(12) Personnel and non-personnel costs shall be paid from the Foundation's funds, insofar as they are not to be assumed by the partner organizations in accordance with Paragraph 1, Sentence 2. The costs to be borne by the Foundation also include outlays for attorneys and counsel whose activity on behalf of persons entitled to payments under Section 11 contributed to the establishment of the Foundation or otherwise were favorable to its creation, particularly by taking part in the multilateral negotiations that preceded the establishment of the Foundation or by filing suits on behalf of claimants under Section 11 between November 14, 1990, and December 17, 1999. There is no legal claim to payments pursuant to Sentence 2. An arbitrator named by the Foundation will determine the allocation of an amount set by the Board of Trustees, based on guidelines that shall be determined and published by the Board of Trustees. Requests for the payments stipulated in Sentence 2 are to be submitted to the Foundation by the attorneys and counsel themselves and on their own behalf within eight months after publication of the guidelines. They must be accompanied by documentation of the outlays claimed. Every attorney and counsel shall make a declaration in the request proceedings to the effect that he waives any claims against his clients upon receipt of a payment under Sentence 2. He is under obligation to advise his clients that he has waived any claims.

(13) For pending litigation concerning matters covered in this Law, court costs shall not be levied.

SECTION 10: DISTRIBUTION OF RESOURCES THROUGH PARTNER ORGANIZATIONS

(1) The approval and disbursal of one-time payments to those persons eligible under Section 11 will be carried out through partner organizations. The Foundation is neither authorized nor obligated in this regard. The Board of Trustees may decide for another mode of payment. The partner organizations shall cooperate with appropriate associations of persecutees and local organizations.

(2) Within two months after entry into force of the Law, the Foundation and its partner organizations are to publicize the possibility of compensation under this Law in an appropriate manner to all groups of eligible people in their respective countries of residency. These publications shall specifically include information about the Foundation and its partner organizations, the conditions on which compensation can be awarded, and application deadlines.

SECTION 11: ELIGIBLE PERSONS

(1) Eligible under this Law are:
1. persons who were detained in a concentration camp as defined in Section 42, Paragraph 2 of the German Indemnification Act or in another place of confinement outside the territory of what is now the Republic of Austria or a ghetto under comparable conditions and were subjected to forced labor;

2. persons who were deported from their homelands into the territory of the German Reich within the borders of 1937 or to a German-occupied area, subjected to forced labor in a commercial enterprise or for public authorities there, and detained under conditions other than those mentioned in Number 1, or were subjected to conditions resembling detention or similar extremely harsh living conditions; this rule does not apply to persons who because their forced labor was performed primarily in the territory of what is now the Republic of Austria can receive payments from the Austrian Reconciliation Foundation;

3. persons who suffered property loss as a consequence of racial persecution with essential, direct, and harm-causing collaboration of German businesses as defined by the laws on indemnification and who could not receive any payment or could not file their claims for restitution or compensation by the deadline because they either did not meet the residency requirements of the Federal Indemnification Act or had their domicile or permanent residence in an area with whose government the Federal Republic of Germany did not maintain diplomatic relations, or because they could not prove that an asset that had been expropriated due to persecution outside the territory of the German Reich in its 1937 borders and could no longer be located there, had been removed to the Federal Republic of Germany, or the proofs of the validity of their claims under the Federal Restitution Act [Bundesrückerstattungsgesetz] and the Federal Indemnification Act [Bundesentschädigungsgesetz] became known and available only due to German reunification, and the filing of the claims under the Law on the Settlement of Open Property Matters or the Law on Indemnification of Victims of Nazism was not allowed, or to the extent that restitution payments for monetary claims expropriated outside Reich territory were denied for lack of the possibility of assessing them, and no payments could be claimed either under the Currency Conversion Act, the Federal Indemnification Act, the Equalization of Burdens Act, or the Reparation Losses Act; that also applies to other persecutees within the meaning of the Federal Indemnification Act; special arrangements within the framework of the International Commission on Holocaust Era Insurance Claims shall remain unaffected.

The partner organizations may also award compensation from the funds provided to them pursuant to Section 9, Paragraph 2 to those victims of National Socialist crimes who are not members of one of the groups mentioned in Sentence 1, Numbers 1 and 2, particularly forced laborers in agriculture. These awards, with reservation as to Section 9, Paragraph 8, must not result in any reduction in the payments to persons eligible under Paragraph 1, Sentence 1, Number 1. The funds provided for in Section 9, Paragraph 4, Sentence 2, Number 2 are intended to compensate property damage inflicted during the National Socialist regime with the essential, direct, and harm-causing participation of German enterprises, but not inflicted for reasons of National Socialist persecution. The funds referred to in Section 9, Paragraph 3, shall be awarded in cases of medical experiments or in the event of the death of or severe damage to the health of a child lodged in a home for children of forced laborers; in cases of other personal injuries they may be awarded.

(2) Eligibility shall be demonstrated by the applicant by submission of documentation. The partner organization shall bring in relevant evidence. If no relevant evidence is available, the claimant's eligibility can be made credible in some other way.

(3) Eligibility cannot be based on prisoner-of-war status.

(4) Payments from the Foundation are exempt from inheritance tax and gift tax.

SECTION 12: DEFINITIONS

(1) Specific characteristics of other places of confinement referred to in Section 11, Paragraph 1, Number 1 are inhumane conditions of detention, insufficient nutrition, and lack of medical care.

(2) German enterprises referred to in Sections 11 and 16 are those that had their headquarters within the 1937 borders of the German Reich or have their headquarters in the Federal Republic of Germany, as well as their parent companies, even when the latter had or have their headquarters abroad. Enterprises situated outside the 1937 borders of the German Reich in which during the period between January 30, 1933, and the entry into force of this Law, German enterprises as described in Sentence 1 had a direct or indirect financial participation of at least 25 percent are also considered German enterprises.

SECTION 13: APPLICATION ELIGIBILITY

(1) Awards under Section 11, Paragraph 1, Sentence 1, Numbers 1 or 2, or Sentence 2 or Sentence 5 are strictly personal and individual and must be applied for in one's own name. In a case where the eligible person has died after February 15, 1999, or where an award under Section 11, Paragraph 1, Number 3 or Sentence 4 is being applied for, the surviving spouse and children shall be entitled to equal shares of the award. If the eligible person left neither a spouse nor children, awards may be applied for in equal shares by the grandchildren, or if there are no grandchildren living, by the siblings. If no application is filed by these persons, the heirs named in a will are entitled to apply. Special arrangements within the framework of the International Commission on Holocaust Era Insurance Claims shall remain unaffected. The claim to payment cannot be ceded or attached.

(2) Juridical persons shall not be eligible. They can file applications as representatives of their shareholders eligible under this Law if specifically authorized by these shareholders. If a religious community or organization suffered property losses with the essential, direct, and harm-causing participation of German enterprises, Sentence 1 does not apply to them or their legal successors.

SECTION 14: CUT-OFF DATES

(1) Eligibility pursuant to Section 11 can no longer be determined if an application has not been received by a partner organization by the end of 31 December 2001. This shall also apply if upon conclusion of processing by the respective partner organization within the meaning of Section 9, Paragraph 9, Sentence 2 the application forms, documentation and evidence required to take a decision on the application have not been received.

(2) Applications that are received directly by the Foundation or by an inappropriate partner organization shall be forwarded to the appropriate partner organization. Special arrangements within the framework of the International Commission on Holocaust Era Insurance Claims shall remain unaffected.

(3) If an application has been filed within the application period specified in Paragraph 1 and if within six months after the death of the eligible person none of the persons eligible as legal successors pursuant to Section 13, Paragraph 1, Sentences 2 through 4 have notified the partner organization of their legal succession, the eligibility for an award shall expire. Paragraph 2 shall apply to the notification of legal succession mutatis mutandis.

(4) Any eligibility under Section 11 will expire after September 30, 2006. If it is within the responsibility of the partner organization that performance could not be made within the period stated then payment can be made until December 31, 2006 despite the expiration of eligibility under Sentence 1. The partner organizations are obliged to announce the expiration of eligibility in an appropriate way for the first time 12 months prior to this expiration date and repeatedly latest six months prior to this expiration date.

SECTION 15: TREATMENT OF OTHER PAYMENTS

(1) Payments for injustices suffered under National Socialism are supposed to benefit the persons eligible and not lead to a reduction of income received from the social security or health care system.

(2) Payments made earlier by enterprises in compensation for forced labor and other National Socialist injustices, even if made through third parties, shall be counted against payments under Section 9, Paragraph 1. Special arrangements within the framework of the International Commission on Holocaust Era Insurance Claims shall remain unaffected.

SECTION 16: EXCLUSIONS FROM CLAIMS

(1) Payments from public funds, including social security, and from German business enterprises for injustice suffered under National Socialism as defined in Section 11 may be claimed only under the terms of this Law. Any further claims in connection with National Socialist injustices are excluded. This applies also to cases in which claims have been transferred to third persons by operation of law, transition, or a legal transaction.

(2) Each claimant shall provide a statement within the framework of the application procedure irrevocably renouncing, without prejudice to Sentences 3 through 5, after receipt of a payment under this Law any further claim against the authorities for forced labor and property damage, all claims against German enterprises in connection with National Socialist injustice, and forced-labor claims against the Republic of Austria or Austrian enterprises. The renunciation becomes effective upon receipt of a payment under this Law. Accepting payments for personal damage under Section 11, Paragraph 1, Sentence 1, Number 1 or 2, or Sentence 2 or Sentence 5 shall not mean the renunciation of payments for insurance or other property damage in accordance with Section 11, Paragraph 1, Sentence 1, Number 3, or Sentence 4, and vice versa. Sentence 1 does not apply to claims arising from National Socialist injustice committed by foreign parent companies with headquarters outside the 1937 borders of the German Reich without having any connections with their German subsidiaries and the latter's involvement in National Socialist injustice. Sentence 1 also does not apply to any claims to restitution of artworks, insofar as the applicant undertakes to pursue this claim in Germany or the country from which the artwork was taken. The renunciation also pertains to compensation of legal costs for the prosecution of the claim, insofar as Section 9, Paragraph 12, does not provide otherwise. The details of the procedure shall be determined by the by-laws.

(3) More extensive compensation arrangements and settlements of the consequences of war at the public expense shall not be prejudiced by the above.

SECTION 17: TRANSFER OF FUNDS

(1) The Foundation is to make funds available quarterly to the partner organizations according to their documented need as outlined in Section 9, Paragraphs 2 and 3. The utilization of funds will be appropriately monitored by the Foundation.

(2) The first allocation of funds to the Foundation requires as a precondition the entry into force of the German-American Intergovernmental Agreement Concerning the Foundation "Remembrance, Responsibility and Future," and the establishment of adequate legal security for German enterprises. The German Bundestag shall determine whether these preconditions exist.

SECTION 18: REQUESTS FOR INFORMATION

(1) The Foundation and its partner organizations are authorized to receive information from agencies and other public bodies that is necessary for the fulfillment of their responsibilities. Information will not be provided if this would be contrary to specific official regulations on the use of the information, or when justifiable protection of the interests of the party concerned outweighs the general interest favoring disclosure.

(2) The information received may be used only for the purpose of carrying out the goals of the Foundation, and an applicant's personal data may be used only for the grant procedure under Section 11. The use of these data for other purposes is admissible only with the express consent of the applicant.

(3) Applicants under this Law may request information from enterprises in Germany for which or for whose legal predecessors they performed forced labor, insofar as this is requisite for determining their eligibility for awards.

SECTION 19: APPEALS PROCESS

The partner organizations are to create appeals organs that are independent and subject to no outside instruction. The appeals process itself is to be free of charge. However, costs incurred by the applicant are not to be reimbursed.

SECTION 20: ENTRY INTO FORCE

This Law enters into force on the date after its promulgation. Section 14 in the version of the Law of August 4, 2001 shall enter into force at the latest as of August 11, 2001.

ANNEX 2

JOINT STATEMENT ON OCCASION OF THE FINAL PLENARY MEETING CONCLUDING INTERNATIONAL TALKS ON THE PREPARATION OF THE FOUNDATION "REMEMBRANCE, RESPONSIBILITY AND THE FUTURE"

The Governments of the Republic of Belarus, the Czech Republic, the State of Israel, the Republic of Poland, the Russian Federation and Ukraine,

the Governments of the Federal Republic of Germany and the United States of America,

The German companies that founded the initiative to establish a foundation, which have since been joined by thousands of other German companies, and

As further participants, the Conference on Jewish Material Claims Against Germany, Inc. and the undersigned attorneys,

Recalling the proposal presented to the Chancellor of the Federal Republic of Germany by German companies on February 16, 1999, to send, as the century draws to a close, "a conclusive humanitarian signal, out of a sense of moral responsibility, solidarity and self-respect,"

Acknowledging the intention of both the Government of the Federal Republic of Germany and German companies to accept moral and historical responsibility arising from the use of slave and forced laborers, from property damage suffered as a consequence of racial persecution and from other injustices of the National Socialist era and World War II,

Recalling with appreciation the December 17, 1999, statement of the President of the Federal Republic of Germany paying German-American Agreement tribute to those who were subjected to slave and forced labor under German rule, recognizing their suffering and the injustices done to them, and begging forgiveness in the name of the German people,

Affirming the consensus reached by all participants on December 17, 1999, at the 7th plenary meeting in Berlin on the establishment of the Foundation "Remembrance, Responsibility and Future,"

Understanding that the Foundation is a sign of solidarity with the victims living in Central and Eastern European states and also a means of providing funds for victims from Central and Eastern Europe, most of whom benefited little from prior German compensation and restitution programs,

Understanding that insofar as the sum of DM to billion to be made available by the German public sector and the German companies for the Foundation "Remembrance, Responsibility and Future" is concerned, that sum is both a ceiling and the final amount and that all payments made towards former National Socialist slave and forced laborers, for other personal injury, for damage to property and for the Future Fund envisaged as part of the Foundation, as well as other costs incurred in connection with the Foundation, shall be financed from this sum, from any contributions from others, and the interest thereon,

Understanding that additional contributions by others for use by the Foundation are welcomed,

Recognizing that the Foundation will provide dignified payments to hundreds of thousands of survivors and to others who suffered from wrongs during the National Socialist era and World War II,

Accepting the common objective that German companies (including parents and subsidiaries as defined in Annex A) receive all embracing and enduring legal peace,

Recognizing that it would be in the participants' interests for the Foundation to be the exclusive remedy and forum for the resolution of all claims that have been or may be asserted against German companies arising out of the National Socialist era and World War II,

Recognizing that the establishment of the Foundation does not create a basis for claims against the Federal Republic of Germany or its nationals,

Declare as follows:

1. All participants welcome and support the Foundation "Remembrance, Responsibility and the Future" and declare their agreement with its elements, including the annexed distribution plan (Annex B). The interests of the former forced laborers, other victims and heirs have been duly taken into account. Based on the circumstances, all participants consider the overall result and the distribution of the Foundation funds to be fair to the victims and their heirs. The Foundation opens up the prospect of payment being made, even if, 55 years after the end of the war, the wrongdoer can no longer be traced or is no longer in existence. The Foundation is also a means of providing funds for forced laborers in addition to payments made by Germany so far.

2. Given the advanced age of the victims concerned, the primary humanitarian objective of the Foundation "Remembrance, Responsibility and Future" is to show results as soon as possible. All participants will work together with the Foundation in a cooperative, fair and non-bureaucratic manner to ensure that the payments reach the victims quickly.

3. Payments are to be made to applicants on behalf of the Foundation "Remembrance, Responsibility and Future" irrespective of their race, religion and nationality. Insofar as the participants themselves distribute funds, they will base their decisions on the criteria of eligibility set out in the German law establishing the Foundation and will act justly in this regard.

4. The participating Governments and other participants will proceed as follows:

   a) The Government of the Federal Republic of Germany ("Germany") and the German companies shall each contribute DM 5 billion to the Foundation "Remembrance, Responsibility and Future."

   b) Germany and the Government of the United States of America ("United States") will sign an Executive Agreement. Such agreement contains the obligation undertaken by the United States to assist in achieving all — embracing and enduring legal peace for German companies.

   c) The Governments of the participating Central and Eastern European States and Israel will implement the necessary specific measures within the framework of their national legal systems to achieve all — embracing and enduring legal peace.

   d) Assuming the request for a transfer referred to in paragraph (e) is granted, the DM 5 billion contribution of German companies shall be due and payable to the Foundation and payments from the Foundation shall begin once all lawsuits against German companies arising out of the National Socialist era and World War II pending in U.S. courts including those listed in Annex C and D are finally dismissed with prejudice by the courts. The initial portion of the DM 5 billion German Government contribution will be made available to the Foundation by October 31, 2000. The remainder of the German Government contribution will be made available to the Federal Foundation by December 31, 2000. Contributions from the German Government will begin earning interest for the benefit of the Foundation immediately. The German Government may advance some of its contribution to the partner organizations for certain startup costs before the lawsuits are finally dismissed. The German companies will make available reasonable advanced funding to provide appropriate publicity of the upcoming availability of Foundation benefits. German company funds will continue to be collected on a schedule and in a manner that will ensure that the interest earned thereon before and after their delivery to the Foundation will reach at least 100 million DM.

   e) Counsel for German company defendants and counsel for plaintiffs (each seeking to assemble at least a substantial majority of defendants' and plaintiffs' counsel respectively) have filed requests with the Multidistrict Litigation Panel seeking a transfer under appropriate conditions to a mutually agreeable federal judge of the federal district court cases listed in Annexes C and D, for the purpose of implementing the other steps in this Joint

Statement and in order to facilitate carrying out the objectives of the Executive Agreement by dismissing with prejudice the transferred cases and any later filed cases thereafter to be transferred as "tag-along" cases.

f) Germany will immediately establish a preparatory committee for the Foundation. The preparatory committee, after consulting with victims' representatives, will provide the publicity envisaged in paragraph (d) prior to the formal establishment of the Foundation, and, in consultation with partner organizations, prepare for the collection of applications for payment by the partner organizations.

g) The counsel for the plaintiffs will file motions or stipulations to dismiss with prejudice all lawsuits they have filed currently pending in U.S. courts against German companies arising out of the National Socialist era and World War II, including those listed in Annex C. They will also cooperate in seeking dismissal with prejudice by the courts of all other such lawsuits, including those listed in Annex D.

h) Germany and the United States will bring into force the Executive Agreement and the United States will thereupon file the Statement of Interest as provided therein.

i) The German Government will encourage German companies to open their archives relating to the National Socialist era and World War II.

Done at Berlin on the seventeenth day of July of the year Two Thousand in a single original, copies of which will be made available to interested parties.

V. N. Gerassimovitch
For the Government of the Republic of Belarus

Jiří Šitler
For the Government of the Czech Republic

Benjamin Shalev
For the Government of the State of Israel

Jerzy Kranz
For the Government of the Republic of Poland

V. A. Kopteltsev
For the Government of the Russian Federation

Oleksandr Maidannyk
For the Government of Ukraine

Stuart E. Eizenstat
For the Government of the United States of America

Dr. Otto Graf Lambsdorff
For the Government of th Federal Republic of Germany

Dr. Manfred Gentz
For the Foundation Initiative of German Enterprises

Israel Miller Gideon Taylor
For the Conference on Jewish Material Claims Against Germany, Inc.

Lawrence Kill
Linda Gerstel
Lawrence Kill
for Anderson, Kill st Olick, P.C.

Stephen A. Whinston Edward W. Millstein
Edward W. Millstein
Stephen A. Whinston
for Berger and Montague, P.C.

Richard E. Shevitz
Irwin B. Levin
Richard E. Shevitz
for Cohen & Malad, P.C.

Michael D. Hausfeld
for Cohen, Milstein, Hausfeld & Toll, P.L.L.C.

Edward Fagan
for Fagan & Associates

Carey D'Avino

Barry Fisher
for Fleishman & Fisher

Dennis Sheils
Robert Swift
for Kohn, Swift st Graf, P.C.

Morris A. Ratner
for Lieff, Cabraser, Heimann & Bernstein, L.L.P.

Martin Mendelsohn
for Verner, Liipfert, Bernhard, Mc Pherson
and Hand

Deborah M. Sturman
Melvyn I. Weiss
for Milberg, Weiss, Bershad, Hynes & Lerach, L.L.P.

J. Dennis Faucher
for Miller, Faucher, Cafferty st Wexler, L.L.P.

Burt Neuborne
New York University School of Law

Myroslaw Smorodsky

Melvyn Urbach
Stanley M. Chesley
for Waite, Schneider, Bayles & Chesley

Michael Witti

ANNEX A

to the Joint Statement on occasion of the final plenary meeting concluding international talks on the preparation of the Federal Foundation "Remembrance, Responsibility and Future,"

done at Berlin, 17 July 2000

Definition of "German companies"

"German companies" are defined as in Sections 12 and 16 of the legislation establishing the Foundation "Remembrance, Responsibility and Future," as follows:

1. Enterprises that had their headquarters within the 1937 borders of the German Reich or that have their headquarters in the Federal Republic of Germany, as well as their parent companies, even when the latter had or have their headquarters abroad.

2. Enterprises situated outside the 1937 German-American Agreement borders of the German Reich in which during the period between January 30, 1933, and the entry into force of the legislation establishing the Foundation "Remembrance, Responsibility and the Future," German enterprises as described in Sentence (1) had a direct or indirect financial participation of at least 25 percent.

3. "German companies" does not include foreign parent companies with headquarters outside the 1937 borders of the German Reich in any case in which the sole alleged claim arising from National Socialist injustice or World War II has no connection with the German affiliate and the latter's involvement in National Socialist injustice, unless there is pending a discovery request by plaintiff(s), of which the United States is provided notice by the defendant with copy to plaintiff(s), seeking discovery from or concerning World War II or National Socialist era actions of the German affiliate.

ANNEX B

to the Joint Statement on occasion of the final plenary meeting concluding international talks on the preparation of the Federal Foundation "Remembrance, Responsibility and the Future,"

done at Berlin, 17 July 2000

[This annex contains a Distribution Plan of the Foundation's funds (Joint Chairmen's Proposal) for the proposed partner organizations.]

ANNEX C

to the Joint Statement on occasion of the final plenary meeting concluding international talks on the preparation of the Federal Foundation "Remembrance, Responsibility and Future,"

done at Berlin, 17 July 2000

[This annex contains a list of known World War II and National Socialist era cases against German companies pending in U.S. courts filed by plaintiffs' counsel participating in the negotiations.]

ANNEX D

to the Joint Statement on occasion of the final plenary meeting concluding international talks on the preparation of the Federal Foundation "Remembrance, Responsibility and Future,"

done at Berlin, 17 July 2000

[This annex contains a list of known World War II and National Socialist era cases against German companies pending in U5. courts filed by plaintiffs' counsel not participating in the negotiations.]

For the sake of brevity the full text of Annexes B–D to the Joint Statement are not included here. The complete document is on file with the EVZ Foundation.

ANNEX 3

AGREEMENT BETWEEN THE GOVERNMENT OF THE UNITED STATES OF AMERICA AND THE GOVERNMENT OF THE FEDERAL REPUBLIC OF GERMANY CONCERNING THE FOUNDATION "REMEMBRANCE, RESPONSIBILITY AND FUTURE"

The Government of the United States of America
and
the Government of the Federal Republic of Germany —

Intending to shape relations between their two States in a spirit of friendship and cooperation for the future and to successfully resolve issues stemming from the past,

Recognizing that the Federal Republic of Germany has, building on Allied legislation and in close consultation with victims' associations and interested Governments, provided, in an unprecedented manner, comprehensive and extensive restitution and compensation to victims of National Socialist persecution,

Noting the historic announcement on February 16, 1999, made by the Federal Chancellor and German companies, in which the companies stated their intention to establish a foundation to compensate forced laborers and others who suffered at the hands of German companies during the National Socialist era and World War II,

Noting that, by means of the Foundation Initiative, its member companies wish to respond to the moral responsibility of German business arising from the use of forced laborers and from damage to property caused by persecution, and from all other wrongs suffered during the National Socialist era and World War II,

Recognizing as legitimate the interest German companies have in all-embracing and enduring legal peace in this matter, and further recognizing that such interest was fundamental to the establishment of the Foundation Initiative,

Noting that the two Governments announced that they welcomed and support the Foundation Initiative,

Noting that the Federal Republic of Germany and German companies have since agreed on the creation of a single Foundation, "Remembrance, Responsibility and Future" (the "Foundation"), formed under German federal law as an instrumentality of the Federal Republic of Germany and funded by contributions from the Federal Republic of Germany and the German companies,

Recognizing that German business, having contributed substantially to the Foundation, should not be asked or expected to contribute again, in court or elsewhere, for the use of forced laborers or for any wrongs asserted against German companies arising from the National Socialist era and World War II,

Recognizing that it is in the interest of both parties to have a resolution of these issues that is non-adversarial and non-confrontational, outside of litigation,

Recognizing that both parties desire all-embracing and enduring legal peace to advance their foreign policy interests,

Noting in this regard the June 16, 2000, letter of the Assistant to the President of the United States for National Security Affairs and the Counsel to the President of the United States and the July 5, 2000, letter of the Foreign Policy and Security Advisor of the Chancellor of the Federal Republic of Germany, copies of which have been made public,

Having worked as partners, in consultation with other interested parties and governments, to assist German companies to achieve wide support for the total amount of funds and the eligibility criteria of the Foundation and for the establishment of all-embracing and enduring legal peace,

Noting that the Foundation will assure broad coverage of victims and broad participation by companies which would not be possible through judicial proceedings,

Believing that the Foundation will provide as expeditious as possible a mechanism for making fair and speedy payments to now elderly victims,

Having in mind that the Foundation covers, and that it would be in the interests of both parties for the Foundation to be the exclusive remedy and forum for addressing, all claims that have been or may be asserted against German companies arising from the National Socialist era and World War II,

Recalling that for the last 55 years the parties have sought to work to address the consequences of the National Socialist era and World War II through political and governmental acts between the United States and the Federal Republic of Germany,

Noting that this Agreement and the establishment of the Foundation represent a fulfillment of these efforts,

Recognizing that the German Government has tabled a Bill before the German Federal Parliament ("Bundestag") to establish the Foundation —

Have agreed as follows:

ARTICLE 1

(1) The parties agree that the Foundation "Remembrance, Responsibility and the Future" covers, and that it would be in their interests for the Foundation to be the exclusive remedy and forum for the resolution of, all claims that have been or may be asserted against German companies arising from the National Socialist era and World War II.

(2) The Federal Republic of Germany agrees to ensure that the Foundation shall provide appropriately extensive publicity concerning its existence, its objectives and the availability of funds.

(3) Annex A sets forth the principles that shall govern the operation of the Foundation. The Federal Republic of Germany assures that the Foundation will be subject to legal supervision by a German governmental authority; any person may request that the German governmental authority take measures to ensure compliance with the legal requirements of the Foundation.

(4) The Federal Republic of Germany agrees that insurance claims that come within the scope of the current claims handling procedures adopted by the International Commission of Holocaust Era Insurance Claims ("ICHEIC") and are made against German insurance companies shall be processed by the companies and the German Insurance Association on the basis of such procedures and on the basis of additional claims handling procedures that may be agreed among the Foundation, ICHEIC, and the German Insurance Association.

ARTICLE 2

(1) The United States shall, in all cases in which the United States is notified that a claim described in article 1 (1) has been asserted in a court in the United States, inform its courts through a Statement of Interest, in accordance with Annex B, and, consistent therewith, as it otherwise considers appropriate, that it would be in the foreign policy interests of the United States for the Foundation to be the exclusive remedy and forum for resolving such claims asserted against German companies as defined in Annex C and that dismissal of such cases would be in its foreign policy interest.

(2) The United States, recognizing the importance of the objectives of this agreement, including all-embracing and enduring legal peace, shall, in a timely manner, use its best efforts, in a manner it considers appropriate, to achieve these objectives with state and local governments.

ARTICLE 3

(1) This agreement is intended to complement the creation of the Foundation and to foster all-embracing and enduring legal peace for German companies with respect to the National Socialist era and World War II.

(2) This agreement shall not affect unilateral decisions or bilateral or multilateral agreements that dealt with the consequences of the National Socialist era and World War II.

(3) The United States will not raise any reparations claims against the Federal Republic of Germany.

(4) The United States shall take appropriate steps to oppose any challenge to the sovereign immunity of the Federal Republic of Germany with respect to any claim that may be asserted against the Federal Republic of Germany concerning the consequences of the National Socialist era and World War II.

ARTICLE 4

Annexes A, B and C shall be an integral part of this Agreement.

ARTICLE 5

This Agreement shall enter into force on the date on which the parties agree by exchange of notes.

DONE at Berlin on the 17th day of July, 2000, in duplicate in the German and English languages, both texts being equally authentic.

For the Government of the United States of America	For the Government of the Federal Republic of Germany
John Kornblum	Wolfgang Ischinger

ANNEX A

of the Agreement between the Government of the United States of America and the Government of the Federal Republic of Germany concerning the Foundation "Remembrance, Responsibility and Future"

Principles Governing the Operation of the Foundation

Article 1, Paragraph 3 of the Agreement provides that the principles governing the operation of the Foundation will be set forth in Annex A. This Annex reflects key elements of the Foundation that form a basis for the Parties' mutual commitments in the Agreement.

1. The Foundation legislation will state that the purpose of the Foundation is to make payments through partner organizations to those who suffered as private and public sector forced or slave laborers and those who suffered at the hands of German companies during the National Socialist era and to establish a "Remembrance and Future Fund" within the Foundation. It will state that the permanent task of the "Remembrance and Future Fund" is to support projects that (a) serve to promote understanding between nations, and serve social justice and international cooperation in the humanitarian sector; (b) support youth exchange programs and keep alive the memory of the Holocaust and the threat posed by totalitarian, unlawful regimes and tyranny; and (c) also benefit the heirs of those who have not survived.

2. The Foundation legislation will provide for a Board of Trustees that consists of an equal number of members appointed by the German Government and German companies and by other governments and victims' representatives, except that the Chairman shall be a person of international stature appointed by the Chancellor of the Federal Republic of Germany. The Board may be reduced in size after four years, but the balance of the membership will continue, to the extent appropriate. The Board will adopt by-laws by a two-thirds majority vote. All Foundation operations will be transparent and by-laws and similar procedures will be made public.

3. The Foundation legislation will provide that the Foundation will be audited by the Federal Accounting Office and that all partner organizations will also be audited.

4. The Foundation legislation will provide that persons who were held in concentration camps as defined under the Federal Compensation Law ("BEG") or in another place of confinement or ghetto under comparable conditions and were subject to forced labor ("slave laborers") will be eligible to receive up to DM 15,000 each. The Foundation legislation will also provide that persons who were deported from their homelands into the territory of the 1937 borders of the German Reich or to a German-occupied area, and were held in prison-like or extremely harsh living conditions ("forced laborers") not covered by the above definition

will be eligible to receive up to DM 5,000 each. In addition, from the allocated funds to make payments to forced laborers, partner organizations will be authorized to make payments to others who were forced to work during the National Socialist era. These other forced laborers will receive up to DM 5,000 each. The eligibility of all laborers covered by the Foundation will be limited to survivors and heirs, as defined under paragraph 8, of those who died after February 15, 1999. In addition, victims of "other non-labor personal injury wrongs," including, but not limited to, medical experimentation and Kinderheim cases, will be eligible to receive payments, within the limits of the amount allocated for that purpose. Victims of medical experimentation and Kinderheim cases are given priority over other non-labor personal injury wrongs. The eligibility of a victim to receive benefits for all "other non-labor personal injury wrongs" will not be affected by whether or not he or she also receives benefits for forced labor. The funds allocated for "other non-labor personal injury wrongs" will constitute a separate allocation. The partner organizations will receive, review, and process applications for payments from the amount allocated for "other personal injury." At the request of a partner organization, the property committee referred to in paragraph 11 will appoint an independent arbitrator to review and process applications to the particular partner organization. The amount allocated will be distributed to each partner organization so that each approved applicant is provided a pro-rata amount of the total amount for all approved "other personal injury" applicants. The decisions of the partner organizations and any arbitrator that may be appointed will be based on uniform standards approved by the Board of Trustees. The Foundation legislation will provide that any costs associated with reviewing and processing applications, including those associated with an arbitrator (if selected), will be drawn from the allocations for each partner organization. Excess amounts in the labor category allocated to any partner organization under the distribution plan annexed to the Joint Statement will be reallocated to labor, with the aim of reaching equal levels of payments to former slave and forced laborers wherever they reside. The Board of Trustees will be entitled to authorize payments above per capita ceilings should circumstances warrant.

5. The Foundation legislation will provide that a slave or forced laborer will not be able to receive payments for the same injury or wrong from both the Foundation and the Austrian Foundation for Reconciliation, Peace and Cooperation.

6. The Foundation legislation will provide that persons who suffered loss of or damage to property during the National Socialist era as a result of racial persecution directly caused by German companies are eligible to recover under the payment system set forth in paragraph 11. The eligibility of such persons will be limited to those who could not receive any payment under the BEG or Federal Restitution Law ("BRueckG") because they did not meet the residency requirement or could not file their claims by the deadline because they lived under a government with which the Federal Republic of Germany did not have diplomatic relations, those whose claims were rejected under the BEG or BRueckG where legal proof became available only after the reunification of the Federal Republic of Germany, provided the claims were not covered by post-reunification restitution or compensation

legislation, and those whose racially-motivated property claims concerning moveable property were denied or would have been denied under the BEG or BRueckG because the claimant, while able to prove a German company was responsible for seizing or confiscating property, was not able to prove that the property was transferred into then-West Germany (as required by law) or, in the case of bank accounts, that compensation was or would have been denied because the sum was no longer identifiable, where either (a) the claimant can now prove the property was transferred into then-West Germany or (b) the location of property is unknown.

7. The Foundation legislation, by making available the amount of 50 million DM, will provide a potential remedy for all non-racially motivated wrongs of German companies directly resulting in loss of or damage to property during the National Socialist era. The Foundation will refer such matters for review and processing to the committee referred to in paragraph 11. All funds allocated to payment for property matters will be distributed within those categories.

8. The Foundation legislation will provide that the heirs eligible to receive payments under paragraphs 6 and 7 consist of the spouse or children. In the absence of the victim, spouse and children, then payments under these paragraphs will be available to grandchildren, if alive; if not, to siblings, if alive; and if there are neither grandchildren nor siblings, to the individual beneficiary named in a will.

9. The Foundation legislation will provide that all eligibility decisions will be based on relaxed standards of proof.

10. The Foundation legislation will provide that legal persons will be allowed to make claims on behalf of individuals when those individuals have given powers of attorney. The Foundation legislation will also provide that where an identifiable religious community has suffered damage to or loss of community property, as distinct from individual property, resulting directly from the wrongs of a German company, a duly authorized legal successor may apply for payment to the committee referred to in paragraph 11.

11. The Foundation legislation will establish a three-member committee for property matters (paragraphs 6 and 7). The United States and the Federal Republic of Germany will each appoint one member; these two members will appoint a Chairman. A secretariat will be largely responsible for the initial review of applications. The Foundation legislation will require the Committee to establish simplified procedures, including simplified and expedited internal appeals. The Committee will not have the authority to reopen any case that has been finally decided by a German court or administrative body, or that could have been decided by application in time, except as specified in paragraph 6. All of the Committee's expenses will be funded from the amount allocated for property claims and the funds will be subject to audit.

12. The Foundation legislation will provide that the Committee referred to in paragraph 11 will distribute the funds allocated to it on a pro-rata basis.

13. The Foundation legislation will make clear that receipt of payment from Foundation funds will not affect the recipient's eligibility for social security or other public benefits. There will be offsets for prior compensation payments made by German companies for forced labor and other National Socialist era injustices, even if made through third parties, but there will be no offsets for any prior Government payments.

14. The Foundation legislation will provide that each applicant for a Foundation payment will be required to state that, upon receipt of a payment from the Foundation, he or she will waive any and all alleged National Socialist era claims against German companies and all National Socialist era labor and property damage claims against the German Government. Such a waiver will not preclude applicants from being eligible to receive payments under the Foundation legislation for other wrongs, for example other personal injuries or loss of property, or any combination thereof. Such a waiver also will not preclude an applicant from bringing an action against a specific German entity (i.e., Government agency or company) for the return of a specifically identified piece of art if the action is filed in the Federal Republic of Germany or in the country in which the art was taken, provided that the applicant is precluded from seeking any relief beyond or other than the return of the specifically identified piece of art.

15. The Foundation legislation will provide that each partner organization will create an internal appeals procedure.

16. The Foundation legislation will require that the Foundation provide appropriately extensive publicity concerning the benefits that the Foundation will offer and how to apply. The Board of Trustees, in consultation with the partner organizations, will determine the form and content of such publicity.

17. The Foundation legislation will allow applications to be made to the partner organizations for at least eight months after the enactment of the Foundation law.

18. The Foundation legislation will authorize the Foundation and its partner organizations to receive information from German Government agencies and other public bodies that is necessary for the fulfillment of their responsibilities, in so far as this is not contrary to particular statutes or regulations or the legitimate interests of the persons concerned.

19. The Foundation legislation will enter into force no later than when the funds of the Foundation are made available to it.

ANNEX B

of the Agreement between the Government of the United States of America and the Government of the Federal Republic of Germany concerning the Foundation "Remembrance, Responsibility and Future"

Elements of U.S. Government Statement of Interest

Pursuant to Article 2, Paragraph 1, the United States will timely file a Statement of Interest and accompanying formal foreign policy statement of the Secretary of State and Declaration of Deputy Treasury Secretary Stuart E. Eizenstat in all pending and future cases, regardless of whether the plaintiff(s) consent(s) to dismissal, in which the United States is notified that a claim has been asserted against German companies arising from the National Socialist era and World War II.

The Statement of Interest will make the following points:

1. As indicated by his letter of December 13, 1999, the President of the United States has concluded that it would be in the foreign policy interests of the United States for the Foundation to be the exclusive forum and remedy for the resolution of all asserted claims against German companies arising from their involvement in the National Socialist era and World War II, including without limitation those relating to slave and forced labor, aryanization, medical experimentation, children's homes/Kinderheim, other cases of personal injury, and damage to or loss of property, including banking assets and insurance policies.

2. Accordingly, the United States believes that all asserted claims should be pursued (or in the event Foundation funds have been exhausted, should timely have been pursued) through the Foundation instead of the courts.

3. As the President said in his letter of December 13, 1999, dismissal of the lawsuit, which touches on the foreign policy interests of the United States, would be in the foreign policy interests of the United States. The United States will recommend dismissal on any valid legal ground (which, under the U.S. system of jurisprudence, will be for the U.S. courts to determine). The United States will explain that, in the context of the Foundation, it is in the enduring and high interest of the United States to support efforts to achieve dismissal of all National Socialist and World War II era cases against German companies. The United States will explain fully its foreign policy interests in achieving dismissal, as set forth below.

4. The United States' interests include the interest in a fair and prompt resolution of the issues involved in these lawsuits to bring some measure of justice to the victims of the National Socialist era and World War II in their lifetimes; the interest in the furtherance of the close

cooperation this country has with our important European ally and economic partner, Germany; the interest in maintaining good relations with Israel and other Western, Central, and Eastern European nations, from which many of those who suffered during the National Socialist era and World War II come; and the interest in achieving legal peace for asserted claims against German companies arising from their involvement in the National Socialist era and World War II.

5. The Foundation is a fulfillment of a half-century effort to complete the task of bringing justice to victims of the Holocaust and victims of National Socialist persecution. It complements significant prior German compensation, restitution, and pension programs for acts arising out of the National Socialist era and World War II. For the last 55 years, the United States has sought to work with Germany to address the consequences of the National Socialist era and World War II through political and governmental acts between the United States and Germany.

6. The participation in the Foundation not only by the German Government and German companies that existed during the National Socialist era, but also by German companies that did not exist during the National Socialist era, allows comprehensive coverage of slave and forced laborers and other victims.

7. Plaintiffs in these cases face numerous legal hurdles, including, without limitation, justiciability, international comity, statutes of limitation, jurisdictional issues, forum non conveniens, difficulties of proof, and certification of a class of heirs. The United States takes no position here on the merits of the legal claims or arguments advanced by plaintiffs or defendants. The United States does not suggest that its policy interests concerning the Foundation in themselves provide an independent legal basis for dismissal, but will reinforce the point that U.S. policy interests favor dismissal on any valid legal ground.

8. The Foundation is fair and equitable, based on: (a) the advancing age of the plaintiffs, their need for a speedy, non-bureaucratic resolution, and the desirability of ex-pending available funds on victims rather than litigation; (b) the Foundation's level of funding, allocation of its funds, payment system, and eligibility criteria; (c) the difficult legal hurdles faced by plaintiffs and the uncertainty of their litigation prospects; and (d) in light of the particular difficulties presented by the asserted claims of heirs, the programs to benefit heirs and others in the Future Fund.

9. The structure and operation of the Foundation will assure (or has assured) swift, impartial, dignified, and enforceable payments; appropriately extensive publicity has been given concerning its existence, its objectives, and the availability of funds; and the Foundation's operation is open and accountable.

ANNEX C

of the Agreement between the Government of the United States of America and the Government of the Federal Republic of Germany concerning the Foundation "Remembrance, Responsibility and Future"

Definition of "German Companies"

"German companies", as used in Article 1, Paragraph 1 and Article 2, Paragraph 1, are defined as in Sections 12 and 16 of the legislation establishing the Foundation "Remembrance, Responsibility and Future," as follows:

1. Enterprises that had their headquarters within the 1937 borders of the German Reich or that have their headquarters in the Federal Republic of Germany, as well as their parent companies, even when the latter had or have their headquarters abroad.

2. Enterprises situated outside the 1937 borders of the German Reich in which during the period between January 30, 1933, and the entry into force of the legislation establishing the Foundation "Remembrance, Responsibility and Future," German enterprises as described in Sentence (1) had a direct or indirect financial participation of at least 25 percent.

3. "German companies" does not include foreign parent companies with head-quarters outside the 1937 borders of the German Reich in any case in which the sole alleged claim arising from National Socialist injustice or World War II has no connection with the German affiliate and the latter's involvement in National Socialist injustice, unless there is pending a discovery request by plaintiff(s), of which the United States is provided notice by the defendant with copy to plaintiff(s), seeking discovery from or concerning World War II or National Socialist era actions of the German affiliate.

ANNEX 4

STATUTES FOR THE FOUNDATION "REMEMBRANCE, RESPONSIBILITY AND FUTURE"

In accordance with Section 7 of the Law on the Creation of a Foundation, "Remembrance, Responsibility and Future", German Federal Law Gazette I of 2 August 2000, p. 1263, hereinafter called Foundation Law, the Foundation "Remembrance, Responsibility and Future" draws up for itself the following Statutes (last amended on 28 June 2012):

SECTION 1

Name, legal form, head office

In accordance with Section 1 of the Foundation Law, the Foundation "Remembrance, Responsibility and Future" is a foundation with legal capacity under public law with its head office in Berlin.

SECTION 2

Purpose of the Foundation

The purpose of the Foundation arises from Section 2 of the Foundation Law.
In realizing the purpose of the Foundation, the Foundation will work to support the implementation and maintenance of the objectives of the Joint Statement of 17 July 2000 on occasion of the final plenary session of the preparatory committee for the establishment of the Foundation "Remembrance, Responsibility and Future".

SECTION 3

Foundation assets

The Foundation will receive foundation resources of five billion deutschmarks each from the institutions named in Section 3 (2) of the Foundation Law. The Foundation assets can be increased by contributions from third parties (Section 3 (4) Sentences 1 and 2 of the Foundation Law). Any resources that are not used must be safely and profitably invested by the Foundation. The Foundation must render accounts about this.

The assets of the "Remembrance and Future" Fund must be kept separately from the assets of the Foundation and be invested in accordance with paragraph 1 of this section. Sponsored projects, which serve to fulfil the tasks assigned to the Fund in accordance with Section 2 (2) of the Foundation Law, must only be financed from the income from these resources. Section 9 (7) Sentence 2 of the Foundation Law remains unaffected. The Foundation strives to preserve the real value of its assets (adjustment for inflation). The original capital of the Foundation shall remain untouched in all cases.

SECTION 4

Organs of the Foundation

In accordance with Section 4 of the Foundation Law, organs of the Foundation are:

- the Board of Trustees and
- the Board of Management.

On assuming their office, the members of the Foundation Board of Trustees and Board of Management undertake to fulfil the intention of the donors, as expressed in the Foundation Law and in these Statutes, to the best of their knowledge and belief and to do everything to promote the interests of the Foundation and to omit any action which could damage the Foundation. They watch over the thrifty and economical use of resources. They undertake to maintain the confidentiality of personal data to which they become privy as part of their Foundation work.

SECTION 5

The Board of Trustees

1. Subject to a decision in accordance with Section 5 (1) Sentence 4 of the Foundation Law, the Board of Trustees consists of the 27 members named in Section 5 (1) Nos. 1–18 of the Foundation Law. The Federal Chancellor may name a deputy for the chairman of the Board of Trustees.

2. The period in office of the members of the Board of Trustees is four years. They may be reappointed. If a member retires before the end of his term of office, a successor may be appointed. The members of the Board of Trustees may be recalled by the institution sending them at any time.

3. The Board of Trustees will draw up standing orders for itself.

SECTION 6

Rights, duties and tasks of the Board of Trustees

1. The Board of Trustees decides on all fundamental questions which are part of the responsibilities of the Foundation; in particular, the Board of Trustees is exclusively responsible for the following tasks:

    - issuing guidelines on the use of Foundation resources in accordance with Section 5 (7) of the Foundation Law and putting into concrete terms the provisions contained in Section 9 of the Foundation Law. The Board of Trustees may change the guidelines as necessary by a majority of its members;

    - deciding on the basis of the legal definition of Section 12 (1) of the Foundation Law on the recognition of "another place of liability" within the meaning of Section 11 (1) No. 1 of the Foundation Law and also the agreement of the sub-categories to be determined by the partner organisations in accordance with Section 9 (8) of the Foundation Law. The Board of Trustees will make a decision after hearing arguments from the partner organisation concerned;

    - appointment of the members of the Foundation Board of Management for a period of up to four years each; re-appointment is permitted; the members of the Board of Management may be dismissed by the Board of Trustees at any time for cause.

    - monitoring the activities of the Foundation Board of Management. For this purpose the Board of Trustees in the person of its chairman can at any time demand information about the activities of the Foundation Board of Management and access to all business documents. The Board of Trustees can also instruct one or several members to undertake this task;

    - approving the budget drawn up by the Board of Management and the annual accounts, as well as discharging the Foundation Board of Management;

    - approving the remuneration of the members of the Board of Management on the basis of the remuneration system under public law and conclusion of the corresponding employment contracts.

    - the naming of a person as arbitrator in accordance with Section 9 (12) of the Foundation Law.

2. The Board of Trustees shall take decisions concerning focus areas and funding programmes based on proposals submitted by the Board of Directors. A corresponding financing volume shall be approved for each funding programme.

3. Based on proposals submitted by the Board of Directors, the Board of Trustees shall take decisions on project applications for funding of more than EUR 100,000 or applications for projects whose project executing agencies are either members of the Board of Trustees or organisations associated with members of the Board. If a member of the Board of Trustees or his/her delegating institution is participating in the implementation of a project, this member shall not be entitled to vote in the respective decision-making process.

4. On the basis of a majority decision, the Board of Trustees can request the Board of Directors to re-examine applications which the Board of Trustees has rejected and to re-submit these for decision-making.

5. The Foundation reimburses the necessary expenses of the members of the Board of Trustees who excercise their right to vote, acting on an honorary basis.

SECTION 7

Foundation Board of Management

1. In accordance with Section 6 (1) Sentence 1 of the Foundation Law, the Foundation Board of Management consists of one chairman as well as two further board members.

The chairman of the Board of Management issues invitations to attend meetings of the Board of Management. He is obliged to do this if a member of the Board of Management makes such a demand in writing.

The Board of Management is quorate if two board members participate in the vote following proper invitation. The Board of Management adopts its resolutions by a majority of the votes cast.

Resolutions of the Foundation Board of Management may also be adopted in written or telexed procedures if all the members of the Foundation Board of Management agree to this in writing or by telex or if a decision by the Foundation Board of Management cannot be achieved in any other way. In this respect, the members of the Foundation Board of Management must ensure their ability to act through the relevant technical facilities.

2. Minutes must be kept of the resolutions adopted by the Foundation Board of Management, to be signed by the chairman of the meeting and the secretary to be appointed on each occasion, and sent to the chairman of the Board of Trustees who will inform members of the Board of Trustees about important decisions.

3. The Board of Management can draw up standing orders for itself which require approval by the Board of Trustees.

SECTION 8

Rights, duties and tasks of the Foundation Board of Management

1. In accordance with Section 6 (3) Sentence 4 of the Foundation Law, the Foundation Board of Management represents the Foundation in legal and non-legal matters. Two members respectively of the Foundation Board of Management jointly represent the Foundation. Each member of the Foundation Board of Management may be represented by another member, multiple representation is not permitted.

2. The Board of Management administers the Foundation and conducts its business in accordance with the purpose of the Foundation as expressed in the Foundation Law as well as with these Statutes and the resolutions of the Board of Trustees. In this context it is also responsible implementing the resolutions of the Board of Trustees as well as dealing with the tasks transferred to it by the Board of Trustees.

The Foundation Board of Management is responsible in particular for:

- the management of the ongoing business of the Foundation in accordance with Section 6 (3) Sentence 1 of the Foundation Law, in which it is responsible for the preparation and conclusion of all legal transactions binding on the Foundation;

- the preparation of the resolutions of the Board of Trustees;

- conclusion of contracts with the partner organisations

- conclusion and settlement of the contract with ICHEIC with the inclusion of the insurance service

- monitoring the economical use of Foundation resources in accordance with their intended purpose by the partner organisations, particularly adherence to the stipulations of the Foundation Law as well as of contracts concluded with the partner organisations;

- regular reports to the Board of Trustees about control of the implementation of contracts concluded with partner organisations;

- the management and administration of the "Remembrance and Future" Fund set up within the Foundation as well as the use of its resources in accordance with the statutes;

- drawing up the annual budget and the annual accounts (management report) as well as seeking the approval of the Federal Finance Ministry in accordance with Section 8 (2) Sentence 2 of the Foundation Law.

3. For the purpose of strengthening the capital assets of the Foundation and also for cofinancing individual programmes and projects, the Foundation seeks to mobilise further endowments and grants.

4. Within the framework of the statutory Purpose of the Foundation (Section 2, Para. 2 of the Law on the Creation of a Foundation "Remembrance Responsibility and Future") and the Central Themes adopted by the Board of Trustees on 20 January 2005, the Board of Directors shall develop focus areas and funding programmes and submit these to the Board of Trustees for approval. The objectives, criteria and procedures for the selection and configuration of the individual projects shall be determined within the funding programmes. The funding programmes shall be publicly announced.

5. Board of Directors is authorised to decide on applications for funding of up to EUR 100,000 for projects whose project executing agencies are neither members of the Board of Trustees nor organisations associated with members of the Board. Should the Board of Directors take a decision on its own responsibility outside the funding programmes, a maximum amount of 15% of the annual approvals volume shall not be exceeded. In cases of exception, individual projects may be supported within the framework of the focus areas in addition to the publicly announced funding programmes. This applies in particular to pilot projects implemented in preparation for new funding programmes.

6. The Board of Directors shall report to the Board of Trustees at the meetings of the Board of Trustees, in which it participates in an advisory capacity, and at least every six months on the development of the funding programmes and their evaluation, as well as on the financial situation of the Foundation. The Board of Directors shall inform the Board of Trustees of approved and rejected applications in tabluar form.

7. In administering the Foundation, the Board of Management can employ suitable staff for support as it deems fit and as permitted by the budget; it can grant them authorities as part of their respectively allocated tasks.

SECTION 9

Foundation partners

As further institutions in the area of responsibility covered by the Foundation,

1. seven partner organisations and appeal bodies to be set up by them
2. a Commission for economic loss and damage to health
3. the International Commission of Holocaust Era Insurance Claims (ICHEIC)

will assume functions assigned to them by the Foundation Law and relevant contracts. They are not organs of the Foundation, which will work together with them to fulfil the purpose of the Foundation and which will seek to achieve the thrifty and economical use of resources.

SECTION 10

Budget and annual accounts

The Board of Management must draw up a budget at least three months before the start of each financial year and present it to the Board of Trustees for approval. The budget approved by the Board of Trustees requires approval by the Federal Finance Ministry.

The Foundation is subject to audit by the Federal Audit Office (Section 80 ff. in connection with Section 105 Federal Budget Code (*Bundeshaushaltsordnung*)). Regardless of this, the accounting, budgeting and administration of the Foundation will be audited by the Federal Office for Central Services and Unresolved Property Issues. The auditing authorities are entitled to request and inspect all relevant documents for budgeting and administration. The Board of Trustees will be informed of the findings of the auditing authorities. After notification of the members of the Board of Trustees, the Board of Management can request, in accordance with Sentence 6, to be discharged by the Board of Trustees in respect of its activities for the year ended.

The budgetary year is the calendar year.

SECTION 11

Amendment of the Statutes

The Board of Trustees can amend the Statutes with a two thirds majority in accordance with Section 7 (3) of the Foundation Law.

SECTION 12

Entry into force and publication

The Statutes or amendments thereto enter into force on resolution of the Board of Trustees.

The Statutes or amendments thereto are published in the Federal Gazette.

ANNEX 5

OVERALL FUNDING FOR THE COMPENSATION PROGRAM FOR FORCED LABOR

Forced Labor Compensation Program Funds		
	Total assets	5,585 million Euros
of which	Compensation programs (all program lines)	5,227 million Euros
	"Remembrance and Future Fund	358 million Euros

Table A-1: Overall funding for the compensation program for forced labor. Note: In addition to the amounts allocated by the Foundation Law, these numbers include additional income from accrued interest and donations received during the course of the program.

ANNEX 6

PAYMENTS BY PARTNER ORGANIZATIONS TO BENEFICIARIES

Partner Organization	Number of Recipients	Total Payment (Million Euros)
Belarus *including* — Belarus — Estonia	129,485	345
Czech Republic	75,769	208
IOM	88,784	376
JCC	158,097	1,148
Poland	483,287	974
Russia *including* — Russia — Latvia — Lithuania — CIS States	252,543	421
Ukraine	471,167	866
All partner organizations	**1,659,132**	**4,338**

Table A-2: Total payments by partner organizations to beneficiaries. Note: Euro amounts are rounded and exclude administration and leftover funds (for total funds of partner organizations see Chapter 3, Table 2).

ANNEX 7

NUMBER OF RECIPIENTS OF FORCED LABOR COMPENSATIONS BY COUNTRY (INCLUDING PAYMENTS TO LEGAL SUCCESSORS)

Country or region	Number of recipients
Abkhazia (Georgia)	7
Adjara (Georgia)	1
Albania	247
Algeria	4
Argentina	814
Armenia	116
Aruba (The Netherlands)	2
Australia	12,044
Austria	1,050
Azerbaijan	110
Bahamas	1
Belarus	119,699
Belgium	3,893
Bolivia	19
Bosnia and Herzegovina	3,879
Brazil	1,309
Bulgaria	426
Canada	14,481
Chagos Islands (United Kingdom)	1
Chile	141
China	2
Colombia	32
Costa Rica	26
Croatia	2,659

Country or region	Number of recipients
Cuba	2
Cyprus	3
Czech Republic	75,804
Denmark	986
Dominican Republic	2
Ecuador	20
Estonia	9,295
Faroe Islands (Denmark)	1
Finland	176
France	8,475
French Polynesia (France)	1
Georgia	344
Germany	9,763
Greece	1,998
Guatemala	8
Hungary	15,040
India	1
Iceland	1
Indonesia	2
Ireland	9
Israel	78,744
Italy	3,395
Ivory Coast	2
Japan	3
Kazakhstan	3,653

Country or region	Number of recipients
Kyrgyzstan	345
Latvia	13,340
Lebanon	1
Lithuania	13,340
Luxembourg	149
Macedonia	37
Malaysia	1
Malta	1
Mexico	70
Moldavia	1,665
Monaco	5
Morocco	5
Nepal	1
The Netherlands	4,500
Netherlands Antilles (The Netherlands)	1
New Caledonia (France)	1
New Zealand	171
Norway	1,366
Pakistan	1
Panama	3
Paraguay	10
Peru	32
Philippines	2
Poland	484,025
Portugal	7

Country or region	Number of recipients
Puerto Rico (United States of America)	1
Romania	6,299
Russia	227,685
Serbia and Montenegro	8,604
Slovakia	1,557
Slovenia	10,852
South Africa	130
Spain	147
Sweden	1,993
Switzerland	384
Tajikistan	40
Thailand	1
Tunisia	12
Turkey	19
Turkmenistan	64
Ukraine	465,672
United Kingdom	3,633
United States of America	48,804
Uruguay	149
Uzbekistan	658
Venezuela	240
Vietnam	1
Zambia	2
Zimbabwe	4
Information not available	615
Total	1,665,690

Table A-3: Number of recipients by country. Note: The data for this table is based on information available on 31 December 2006. The official number of recipients of the program is 1,659,132.

ANNEX 8

EXAMPLE OF CLAIM FORM AND GUIDELINES FOR CLAIMANTS, PROVIDED BY IOM.

INTERNATIONAL ORGANIZATION FOR MIGRATION (IOM)

**CLAIM FORM FOR
SLAVE LABOUR, FORCED LABOUR,
PERSONAL INJURY OR DEATH OF A CHILD**

German Forced Labour Compensation Programme
REMEMBRANCE, RESPONSIBILITY and FUTURE

Please read the attached guidelines carefully before you begin. This **IOM claim form** is for claimants who are **not Jewish** and who do **not live** in one of following countries: the Czech Republic, Poland, the Russian Federation or a country that was a republic of the former Soviet Union. Type or neatly print all requested information in black or blue ink. Attach photocopies, not originals, of any requested documents. Please submit to the IOM one original and one copy of the claim form and two copies of all attached documents.

CLAIMANT'S PERSONAL INFORMATION

1. Claimant's Last Name	2. Claimant's First Names

3. Claimant's Maiden Name, if applicable	4. Sex Male ☐ Female ☐

5. Current Citizenship	6. Citizenship at Birth	7. Ethnic Origin

Other names used by claimant during the Nazi era, if applicable

8. Last Name	9. First Names

| 10. Date(s) of birth — Enter any birth date used during the Nazi era Year / Month / Day | 11. City of birth as known at that time |
| | 12. Country of birth as known at that time |

Permanent Residence

13. Street name and number, apartment number	14. City, Town or Village

15. Province or State	16. Country	17. Postal Code

18. Telephone-home	19. E-mail

20. State your Country of permanent residence on 16 February 1999, if different from Country at number 16

Mailing Address, if different from Permanent Residence

21. Street name and number, apartment number	22. City, Town or Village

23. Province or State	24. Country	25. Postal Code

26. Telephone-home	27. E-mail

28. Are you claiming for a former slave labourer, forced labourer, personal injury victim or parent of a deceased child who died on or after 16 February 1999? Yes ☐ No ☐

29. If "Yes", what is your relationship to the deceased? ☐ spouse ☐ child ☐ grandchild ☐ sibling ☐ heir under a will

30. If "Yes", have you attached proof of relationship to deceased by submitting a copy of a marriage certificate, birth certificate, family registration booklet, will, etc.? Yes ☐ No ☐

31. Were you (or the deceased) a prisoner of war (POW) at any time from 1939–45? Yes ☐ No ☐

32. If "Yes", you may file a claim only if you (or the deceased) were sent to a concentration camp or were discharged as a POW

POW Date of Discharge		
Year	Month	Day

IOM · OIM

CID 1

Claimant's name ....

German Forced Labour Compensation Programme
REMEMBRANCE, RESPONSIBILITY and FUTURE

INFORMATION ABOUT DECEASED PERSON

You need to fill in this page only if you are claiming for a deceased person who died on or after 16 February 1999. If you are claiming on your own behalf, please go to next page.

33. Last Name of deceased	34. First Names of deceased	
35. Maiden Name of deceased, if applicable		36. Sex of deceased Male ☐ Female ☐
37. Citizenship of deceased at birth	38. Ethnic Origin	

Other names used by deceased during the Nazi era

39. Last Name of deceased	40. First Names of deceased

41. Date(s) of birth of deceased Enter any birth date used during the Nazi era	43. City of birth of deceased as known at that time
Year / Month / Day	44. Country of birth of deceased as known at that time
42. Date of death Year / Month / Day	45. Country where deceased died

46. You must attach a copy of the death certificate. Is a copy attached? Yes ☐ No ☐	*For official IOM use* *Please leave blank* Y ☐ N ☐

INFORMATION ABOUT PERSONS OTHER THAN CLAIMANT WHO ARE CLAIMING FOR DECEASED

Each person claiming must submit proof of relationship to the deceased by submitting a copy of a marriage certificate, birth certificate, family registration booklet, will, etc. If more space is required, please attach additional sheets.

	Second Person Claiming (other than claimant)	Third Person Claiming (other than claimant)	Fourth Person Claiming (other than claimant)
47. Last Name			
48. First Name			
49. Street name and number, apartment number			
50. City, Town or Village			
51. Province or State			
52. Country			
53. Postal Code			
54. Relationship to deceased	☐ spouse ☐ child ☐ grandchild ☐ sibling ☐ heir under will	☐ spouse ☐ child ☐ grandchild ☐ sibling ☐ heir under will	☐ spouse ☐ child ☐ grandchild ☐ sibling ☐ heir under will
55. Is proof of relationship to deceased attached?	Yes ☐ No ☐	Yes ☐ No ☐	Yes ☐ No ☐

IOM · OIM

HID 2

Claimant's name ....

German
Forced Labour
Compensation Programme
REMEMBRANCE, RESPONSIBILITY and FUTURE

SLAVE LABOUR

You need to fill in this page only if you, or the deceased for whom you are claiming, were held in a concentration camp, ghetto or another place of confinement under comparable conditions and were subjected to slave labour. Comparable conditions include inhumane prison conditions, insufficient nutrition and lack of medical care. Otherwise please go to next page.

56. Indicate the types of place(s) where you (or the deceased) were held		
☐ Concentration camp	☐ Ghetto	☐ Other place of confinement

Name the place(s) where you (or the deceased) were held and indicate for which time periods

57. Concentration Camp	58. From		59. To	
	Year	Month	Year	Month
a.				
b.				

60. Ghetto	61. From		62. To	
	Year	Month	Year	Month
a.				
b.				

63. Other place of confinement	64. From		65. To	
	Year	Month	Year	Month
a.				
b.				

66. Name the company(ies) for which you (or the deceased) performed slave labour, if known		
a.	c.	
b.	d.	

Indicate which documents you have provided in support of your claim

For official IOM use Please leave blank	67. Document (photocopies only)	68. Number on document
a. ☐	☐ Liberation certificate	
b. ☐	☐ Repatriation document	
c. ☐	☐ Displaced persons card	
d. ☐	☐ Prison record *(Personalakte)*	
e. ☐	☐ Search result from the International Tracing Service *(Internationaler Suchdienst, Bad Arolsen)*	
f. ☐	☐ Other (please specify)	

SLA 3

Claimant's name ....

German
Forced Labour
Compensation Programme
REMEMBRANCE, RESPONSIBILITY and FUTURE

FORCED LABOUR

You need to fill in this page only if you, or the deceased for whom you are claiming, were deported to Germany or a German-occupied area and were subjected to forced labour and were held in extremely harsh living conditions. Otherwise please go to next page.

Where were you (or the Deceased) deported **from**	69. Town/City deported from		70. Country deported from	
Where were you (or the Deceased) deported **to**	71. Town/City deported to		72. Country deported to	
73. Date deported		74. Date released		
Year	Month	Year		Month

75. Did you perform forced labour for a company or public authority?		Yes ☐ No ☐
76. Did you perform forced labour in agriculture?		Yes ☐ No ☐
77. Were you held at anytime in a Work Reform Camp (*Arbeitserziehungslager*)?		Yes ☐ No ☐
78. Were you occasionally (for example on Sundays) allowed to move in the village or town or city where you were held?		Yes ☐ No ☐
79. Were you held under guard and subjected to constant searches and controls by guards or police both during and outside working hours?		Yes ☐ No ☐

Fill in numbers 80-81, if you performed forced labour for a **company or public authority**

80. Name the company(ies) or public authority(ies) for which you (or the deceased) performed forced labour
a.   b.

81. Name the Work Reform Camp (*Arbeitserziehungslager*) or forced labour camp(s) or other place(s) where you (or the deceased) were held
a.   b.

Fill in number 82, if you performed forced labour in **agriculture**

82. Name the person or entity for whom you (or the deceased) performed forced labour in agriculture, if known
a.   b.

Indicate which documents you have provided in support of your claim

For official IOM use Please leave blank		83. Document (photocopies only)	84. Number on document
a.	☐	☐ Work book for foreigners (*Arbeitsbuch für Ausländer*)	
b.	☐	☐ Work card (*Arbeitskarte*)	
c.	☐	☐ Company work record (*Arbeitsbescheinigung*)	
d.	☐	☐ Work requisition labour office (*Arbeitsamt*)	
e.	☐	☐ Deportation card or attestation	
f.	☐	☐ Prison record (*Personalakte*)	
g.	☐	☐ Discharge certificate (*Entlassungsschein*)	
h.	☐	☐ Repatriation document	
i.	☐	☐ Displaced persons card	
j.	☐	☐ Search result from the International Tracing Service (*Internationaler Suchdienst, Bad Arolsen*)	
k.	☐	☐ Passport for foreigners (*Fremdenpass*)	
l.	☐	☐ Other (please specify)	

FLA 4

Claimant's name ....

German
Forced Labour
Compensation Programme
REMEMBRANCE, RESPONSIBILITY and FUTURE

You need to fill in this page only if you are claiming for a personal injury or death of a child. Otherwise please go to next page.

PERSONAL INJURY – Medical Experiments

85. Were you (or the deceased) subjected to medical experiments under the Nazi regime? If No, go to number 88.		Yes ☐ No ☐
86. Name the Camp where the medical experiments were conducted		

Indicate which documents you have provided in support of your claim

For official IOM use Please leave blank	87. Document (photocopies only)
☐	☐ Medical certificate
☐	☐ Other (please specify)

PERSONAL INJURY – Child Lodged in Home for Children of Slave or Forced Labourers

88. Were you (or the deceased) lodged in a home for children of slave or forced labourers and was your (or the deceased's) health, either mental or physical, severely damaged? If No, go to number 94.		Yes ☐ No ☐
89. Date placed in home for children	90. Name the camp where children's home was situated	
Year Month		
91. Date released from home for children	92. Name the home for children, if known	
Year Month		

Indicate which documents you have provided in support of your claim

For official IOM use Please leave blank	93. Documents (photocopies only)
☐	☐ Medical certificate
☐	☐ Other (please specify)

DEATH OF CHILD – Child Lodged in Home for Children of Slave or Forced Labourers

94. Are you (or was the deceased) the parent of a child who died while lodged in a home for children of slave or forced labourers?		Yes ☐ No ☐
95. Child's Last Name	96. Child's First Names	
97. Name the camp where children's home was situated	98. Name the home for children, if known	

99. Date of birth of child			100. Date of death of child			101. Date placed in home for children	
Year	Month	Day	Year	Month	Day	Year	Month

Indicate which document you have provided in support of your claim

For official IOM use Please leave blank	102. Document (photocopies only)
☐	Please specify

OTHER PERSONAL INJURY

103. Did you suffer other personal injury in connection with National Socialist wrongs?		Yes ☐ No ☐

Indicate which document you have provided in support of your claim

For official IOM use Please leave blank	104. Document (photocopies only)
☐	☐ Medical certificate
☐	☐ Other (please specify)

PIN 5

ANNEX 8 ■ 245

Claimant's Name ....

PARTICIPATION IN ANOTHER GOVERNMENT PROGRAMME

German
Forced Labour
Compensation Programme
REMEMBRANCE, RESPONSIBILITY and FUTURE

Please indicate below whether you (or the deceased) participated in another Government programme. Information about whether you (or the deceased) participated in another programme may help IOM process your claim faster. Any money previously received from such a programme **will not be deducted** from any payment made by IOM.

105. Government Programme	106. Your (or deceased's) Programme Identification Number
a. ☐ Germany, Federal Indemnification Law – *Bundesentschädigungsgesetz/BEG*	
b. ☐ Germany, Hardship Fund – *HNG Fonds*	
c. ☐ Germany, Hardship Fund – *Wiedergutmachungs–Dispositions-Fonds*	
d. ☐ Germany, Hardship payments for medical experiments	
e. ☐ Belgium, granted status of *Prisonnier Politique*	
f. ☐ Belgium, granted status of *Déporté pour le Travail Obligatoire*	
g. ☐ France, granted status of *Déporté Résistant* or *Déporté Politique*	
h. ☐ France, granted status of detainee in Work Reform Camp *(Arbeitserziehungslager/AEL)*	
i. ☐ France, granted status of *Personne Contrainte au Travail (PCT)*	
j. ☐ Italy, granted status under Law 791	
k. ☐ Italy, confirmed as *Internato Militare Italiano (IMI)*	
l. ☐ Slovenia, granted status under the Law on Victims of War – *ZZVN*	
m. ☐ Other (please specify)	

POTENTIAL ENTITLEMENT UNDER THE HOLOCAUST VICTIM ASSETS LITIGATION (SWISS BANKS)

You may be entitled to further payment pursuant to a settlement under the Holocaust Victim Assets Litigation (Swiss Banks) that was brought before the United States District Court, Eastern District of New York. Please answer the questions below so that IOM may send you the necessary information when it becomes available.

107. Were you (or the deceased) a Jehovah's Witness, Roma, homosexual or disabled and were you (or the deceased) held in a concentration camp, ghetto, another place of confinement, forced labour camp, prison, SS brigade, or a similar place and forced to work?	Yes ☐ No ☐
108. Were you (or the deceased) forced to work for a Swiss company, or a German company owned by a Swiss company, during the Nazi era?	Yes ☐ No ☐
109. If "Yes", name the Company for which you worked	
110. Were you (or the deceased) a Jehovah's Witness, Roma, homosexual or disabled and were you (or the deceased) either i) denied entry into or expelled from Switzerland by the Swiss authorities or ii) admitted into Switzerland as a refugee and detained, mistreated or abused by the Swiss authorities?	Yes ☐ No ☐

PAYMENT INFORMATION

111. If your claim is approved by the IOM, indicate how you would like to receive payment. Please note that heirs awarded compensation for the deceased will only be sent cheques in their own name for equal shares of the award.

☐ Cash (distributed by **IOM offices only**)   ☐ Cheque   ☐ Bank transfer (if bank transfer, provide banking information below)

Banking Information and Address

112. Bank	113. Account holder's name	114. Bank account number
115. Bank street name and number		116. Town or City
117. Province or State	118. Country	119. Postal Code
120. Bank telephone number	121. Bank routing number	

OTH 6

Claimant's name ....

PERSONAL STATEMENT

German
Forced Labour
Compensation Programme
REMEMBRANCE, RESPONSIBILITY and FUTURE

> Please provide a brief description below of what happened to you, or the deceased for whom you are claiming, during the period That you (or the deceased) were a **slave labourer** or **forced labourer**. Describe the conditions in which you (or the deceased) were held.
>
> If you are claiming for **medical experiments**, describe the nature and impact of the experiments on your health (or that of the Deceased). If you are claiming for **severe damage to health** while lodged in a home for children of slave or forced labourers, Describe your (or the deceased's) injuries. If you are claiming for the **death of a child** while lodged in a home for children of Slave or forced labourers, describe the circumstances of the child's death. If you are claiming for **other personal injury**, Describe the specific National Socialist wrong that caused the other personal injury.

PER 7

Claimant's name ....

SIGNATURE, CONSENT AND WAIVER

German
Forced Labour
Compensation Programme
REMEMBRANCE, RESPONSIBILITY and FUTURE

Please sign where indicated. You must sign the official IOM claim form before a notary public or other official authorized to attest to the authenticity of signatures and documents. If you are homebound, you may sign the IOM claim form before an attending physician.

a) If you received compensation after 1945 from a **German company** for Nazi injustice, please indicate the name of the company and the amount below. This previously received compensation **will be deducted** from any payment that may be awarded to you by IOM. However, the information you provide here may help IOM process your claim faster.
Name of   Amount
Company 122... Currency 123................. Received 124......................................

b) I understand that my entitlement to receive payment under the German Forced Labour Compensation Programme is dependent on the conditions specified in the German Law.

c) I (or the deceased) have not applied for or received any payments under this Programme for the same Nazi injustice for which I claim on this claim form.

d) I (or the deceased) have not applied for or received a payment from the Austrian Reconciliation Fund for the same Nazi injustice for which I claim on this claim form.

e) I agree that in connection with the processing and checking of this claim my data and that of the deceased will be kept in a central database and a check will be made for claims that may have been filed by me with the other partner organizations.

f) I authorize the IOM to inspect all relevant third party files and databases to verify my claim, for example, German Government archives, Red Cross International Tracing Service archives, etc.

g) I waive irrevocably on **receipt of a payment** under the German Forced Labour Compensation Programme the assertion of any of the following claims **outside the German Law:**
   i.   Against the Federal Republic of Germany, German Federal States and other German public institutions in respect of slave labour, forced labour or property losses.
   ii. Against German companies with regard to all claims connected with National Socialist injustice.
   iii. Against the Republic of Austria and Austrian companies in respect of slave labour or forced labour.

   This waiver does not apply to claims and payments to be made under German laws on the consequences of war or Indemnification measures or to any claims relating to the return of works of art. The latter may only be asserted, however, in Germany or in the country from which the work of art was taken.

h) I attest that the information provided in support of this claim is true and made to the best of my knowledge. I am aware that false information may lead to action for the return of any payment made and further legal action.

Signature of claimant ....

Type of current   Number of current
Identification document 125.. Identification document 126...

I have verified the claimant's identification card or passport and documentation of the claimant's permanent residence as of 16 February 1999. Where applicable, I have verified the relationship of the claimant to the deceased.

Stamp and signature of notary public/other official/attending physician

Date .... City ....
Printed name of notary public/other official/attending physician

....
Last Name   First Name

Address of notary public/other official/attending physician ....

....

Telephone number of notary public/other official/attending physician...

SIG 8

INTERNATIONAL ORGANIZATION FOR MIGRATION (IOM)

GUIDELINES FOR CLAIM FORM FOR
SLAVE LABOUR, FORCED LABOUR,
PERSONAL INJURY OR DEATH OF A CHILD

German
Forced Labour
Compensation Programme
REMEMBRANCE, RESPONSIBILITY and FUTURE

On 12 August 2000, a German Law came into force designating seven organizations, including the International Organization for Migration (IOM), to make payments to former slave and forced labourers and certain other victims of National Socialist (Nazi) injustice. The German Government and German companies are providing the funds in equal parts. The German Law recognizes that the injustice committed and the human suffering caused cannot be truly compensated by financial payments and that the Law comes too late for those who lost their lives as victims of the Nazi regime or have died in the meantime.

IOM HELPLINE

If you have any questions after reading these Guidelines, please contact the IOM at one of the IOM telephone numbers on page 4.

WHO MAY FILE ON THIS IOM CLAIM FORM

Slave Labourers

Persons who were held inside or outside their own country in a concentration camp, ghetto, or another place of confinement under comparable conditions and were subjected to slave labour. Comparable conditions include inhumane prison conditions, insufficient nutrition and lack of medical care. Slave labourers may receive up to DEM15,000.

Forced Labourers for a Company or Public Authority

Persons who were deported from their own country into Germany or a German-occupied area and were subjected to forced labour for a company or public authority and were held in extremely harsh living conditions. Persons who were forced to work within their own country, even if occupied by Germany, are not entitled to receive payment.

Not every person who was deported to Germany or a German-occupied area and forced to work there is entitled to compensation under the German Law. Only those who were held in prison-like or similar extremely harsh living conditions may receive compensation. Such conditions generally existed in Work Reform Camps ("Camps de rééducation par le travail" or "Arbeitserziehungslager/AEL") and in other camps where persons were held under guard and were subjected to constant searches and controls by guards or police and where they were not allowed to leave the camp except for transfer to the work site.

Forced labourers may receive up to DEM 5,000.

Please note:

Persons who were deported from France and who were subjected to "Service du Travail Obligatoire en Allemagne (STO)" during the Nazi era and who were subsequently granted the status of "Personne Contrainte au Travail en Pays Ennemi (PCT)" under French legislation, are not entitled to receive payment under the German Forced Labour Compensation Programme unless they were held in prison-like or similar extremely harsh living conditions as described above.

Persons who were deported from Belgium and forced to work in Germany or a German-occupied area during the Nazi era and who were subsequently granted the status of "Déporté pour le Travail Obligatoire" under Belgian legislation, are not entitled to receive payment under the German Forced Labour Compensation Programme unless they were held in prison-like or similar extremely harsh living conditions as described above.

Forced Labourers in Agriculture

Persons who were deported from their own country into Germany or a German-occupied area and were subjected to forced labour in agriculture. Persons who were forced to work in agriculture within their own country, even if occupied by Germany, are not entitled to receive payment. Forced labourers in agriculture may receive up to DEM2,000.

Personal Injury Victims

Persons who were subjected to medical experiments may receive up to DEM15,000.

Persons who were, as a child, lodged in a home for children of slave or forced labourers and whose health, either mental or physical, was severely damaged may receive up to DEM15,000.

Persons who suffered other personal injury in connection with National Socialist wrongs may receive up to DEM15,000.

INTERNATIONAL ORGANIZATION FOR MIGRATION (IOM)

German
Forced Labour
Compensation Programme
REMEMBRANCE, RESPONSIBILITY and FUTURE

Parents of a Deceased Child

Parents of a child who died while lodged in a home for children of slave or forced labourers. The parents together (or one parent if the other is deceased) may receive up to DEM15,000.

Heirs

A surviving spouse and children may file a claim for equal shares of any potential payment that would have been awarded to a victim as described above who died **on or after 16 February 1999**. Under the German Law, heirs of a victim who died **before 16 February 1999** are not entitled to receive payment.

If the deceased left neither a spouse nor children, a claim may be filed by the grandchildren. If there are no grandchildren, the brothers and sisters of the deceased may claim. If the deceased left neither spouse, children, grandchildren, brothers or sisters, then the heirs named in a will may claim. Each person claiming must provide proof of his/her relationship to the deceased by submitting a copy of a marriage certificate, birth certificate, family registration booklet, will or other relevant document.

Only one claim form should be filed on behalf of all persons claiming for a deceased person. The claim form should be filed with the organization that would have been responsible for the deceased's claim had he/she lived. See the section on "Where to File a Claim for Slave Labour, Forced Labour, Personal Injury or a Death of a Child" below.

Prisoners of War (POWs) are not entitled to receive payment

You are not entitled to receive payment if you, or the deceased for whom you are claiming, were a POW. However, if you (or the deceased) were subsequently sent or transferred to a concentration camp, or if you were no longer a POW when you were subjected to forced labour, you may file a claim.

WHERE TO FILE A CLAIM FOR SLAVE LABOUR, FORCED LABOUR, PERSONAL INJURY OR DEATH OF A CHILD

The German Law determines which organization should process which claims based principally on where the claimant lives and whether the claimant is Jewish or not. IOM accepts a person's self-description of himself/herself as either Jewish or not.

This IOM claim form is for claimants who are **not Jewish** and who do **not live** in one of following countries: **The Czech Republic, Poland, the Russian Federation, or a country that was a republic of the former Soviet Union.**

Jewish claimants who do **not** live in one of the countries listed above should obtain and file a claim form with the **Conference on Jewish Material Claims Against Germany** at the addresses on page 4.

Both Jewish and non-Jewish claimants who live in one of the countries listed above should obtain and file a claim form with the **relevant organization** at the addresses on page 4.

Both Jewish and non-Jewish claimants who were held in **Austria** should obtain further information from the **Austrian Reconciliation Fund** at the address on page 4. However, claimants who were held in **Mauthausen and its subcamps or the subcamps of Dachau in Austria** are covered by the German Law. Therefore, **non-Jewish** claimants who were held in these camps should file a claim form with **IOM**. **Jewish** claimants who were held in these camps should obtain and file a claim form with the **Conference on Jewish Material Claims Against Germany** at the addresses on page 4.

COMPLETING THIS IOM CLAIM FORM

Each victim should **fill in a separate IOM claim form** and should complete **only those claim form pages that are applicable to him/her.** Each victim should submit to the IOM one original and one copy of the claim form and two copies of all accompanying documents.

Example A: If you were deported, forced to work and held in a forced labour camp and were then transferred to a concentration camp where you performed slave labour, you should fill in the claim form pages for both Slave Labour as well as Forced Labour. If your claim is approved, you would only receive once the highest amount to which you would be entitled, which in this case would be up to DEM15,000.

Example B: If a wife and husband were each subjected to slave labour in a concentration camp, the wife and husband should each fill in a separate IOM claim form. If they were also each subjected to medical experiments, they should each complete the claim form pages relating to Slave Labour as well as Personal Injury. If the wife's and husband's claims are both approved, they would each receive the amounts for both of the two situations, which in this case would be up to DEM30,000.

INTERNATIONAL ORGANIZATION FOR MIGRATION (IOM)

German
Forced Labour
Compensation Programme
REMEMBRANCE, RESPONSIBILITY and FUTURE

State your name on every attached document and in the space provided for it on the top of the every page of the IOM claim form. This is to help IOM locate documents in the event that they should become detached from one another.

If you are represented by a lawyer or another person, your representative must submit to IOM a written authorization from you. Payment cannot be made to a representative but only to you. IOM will not reimburse lawyers' or any other fees.

All persons, whether represented or not, must sign the IOM claim form themselves before a notary public or other official authorized to attest to the authenticity of signatures and documents. If you are homebound, you may sign the IOM claim form before an attending physician.

Together with the IOM claim form, you should submit photocopies of any documentation you have to support your claim such as a Work card (*Arbeitskarte*), Work book (*Arbeitsbuch*), medical records or other relevant document.

If you have no documentary evidence, you should still submit an IOM claim form. IOM has arranged with the Red Cross International Tracing Service, German Government, and other relevant institutions to try and verify your claim by searching their archives and databases on the condition that you sign the consent page in the IOM claim form.

Please provide a brief description of what happened to you in the space provided on page 7 of the IOM claim form.

DEADLINE FOR FILING IOM CLAIM FORMS

For your claim to be considered, you must complete an official IOM claim form. IOM provides its claim form free of charge. Send the IOM claim form to the address on the pre-addressed envelope that came with your claim form package. If you did not receive a pre-addressed envelope, send your claim form to the IOM office nearest you at the address on page 4. The envelope should be post-marked no later than **11 August 2001**.

PROCESSING OF THE CLAIMS AND PAYMENT

IOM will send you a confirmation of receipt after having received the IOM claim form. The IOM office in Geneva, Switzerland will take a decision on your claim. IOM will advise you in writing whether your claim has been approved or rejected. If your claim is approved, the German Law provides for payments to be made in two instalments. If your claim is rejected, the German Law allows for a right of appeal to an Appeals Body that will be established at the IOM office in Geneva.

PROPERTY LOSSES

Please note that IOM is also responsible for payment of **property losses** suffered under the Nazi regime as a result of **direct participation of German businesses**. **Both Jewish and non-Jewish persons, no matter where the person is resident,** may claim for property losses with **IOM**. Heirs of a person who died at **any time prior to filing** an official IOM claim form for property losses may also claim. To obtain an official IOM claim form for property losses, contact the IOM at the addresses on page 4.

INTERNATIONAL ORGANIZATION FOR MIGRATION (IOM)

German
Forced Labour
Compensation Programme
REMEMBRANCE, RESPONSIBILITY and FUTURE

CONTACT INFORMATION - IOM

International Organization for Migration
Completed Claim Forms should be returned to the IOM/GFLCP Office responsible for the country in which you reside
Web site: www.compensation-for-forced-labour.org

International Organization for Migration – IOM Geneva
German Forced Labour Compensation Programme
17 route des Morillons, P.O.B. 71, CH-1211 Geneva 19, Switzerland
Tel.: + 41 22 717 9230
e-mail: compensation@iom.int
Web site: www.compensation-for-forced-labour.org

CONTACT INFORMATION – OTHER PARTNER ORGANIZATIONS

Conference on Jewish Material Claims Against Germany
15 East 26th Street
New York, NY 10010, USA
Web site: www.claimscon.org

Conference on Jewish Material Claims Against Germany
Sophienstrasse 26
D - 60487 Frankfurt am Main, Germany
Web site: www.claimscon.org

German - Czech Foundation "Fund of the Future"
P.O.B. 47, Legerova 22
120 21 Prague 2, Czech Republic
Tel: + 420 2 24 26 20 40

German - Polish Foundation "German-Polish Reconciliation"
Ul. Krucza 36
00- 921 Warsaw, Poland
Tel: + 48 22 629 73 35

Belarus Foundation
"Understanding and Reconciliation" (also responsible for Estonia)
Ul. Jakuba Kolasa 39a
220013 Minsk, Belarus
Tel: + 375 17 23 27 096

Ukrainian National Foundation
"Understanding and Reconciliation" (also responsible for Moldova)
Wuliza Frunse 15
01080 Kiev, Ukraine
Tel/fax : +380 44 462 50 06

Russian Foundation "Understanding and Reconciliation" (also responsible for countries that were republics of the former Soviet Union except for Belarus, Estonia, Moldova and the Ukraine)
Stolowy pereulok 6
121069 Moscow, Russian Federation
Tel/Fax: + 7 095 291 10 48

CONTACT INFORMATION - AUSTRIAN RECONCILIATION FUND

Office of the Special Representative of the Austrian Federal Government
Dr. Maria Schaumayer
Ballhausplatz 1
1014 Vienna, Austria
Tel. +43 1 53 115 21 60 or 61 or 62

web - en

ANNEX 9

EXCERPT FROM IOM DOCUMENT "EVIDENTIARY GUIDELINES"

This is an excerpt from a document that IOM developed and maintained throughout the processing and verification of the claims. It shows the large variety of different documents that were submitted in support of the claims. In order to ensure consistency in the classification of the documents and in the assessment of their evidentiary value, IOM developed these "Evidentiary Guidelines" which were distributed to all its claims reviewers to be used in the verification of the claims.

Table of content

Introduction	5
I. General procedures	
How to Classify Evidence in the Claims Registration System ("the CRS")	6
Classifying documents in numbers 67.a–67.f of the CRS	7
Classifying documents in Document Type i.	8
Claims filed by Prisoners of War	9
II. Index	**11**
Liberation certificate, 67.a	11
Repatriation document, 67.b	12
Displaced person's card, 67.c	14
Search result from the International Tracing Service, 67.e (Internationaler Suchdienst, Bad Arolsen) and Search result from National Red Cross Office	16
Work book for foreigners (Arbeitsbuch für Ausländer), 83.a	17
Work card (Arbeitskarte) 83.b	18
Company work record 83.c	18
Work Requisition Labour Office (Arbeitsamt) 83.d	20
Deportation card or attestation, 83.e	20
Prison record (Personalakte), 83.f	22
Discharge certificate (Entlassungsschein), 83.g	24
Repatriation document, 83.h	25
Displaced persons card, 83.i	25
Search result from the International Tracing Service (Internationaler Suchdienst, Bad Arolsen), 83.j	25
Passport for foreigners (Fremdenpass), 83.k	27
Document type i.	27

Sufficient documents **stating person was held in an officially recognized slave labour camp in accordance with BEG and German Foundation lists of camps.**

Document type ii.	33
Concentration camp number tatooed on person's arm or as stated in documents or personal statement.	
Document type iii.	33
Official document stating person was a POW or held in a Stalag or Oflag (camp for POWs).	
Document type iv.	35
Victims' Association membership card stating person was held in a camp, forced to work or deported.	
Document type v.	35
Witness Statement stating person was held in a camp, forced to work or deported.	
Document type vi.	35
Books or newspaper articles stating person was held in a camp, forced to work or deported.	
Document type vii.	35
Letters sent to and from person held in a camp from 1933–1945	
Document type viii.	36
Photos showing person was held in a camp, forced to work or deported.	
Document type ix.	36
General travel documents issued after Liberation (7 May 1945)	
Document type x.	36
Certificate/Card issued under Belgian law stating person was Déporté pour le Travail Obligatoire.	
Document type xi.	36
Certificate/Card issued under Belgian law stating person was Prisonnier Politique	
Document type xii.	37
Certificate issued under French law stating person was Personne Contrainte au Travail or Patriote transféré en Allemagne.	
Document type xiii.	38
Certificate/Card issued under French law stating person was Déporté Politique	
Document type xiv.	38
Certificate/Card issued under French law stating person was Déporté Résistant	
Document type xv.	39
Certificate/Card issued under French law stating person was held in Arbeitserziehungslager/AEL (Work Reform Camp)	
Document type xvi.	40
Decision/Pension Statement issued under German Federal Indemnification Law — Bundesentschädigungsgesetz/BEG	
Document type xvii.	41

Certificate issued under Hardship Fund —
Härtefonds für rassisch Verfolgte nicht jüdischen Glaubens/HNG Fonds.
Document type xviii. 41
Certificate issued under Hardship Fund — Wiedergutmachungs-Dispositionsfonds.
Document type xix. 41
Foglio Matricolare
Document type xx. 41
Other documentary evidence stating person was an IMI.
Document type xxi. 42
Personal Statement stating person was an IMI.
Document type xxii. 43
Discharge Certificate for IMI.
Document type xxiii. 43
Certificato di Inscrizione issued under Italian Law 791.
Document type xxiv. 44
Reduce dalla deportazione stating person was a civilian deportee.
Document type xxv. 44
Certificate issued by Arbejdsskadestyrelsen
(Danish National Board of Industrial Injuries)
Document type xxvi. 45
Certificate issued by Kansallisarkisto (Finnish National Archives).
Document type xxvii. 45
Certificate issued by Riksarkivet (Swedish National Archives)
Document type xxviii. 46
Person registered in Norwegian Ottosen database
Document type xxix. 46
Decision issued under Slovenian Law ZZVN stating person held in concentration camp
Document type xxx. 47
Decision issued under Slovenian Law ZZVN stating person was exiled.
Document type xxxi. 47
Decision issued under Slovenian Law ZZVN stating child held in camp
Document type xxxii. 47
Certificate issued under Slovak Law 255/1946

III. Consolidated List of Codes of Documents to be selected in Drop Down Boxes in Claims Registration System
General

AEL-not on Found. nor LRC lists	49
Affidavit-personal	49
Affidavit from witness	49
AUTOBIO	49
BADGE	49

BRÜG	50
CAMPDOC	50
COURTDOC-PERSECUTEE	50
Czech Protectorate Workbook	50
DRAFT	50
Eligible for "Germanization" under NAZI laws	51
German military	51
German Post War Pension Documents	51
HIRSCH	51
ID	52
KGB Archive — Slave Labour	52
KGB Archive — Prison Record	52
KGB Archive — Forced Labour	52
Labour Reform Camp document	52
MAID	53
MISSING	53
NOT DEPORTED	54
PARENTDOC	54
Polish Archives — Slave Labour	54
Polish Archives — Prison Record	54
Polish Archives — Forced Labour	54
Polish Home Army — 4 Oct. 1944	54
POW	55
POW — Post May 1945	55
Reichsarbeitsdienst (RAD)	55
Russian Archives — Slave Labour	55
Russian Archives — Prison Record	56
Russian Archives — Forced Labour	56
STAYDOC	56
Ukrainian Archives — Slave Labour	56
Ukrainian Archives — Prison Record	56
Ukrainian Archives — Forced Labour	56
Ukrainian Help Committee	56
Umsiedler	57
UNHCR	57
Volunteer	57
WS-common knowledge	57

Belgium 57
Prisonnier politique- Prison

Finland 58
KAK Klooga before 9/43
KAK Klooga after 9/43
KAK presence in Germany

France 58
Déporté Politique- Prison
Déporté Résistant- Prison
Interné Politique/Résisitant

Germany 59
VDN

Greece 59
GPA
Greece-Law n°4178/1961 — Slave Labour Camp
Greece-Law n°4178/1961 — Deported & forced labour

Hungary 60
HCKZ
HCD
HCF
HCG
Hungary — SOLDIER
LEVE

Italy 61
CDI-Prison
Italy — Gazzetta Ufficiale 1968 — Slave Labour Camp
Italy — Happacher's list of Bolzano's
Detainees
MOD69
SBANDATO
SUSPECT
Tibaldi Lists — Slave Labour

Jehovah's Witnesses 62
Watchtower — Slave Labour
Watchtower — Prison
Watchtower — Forced Labour

Luxembourg 62
Lux — Certificate from CNR/Grand Duc- Slave Labour Camp
Lux — Livre d'or des camps- Slave Labour Camp
Lux — Livre d'or des prisons- Prisons
Lux — Livre d'or des prisons- Slave Labour Camp
LSTAAT

Norway 63
KIP

Romania 64
Romania — Iron Guard

Slovenia 64
Slovenia-Law ZPIZ — Slave Labour Camp
Slovenia-Law ZPIZ — deported and forced to work
Slovenia-Law ZPIZ — partisan

Sweden 65
Swedish Police report — SL
Swedish Police report — Prison Record
Swedish Police report — FL

United Kingdom 65
UK Administration — SL
UK Administration — FL

Former Republic of Yugoslavia 66
LPDKZ
LPDDP
LPDFW
LPDPA

[...]

BIBLIOGRAPHY

References

Authers, John. "Making Good Again: German Compensation for Forced and Slave Laborers." In *The Handbook of Reparations,* ed. Pablo de Greiff, 420–448. New York: Oxford University Press, 2006.

Borggräfe, Henning. *Zwangsarbeiterentschädigung: Vom Streit um „vergessene Opfer" zur Selbstaussöhnung der Deutschen.* Göttingen: Wallstein Verlag, 2014.

Eizenstat, Stuart E.. *Imperfect Justice: Looted Assets, Slave Labor, and the Unfinished Business of World War.* New York: Public Affairs, 2003.

Engert, Stefan. "Germany-Israel: A Prototypical Political Apology and Reconciliation Process." In *Apology and Reconciliation in International Relations: The Importance of Being Sorry,* eds. Christopher Daase, Stefan Engert, Michel-André Horelt, Judith Renner and Renate Strassner. Abingdon: Routledge, 2016.

Federal Foreign Office. "Compensation for National Socialist Injustice," 2017. Accessed 15 May 2017. www.auswaertiges-amt.de/EN/Aussenpolitik/InternatRecht/Entschaedigung_node.html#doc482342bodyText7.

Feichtlbauer, Hubert. *Forced Labor in Austria 1938–1945.* Wien: Austrian Reconciliation Fund, 2005.

Foundation "Remembrance, Responsibility and Future". *Teaching Human Rights: Funding Programme for Human Rights Education Through History Learning: Information and Selected Projects.* Berlin: Stiftung Erinnerung, Verantwortung und Zukunft, 2013. Accessed 15 May 2017. www.stiftung-evz.de/fileadmin/user_upload/EVZ_Uploads/Handlungsfelder/Handeln_fuer_Menschenrechte/Menschen_Rechte_Bilden/20130820_EVZ_Broschuere_MRB_en.pdf.

De Greiff, Pablo, ed. *The Handbook of Reparations.* Oxford: Oxford University Press, 2006.

De Greiff, Pablo. "Introduction: Repairing the Past: Compensation for Victims of Human Rights Violations," in The Handbook of Reparations, ed. Pablo de Greiff, 1–10. Oxford: Oxford University Press, 2006.

Goschler, Constantin, ed. *Die Entschädigung von NS-Zwangsarbeit am Anfang des 21. Jahrhunderts: Die Stiftung "Erinnerung, Verantwortung und Zukunft" und ihre Partnerorganisationen.* Göttingen: Wallstein-Verlag, 2012.

Von Plato, Alexander, Almut Leh and Christoph Thonfeld, eds. *Hitler's Slaves: Life Stories of Forced Labourers in Nazi-Occupied Europe.* New York, Oxford: Berghahn, 2010.

Wühler, Norbert and Heike Niebergall. *Property Restitution and Compensation: Practices and Experiences of Claims Programmes.* Geneva: International Organization for Migration, 2008. Accessed 13 May 2017. https://publications.iom.int/system/files/pdf/property_restitution_compensation.pdf.

United Nations. *Basic Principles and Guidelines on the Right to a Remedy and Reparation for Victims of Gross Violations of International Human Rights Law and Serious Violations of International Humanitarian Law.* United Nations General Assembly Resolution 60/147, 21 March 2006. Accessed 15 May 2017. www.un.org/ruleoflaw/files/BASICP~1.PDF.

Legal Materials

Laws

Alien Tort Claims Act, 1789. 28 U.S.C. § 1350 (1789)

Federal Compensation Act, 1953. German Federal Law Gazette, Year 1953, Part I, Page 1387.

Law on the Creation of a Foundation "Hilfswerk für behinderte Kinder", 1971. German Federal Law Gazette, Year 1971, Part I, no 131, page 2018.

Draft of the Law on the Creation of a Foundation "Remembrance, Responsibility and Future", 2000. Register of the German Parliament, BT-Drs 14/3206. Accessed 15 May 2017. http://dipbt.bundestag.de/doc/btd/14/032/1403206.pdf.

Law on the Creation of a Foundation "Remembrance, Responsibility and Future", 2000. German Federal Law Gazette Year 2000 Part I, Page 1263.

Polish Law on tax exemptions of compensation payments for victims of Nazi persecution, 2000. Dz. U. 2000 Nr. 93, Poz. 1028.

International Agreements

Agreement between the United States of America and Austria concerning the Austrian Fund "Reconciliation, Peace and Cooperation", 2000. Austrian Federal Law Gazette BGBL III Nr. 221/2000. Accessed 15 May 2017. http://diglib.uibk.ac.at/ulbtirol/content/pageview/1336019.

Agreement between the United States of America and Austria relating to the Agreement of October 24, 2000. Federal Ministry of Foreign Affairs of the Republic of Austria, No 2140.02/0044e-BdSB/2001. Accessed 15 May 2017. https://www.state.gov/documents/organization/129565.pdf.

Court Decisions and Judgements

Court decision of the German Federal Constitutional Court on the "Law on the Creation of a Foundation 'Hilfswerk für behinderte Kinder'", 1976.
BVerfGE 42, 263, 8 July 1976

Ferrini c. Republica Federale di Germania. Judgement, Italian Supreme Court of Cassation, Riv. Dir. Int. 87 (2004) 539, 11 March 2004. Accessed 15 May 2017. http://scienzepolitiche.unipg.it/tutor/uploads/ferrini_c__repubblica_federale_di_germania.pdf.

Court decision of the German Federal Constitutional Court on the "Constitutionality of the Exclusion of Claims by the Foundation Law", 2004. BVerfGE 112, 93, 7 December 2004.

Poznanski and Others v. Germany. Judgment, European Court of Human Rights, HUDOC 25101/05, 3 July 2007. Accessed 15 May 2017. http://hudoc.echr.coe.int/eng#{%22appno%22:[%2225101/05%22],%22itemid%22:[%22001-81724%22]}

Jurisdictional Immunities of the State (Germany v. Italy: Greece intervening). Judgement I.C.J. Reports 2012, p. 99, 3 February 2012. Accessed 15 May 2017. www.icj-cij.org/docket/files/143/16883.pdf.

Reports of the Federal Government of Germany on the Compensation Program

27 November 2001: BT-Drs.14/7728, http://dipbt.bundestag.de/doc/btd/14/077/1407728.pdf;
19 March 2002: BT-Drs.14/8673, http://dipbt.bundestag.de/doc/btd/14/086/1408673.pdf;
30 December 2002: BT-Drs.15/283, http://dipbt.bundestag.de/doc/btd/15/002/1500283.pdf;
25 June 2004: BT-Drs.15/3440, http://dipbt.bundestag.de/doc/btd/15/034/1503440.pdf;
21 July 2005: BT-Drs.15/5936, http://dipbt.bundestag.de/doc/btd/15/059/1505936.pdf;
09 July 2008: BT-Drs.16/9963, http://dipbt.bundestag.de/doc/btd/16/099/1609963.pdf
(all accessed 15 May 2017).

11th Report of the Federal Government of Germany on the Status of Legal Closure for German Companies in the Context of the Foundation "Remembrance, Responsibility and Future" 15.04.2010; BT-Drs 17/1398. Accessed 15 May 2017. http://dipbt.bundestag.de/dip21/btd/17/013/1701398.pdf.

Internet Resources

Homepage of the EVZ Foundation
www.stiftung-evz.de

About the Foundation Initiative of the German Industry
www.wollheim-memorial.de/en/die_stiftungsinitiative_der_deutschen_wirtschaft_1999

Homepages of the partner organizations of the compensation program
Belarus: International Public Organization "Understanding," www.moov.by (successor organization)
Czech Republic: German-Czech Future Fund, www.fondbudoucnosti.cz
International Organization for Migration, www.iom.int
Jewish Claims Conference, www.claimscon.org
Poland: Foundation Polish-German Reconciliation, www.fpnp.pl
Ukraine: International Foundation "Mutual Understanding and Tolerance," www.toleranz.org.ua (successor organization)
Note: The Russian partner organization does not exist anymore.

German National Archives documentation on locations of forced labor camps
www.bundesarchiv.de/zwangsarbeit/haftstaetten/index.php

International travelling exhibition "Forced Labor Under National Socialism"
www.ausstellung-zwangsarbeit.org/homepage/?L=1

German Federal Office for Central Services and Unresolved Property Issues on payments to former Soviet prisoners of war
www.badv.bund.de/EN/UnresolvedPropertyIssues/PaymentToFormerSovietPrisonersOfWar/start.html

Wollheim Memorial
www.wollheim-memorial.de

Austrian Reconciliation Fund
www.versoehnungsfonds.at

EVZ Educational Project "Mit Stempel und Unterschrift"
www.mit-stempel-und-unterschrift.de

INDEX

acceptance of the compensation program for forced labor, 13, 24–25, 48, 188, 191–93
acknowledgement, 181, 182–85, 187, 188, 190–91, 192
additional program lines, 7–8, 10, 89n4, 91n7, 128–40
administrative costs
    of partner organizations, 44–45, 118, 119
    of the EVZ Foundation, 22, 44–45, 57, 167
    and partnership agreements, 45
    See also audit
agriculture
    considered in the opening clause, 28, 30, 33
    and forced labor, 3, 21, 28
Alien Tort Claims Act, 15, 15n1
apology
    as acknowledgement 192
    as a copy together with compensation payments, 113, 192
    of Johannes Rau, 183
    public, 183n4
appeal committees
    organizational structure of, 61, 97–99
    supervision of, 61, 97
    within partner organizations, 64–65
appeals
    calculating amounts of, 46–47
    control of, 121
    deadline of, 62, 97
    of other personal injuries claims, 132
    of property loss claims, 136–37
    process, 92, 99–101
applicants. *See* claimants
applications for compensation. *See* claims
appropriateness, 185–87. *See also* justice
archives
    international, 90–93, 100, 123, 157–58, 184
    research in, 55, 90, 91
    See also German Federal Archives
archiving
    of legal closure waivers, 55, 149
    of payment records, 112, 157–58

audit
	of claims processing, 115–16, 92, 120–22 (*see also* control teams)
	of EVZ Foundation, 54, 116, 117–19
	of partner organizations, 63–64, 86, 102, 116, 120–22
Austria, 8, 8n, 145
	Agreement between the United States of America and, 145n1
Austrian Reconciliation Fund, 8, 8n, 34, 91, 91n7, 91n9

BADV. *See* German Federal Office for Central Services and Unresolved Property Issues
BEG. *See* Federal Compensation Law
Belarus, 20, 60n, 76n6, 158, 168, 177
beneficiaries, 17, 43, 44n3, 45, 46, 50, 70, 104–9, 111–12, 124, 139, 187, 195
	death of, 80, 97. *See also* legal successors
	number of, 7, 15, 17, 22, 33, 40, 74, 138–39, 180
	See also claimants
BMF. *See* German Ministry of Finance
Board of Directors, 29, 57–59, 61–62, 122, 154
Board of Trustees, 19, 29, 44, 48, 53, 55–57, 65–66, 117, 154, 157, 168, 173, 180

category of compensation. *See* eligibility categories
ceiling
	for funds, 22, 37
	for installments, 105, 105n3
	for property losses, 120, 140
Central and Eastern Europe, 3, 5–6, 14, 16, 20, 29, 34, 42, 70, 95, 133, 138, 194
children of forced laborers, 23, 130–31
claim form, 71–74, 88–89, 123, 132n, 134, 157–58
claims
	filing deadline of, 46, 69, 81, 89n5
	rejection of, 35, 61, 79, 92, 99, 121
	submission to partner organizations, 72, 76, 78–81, 102
claims processing 85–102
	and organizational structure, 59–64
claimants
	death of, 36–37, 46, 96–97. *See also* legal successors
	Jewish, 42 (*see also* Conference on Jewish Material Claims against Germany)
	non-Jewish, 74 (see also International Organization for Migration)
	number of, 23, 45, 76
	place of residence of, 21–22
	See also beneficiaries
class action lawsuits. *See under* lawsuits

communication, 49, 65, 70–71, 74–75, 80–83, 90, 96, 102. *See also* outreach
compensation payments
    amount of, 7, 21, 104, 132–33
    cooperation with banks to distribute, 109–110
    in different currencies, 111
    in installments, 7, 45–46, 48, 80, 105, 184
    processing of, 7, 45–46, 86–87, 105–110
completeness of reparations, 189–90
complexity of reparations, 2, 7–8
concentration camps, 3–4, 7, 11, 15, 21, 27–29, 31–32, 130, 132
Conference on Jewish Material Claims against Germany (JCC). *See under* partner organizations
control teams, 95, 115–16, 120–24, 126, 155–56. *See also* audit
court decisions on forced labor 6, 143
currencies, 48–49, 111
cut-off dates, 46, 96, 111, 155. *See also* deadlines
Czech Republic, 20, 76n6, 168, 195

deadlines, 36, 69, 78, 81, 88–89, 97, 99–100, 110, 111–12, 143, 155, 159. *See also* cut-off dates

Eastern Europe. *See* Central and Eastern Europe
education, 161, 171, 173–75. *See also* human rights
eligibility categories
    category A, 7, 29, 31
    category B, 7, 29–31
    category C (*see* opening clause)
eligibility criteria 26–38, 47, 79, 81, 83, 189–90,
    critique of, 73
    for other personal injuries, 131
    for property loss claims, 133–34
    and harsh living conditions, 21, 28–29, 34
    interpretation of, 79, 86, 102, 117–18, 125
    and lawsuits, 149
evidence, 90–91, *See also* standard of proof
    falsified, 123
    IOM's Book of, 93, 93n11
    lack of, 35, 143
    of Nazi persecution, 35, 91, 93–95, 100, 135, 184
EVZ Foundation
    administration of, 22, 44–46, 53, 55
    after ending of compensation program, 155–58
    establishing of, 41–42
    funding programs of, 168–77
    organizational structure of, 53–59

Federal Republic of Germany, 2, 5, 14, 20, 22, 41, 54, 56, 142–44, 148–49, 182, 188
financial management of the compensation fund 9, 48–50, 51, 55, 58, 111,
forced labor in Nazi Germany, 3–6
forced laborers
    numbers of, 3, 13, 17, 28, 150 190
Foundation for Polish-German Reconciliation (FPNP), 21, 31–32, 43, 60, 62–63, 71–74, 77–80, 88—91, 97—98, 100—101, 105—112, 120
Foundation Initiative of the German Industry, 6–7, 16, 16n, 18, 22, 41, 41n2, 146
Foundation Law, 7, 20—22, 28—30, 34, 60, 105, 129, 131, 147, 159
FPNP. *See* Foundation for Polish-German Reconciliation
fraud, 123–124
funding
    allocated to partner organizations, 42–45
    of the compensation program, 15, 18, 40–44, 130, 167
    of additional program lines, 131
fundraising 41–42, 51, 168, 178
Future Fund. *See* "Remembrance and Future" Fund

GDR. *See* German Democratic Republic
German Chancellor, 16, 56, 154
German companies, 2–6, 15, 16, 23, 40–41, 144–46, 148, 165, 183, 186, 188
    boycotts of, 6, 15, 42
    lawsuits against, 6, 14–15, 19–20, 23, 41, 105, 129, 142–46, 188, 192
    negative lists, 42
    See also Foundation Initiative of the German Industry
    See also legal closure
German Democratic Republic (GDR), 4–6
German Federal Archives, 124, 158–60
German Federal Budget Law, 54
German Federal Compensation Law (BEG), 5, 136
German Federal Constitutional Court, 54n1, 147
German Federal Foreign Office, 110, 168
German Federal Office for Central Services and Unresolved Property Issues (BADV), 110n8, 116, 118
German Federal Office of Administration, 119
German Ministry of Finance (BMF), 18n7, 55, 111, 116, 117
German Parliament, 18, 105, 116, 146, 148, 155, 165, 180
German Presidents
    Horst Köhler, 154
    Johannes Rau, 108, 183, 192
    Richard von Weizsäcker, 192
Germany. *See* Federal Republic of Germany
Greece, 95n16, 149—50, 168

harsh living conditions. *See under* eligibility criteria
Hitler, Adolf, 3
human rights
    education, 169–71, 173–75
    European Convention of, 147
    European Court of, 101, 147
    violations of, 13, 20, 142, 182, 19
humanitarian programs, 48, 137, 156, 170, 190, 193. *See also* social programs
individual compensation payments. *See* compensation payments
installments, 7, 45–46, 48, 80, 105, 184. *See under* compensation payments
insurance claims, 7, 129, 160
interest accrued during the program, 22, 41, 43, 44, 44n, 49—50, 55, 133, 167
See also financial management
International Organization for Migration (IOM), 21, 42–43, 60, 63–64, 74–76, 80–83, 87–95, 98–101, 105–10, 112, 119–20, 134–38
Italian Military Internees (IMIs), 35, 79, 100, 117—18, 149
Italy, 35, 149

JCC. *See* Conference on Jewish Material Claims Against Germany
Jewish Claims Conference. *See* Conference on Jewish Material Claims against Germany
Jewish forced laborers
    persecution of, 3, 28, 189
    See also Conference on Jewish Material Claims against Germany
Joint Statement that concluded international negotiations, 20, 145–46
justice, 185–89

lawsuits
    after the compensation program, 159
    against German companies, 6, 14–15, 19–20, 23, 41, 105, 129, 142–46, 188, 192
    against Germany, 14, 142–44, 98, 192
    by Germany against Italy, 149–50
    class action, 6, 6n7, 15, 19, 20, 41, 54, 129, 129n, 143–46, 181
    dismissal of, 105, 145–46, 149 (*see also* legal closure)
lawyers
    fees for, 22, 143
    victims', 6, 13, 91n8
leftover funds, 48, 55, 156, 163
    use of 48, 157, 190
legal closure, 19–20, 25, 142–51, 159, 188
    waivers, 55, 98, 144, 148–49, 159–60, 184, 188

legal successors
    claims, 96–99
    cut-off date for filing claims of, 46, 110, 111–12, 155, 162
    definition of, 36, 96
    eligibility of, 36–37, 187n9
    identifying of, 47, 112
    payments to, 107
    See also claimants: death of
legal supervision of the compensation program, 55, 117–18

media, 15, 42, 58, 72–73, 75–76, 81–82. *See also* outreach
Merkel, Angela, 154
negotiations
    international, 6–8, 13–19
Norbert Wollheim trial, 6, 6n5

opening clause, 21, 30–33, 189. *See also* agriculture
other personal injuries, 7–8, 21–22, 129–32
outreach, 69–84

partner organizations, 21, 43, 59–61, 65–66
    administrative costs of (*see under* administrative costs)
    after ending of compensation program, 155–56
    agreements with, 44–45, 70–62
    Belarusian, 21, 60, 120, 156, 194
    Conference on Jewish Material Claims against Germany (JCC), 21, 43, 60, 70–71, 137, 158
    Czech 21, 43, 60, 70, 120, 156, 158
    International Organization for Migration (*see* International Organization for Migration)
    Polish (*see* Foundation for Polish-German Reconciliation (FPNP))
    Russian, 21, 43, 60, 120, 156, 194
    Ukrainian, 21, 43, 60, 120, 194
Poland, 3, 20, 33, 71–74, 77, 97, 105, 105n4, 109–12, 194
Polish Ministry of Treasury, 61–63
prisoners of war, 17, 33, 117
proof. *See* standard of proof
Property Claims Commission, 134–37
property loss, 23, 108n5, 129–30, 133–37. *See also* additional program lines

queries by claimants, 80–81, 159, 163

racism
    in the forced labor system, 28, 131
"Remembrance and Future" Fund, 8, 23, 130, 165–78, 193
research
    for claims verification, 95, 132, 135–36 (*see also* archives: research in)
    on Nazi history, 161–62
responsibility
    of German companies, 5, 7, 20, 54, 143, 182–83, 188–89,
    of the German State, 6, 7, 20, 54, 183n4, 194
Roma. *See* Sinti and Roma
Russia. *See* Russian Federation
Russian Federation, 20, 60n5, 76n6, 156, 168, 177

Second World War, 3–4, 6n5, 28, 189
Sinti and Roma, 3, 28, 56, 76, 95, 95n17, 106, 106n6, 129, 131, 137–38, 175
social programs, 130, 137–38. *See also* humanitarian programs
Soviet Union, 3–4, 22, 28, 60n, 138, 161
standard of proof, 35–37, 135. *See also* evidence

taxation
    and compensation payments, 110
    of payments to legal successors, 110
Third Reich, 2, 8, 15, 28, 30
tranche, 44n, 46n, 50, 95, 106, 110
transitional justice, 4n, 180–90
trauma, 78, 131
trials
    on forced labor, 6, 6n5, 143
    Norbert Wollheim, 6, 6n5,
    Nuremberg International Military Trials, 4–5

Ukraine, 20, 33, 60n, 76n6, 106, 120, 123, 158, 177
United Nations, 11, 181n
    basic principles and guidelines on reparations, 181n, 186
United States of America
    foreign interests of the, 120, 145
    Government of, 16, 20, 144–46
    lawsuits in the, 14–15, 20, 142–44
US-German Agreement, 20, 116, 144

victims
    associations, 6, 13, 16, 20, 30, 36n, 40, 64–66, 72–75, 81, 194,
    representatives, 13, 17, 165–66, 180–81, 186, 194

waivers. *See* legal closure: waivers
witnesses of forced labor
    contemporary, 167
    and inclusion in claims verification process, 65